NASTASE

Nastase

Richard Evans

AIDAN ELLIS

Photograph acknowledgements
Roy Choudhury—3
Albert Evans—4, 12
Richard Evans—5, 8, 13, 18–21, 24, 25
Ken Hawkins—17
I.P.S.—Italian Photo Service—29
Ed Lacey—14, 15
Arthur and Michael Cole—Le Roye Productions—6, 7, 10, 11, 16, 22–23, 26, 27, 28, 30, 31
T. Macarschi—2
Pietro Scheggi—9
(For picture identification cross-check above numbers with list of illustrations on page 8.)

The publisher would like to thank Alan Little, Librarian at The Wimbledon Lawn Tennis Museum, for his help.

First published in 1978 in the United Kingdom by Aidan Ellis Publishing Limited, Cobb House, Nuffield, Henley on Thames, Oxon RG9 5RU

British Library Cataloguing in Publication Data

Evans, Richard
    Ilie Nastase.
    1. Nastase, Ilie   2. Tennis players—Romania—Biography
    796.34′2′0924   GV994.N/
ISBN 0–85628–058–5

Printed in Great Britain by offset lithography by
Billing & Sons Ltd, Guildford, London and Worcester

In memory of
MY MOTHER
who taught me to care for the written word

CONTENTS

LIST OF ILLUSTRATIONS

INTRODUCTION

This is the story of a flawed and funny man—a supreme athlete; an instinctive artist; a born entertainer. But it is not enough to describe Ilie Nastase as one of the most vividly colourful personalities to have burst upon the sporting world in this or any other age. For deep in his soul lurks a deeper shade of crimson. And when the Balkan blood is stirred by fear, anger or indignation, the emotions that are unleashed erupt with an intensity few of us can comprehend. Embarrassed and shocked by the ranting, raging profanity, we turn away and ask the question that has been posed a thousand times—'Why can't he control his temper and let his talent do the talking?'

But no matter how much we might wish otherwise, there is only one answer. 'You cannot change Nastase,' says his fellow Romanian, Ion Tiriac. 'And if you could, he would not be Nastase.'

Having watched him as a performer and known him as a man for eight years, I know Tiriac is right. It might have been possible once, but not now. Nastase will change naturally with the passage of time, as we all do. But no fundamental change in his behaviour will be brought about by fines or suspensions, lectures or criticism, either in public or in private. He is what he is—lovable, charming and generous; temperamental, arrogant and obscene. Mr Nice'n Nasty one should call him; for his nickname, which he happily accepts as a natural reflection of his image, is only part of the whole.

I have not skirted round the nasty part in this book. To do so would not merely be dishonest but also absurd. Unlike some famous personalities who might have been quiet alcoholics or closet queens, Ilie has no secret vices. Nasty and his nastiness are aired out there on stage for all the world to see. His virtues are more private and if I have emphasized them in the pages that follow it is because I am inclined to heed Mark Antony, who told a Roman throng no less malleable than the ones Nastase has to face at the Foro Italico today, 'The evil that men do lives after them/The good is oft interred with their bones'. It would be sad if Ilie was remembered only for his evil deeds. There is too much good in the man for it to be allowed to pass unnoticed.

9

Nastase

Nastase is no Caesar—Panatta, the current Roman god, would not have it so—and here he will not receive as eloquent a eulogy as Antony might have managed. But I have tried to paint both sides of the portrait and the reader will have to decide which face he wishes to remember. On some occasions I have presented excuses for certain incidents in which I feel Nastase carried an unequal share of the blame.

However, I do think the most serious objection raised against Nastase by those who would like to see him thrown out of the game—namely that he presents an intolerably poor example to youngsters in an age that is already short on discipline—is a valid one. Up to a point. I would qualify that argument by maintaining that no teenager of ordinary talent is going to last very long in the game if he starts imitating Nastase. Nor, as Frew McMillan observes, is it only the bad examples that the kids of today want to emulate. Arthur Ashe and Bjorn Borg also have their disciples.

One change I think we will see in Nastase will occur when he is entrusted with some heavy responsibility. Already he has been approached by young players seeking advice and guidance on the circuit and he is very keen to help in any way he can. Also there is a possibility of his becoming player-coach to one of the World Team Tennis franchises sometime in the future. He jokes about it when the subject is raised but one does not have to peer very hard behind the façade to realize that this is something he would dearly love to do.

In the meantime I prefer to remember the funny face of the outrageous, self-mocking clown who is so game for any new and amusing experience that at the height of his fame he can accept an invitation to serve at table as a waiter. Luis, the Spanish patron of the Costa Brava Restaurant in Stockholm put him up to it and for a whole evening Ilie buzzed around taking orders and generally managing to get the right meal to the right table. Nastase's motivation for doing something like that is no more complicated than a determination to have fun. It is this zany zest for life that drives him on and on ... sometimes right on past the boundaries of good taste and common sense. But almost always it is only on court in the heat of battle that he misses the Halt signs. And once past them a mixture of fear, bewilderment and bloody-minded anger combine to create a fury that is awesome and often ugly to behold. But no matter what other pollution it might pick up along the way, at the source of this angry flood lies nothing more than an uncontrollable excess of a zest for life.

The task of writing about a character as multifaceted as Ilie Nastase has not been easy. I did not, of course, expect it to be. Inevitably I was too often reminded of James Cameron's description of the journalist's living nightmare: 'a deadline, a ringing phone, a thirst and an unquiet mind'.

But whatever problems I encountered were not of Ilie's making, save for the impossibility of his travel schedule during the summer of 1977, which was even tougher on him than it was on me. Given that there is little time left over when one is trying to play matches, practise, make personal appearances and attend business meetings, in at least one, if not three or four, different cities each week, Ilie made himself available to me whenever he could. The rest was up to me. As he was in South America when the final manuscript was sent to the publisher, he did not vet a word. It had never been my intention that he should.

I am, nonetheless, indebted to him for his cooperation. And, of course, there are others to whom I owe a special word of thanks. First, to David Vine of the BBC for suggesting the project and introducing me to Aidan Ellis, who turned out to be a most understanding publisher—a man who has mastered the delicate art of coaxing a writer to greater effort without harrying him to death.

As this book was, of necessity, written on the run, I was continually seeking sanctuary for brief periods and thus imposing myself on friends and relations in such far-flung places as Lausanne, San Francisco, Los Angeles and even Paris, when I needed to escape from my own phone. Without their generous hospitality, Aidan's elastic deadline would have been stretched further still.

And, not least, I wish to remember the devotion of my mother who suffered my absence during a long summer's illness without a word of complaint. The dedication in this book is not lightly given.

On a more technical level I owe thanks to the tennis writer's bible, the BP *World of Tennis Year Book* and its expert editors, John Barrett and Lance Tingay; John Samuel, Sports Editor of the *Guardian*, who allowed me to rummage through his paper's sporting files; David Gray, the *Guardian*'s former Tennis Correspondent who chronicled the life and times of Ilie Nastase with such balanced judgment for so long; and Ron Bookman, editor of *World Tennis* who gave me access to his picture library. And, indeed, to numerous colleagues, amongst whom I should particularly mention Bud Collins, Rex Bellamy, Barry Lorge, Jim Murray and Laurie Pignon, I must offer my appreciation and thanks for the excerpts I have used from their articles, all of which, I feel, will contribute immeasurably to the reader's understanding of the subject.

As much as anybody, of course, I am indebted to the players and members of the international tennis community who gave me their time and their opinions whenever I asked. Without their cooperation this book, truly, would never have been written.

A word, finally, about politics. If I were writing another kind of book I would have plenty to say about the political situation in Romania. But this is a story about a tennis player—and an apolitical one at that. Nastase is not unaware of what goes on in his country and he has his own opinions about it. But he knows he has been placed in a highly privileged position and he genuinely feels he can better serve his family, his friends and himself by maintaining his ties with Romania. His reasons are partly practical and partly emotional. Although he spends very little time there now, he loves Bucharest and he would be a very cold fish indeed if he did not enjoy the adulation with which that love is returned.

Under the present arrangement, a great deal of self-serving pragmatism is being exercised on both sides. But in this particular instance I personally feel it is better that way. No one is harmed by it and the Romanian authorities and Nastase are by no means the only parties to reap the rewards. A great many other people who have little enough in their lives enjoy spin-off benefits as a result of Nastase playing ball with Bucharest. Anyone wishing to blow the whistle should remember that.

Paris, November 1977

RIE

1

EARTHQUAKE

The dogs had been howling for an hour. Even the trams clattering down Marasti Boulevard could not drown the incessant, spine-chilling wails coming from the cage-like kennels underneath the patio at the back of the house.

In the living-room Sandra Groza, an aunt of Ion Tiriac, moved restlessly on the sofa as she watched television. The noise perturbed her. She was worried, of course, that it would wake Ion Alexandru, Tiriac's six-month-old son who was sleeping upstairs.

But her concern ran deeper than that. With Tiriac and Mikette, the tall Austrian blonde of serene beauty who had borne him the child, away in the States, she was responsible for the baby. And now, suddenly, in some indefinable way she was concerned for its safety. Maybe it was just that the noise the two Alsatians were making reminded her a little of the police sirens that she had seen in American gangster movies on television. The rise and fall of that high-pitched wail always signified impending death and disaster. She tried to put it out of her mind. Maybe they were just hungry although, God knows, she had fed them their full ration of raw meat only a few hours before.

A couple of miles away, across the broad, tree-lined avenues and spacious squares that form the picturesque residential sections of Bucharest, the tei trees outside No 8 Andrei Muresanu Street stirred as the first hint of a breeze began to disturb the evening's calm.

It was 9.24 pm on Friday 4 March 1977. Inside the house, Gheorghe Nastase sat slumped in front of the big black and white television set, a large bottle of beer within easy reach on the dining-room table. Although relatives often dropped round to enjoy the largely unused facilities of the five-bed-roomed house Ilie Nastase had bought five years before for himself and his parents, the place this particular evening was practically deserted. While Gheorghe sat engrossed in the movie on television, his wife, Elena, busied herself with a few final household chores in the basement flat below. Unlike Tiriac's aunt, neither felt any premonition of danger.

Until the house started to move.

When he felt the first shudder, Gheorghe Nastase grabbed the dining-table and, still barely comprehending, stared aghast at the ceiling. For a few seconds he heard the house scream as if it was on the rack; every beam and every support tearing and wrenching in its socket; the very foundations jarred by the trembling earth. Like someone in agony, the whole building seemed to cry out.

At the same instant that the nine-foot high sideboard pitched forward, sending glasses, plates and a large selection of Ilie's cups crashing to the floor, Gheorghe was hurled across the room as he tried to get out of his chair. He lay there waiting for the end. But after sixty seconds the earthquake stopped. Fifteen seconds more, it was estimated later, and the house would have come down.

A friend of the Nastases had been walking down a nearby street when the worst disaster in Romania's history sent shock waves through Europe. Later the friend told how he suddenly felt a great gush of hot air round his legs. Then the sky reddened and the earth started to tremble. A hundred yards in front of him a house swayed and then collapsed before his eyes. He fell to his knees and prayed. 'I thought it was the end of the world,' he said with the simplicity and conviction of a man who has seen the face of hell.

Tiriac's aunt had been right, of course. The Alsatians' wails had been a warning siren; plaintive howls from the animal kingdom to uncomprehending man. The dogs had felt the first tremors deep down in the bowels of the earth through their sensitive paws and three weeks later, when a second, minor earthquake struck, they were just as alert. This time Tiriac's relatives acted on the canine instinct and herded everyone into a car, drove it into the middle of the street and waited. Thirty minutes later the earth trembled once again.

But that was little more than a resettlement of disturbed rock formations which registered 4.5 on the Richter scale and did little further damage. The main earthquake was a 9.6 blockbuster that totally destroyed the town of Craiovo and wrecked parts of Bucharest.

As with Nastase's house, Tiriac's three-storey villa survived the catastrophe, although great cracks were visible high up on the walls of both buildings. Like Ilie's father, Tiriac's aunt was also hurled across the room as she rushed for the stairs, but neither she nor the baby was hurt.

Officially, 1,500 people died as a result of the earthquake but more realistic estimates put the number at 4,000. By the time a new day dawned over Romania, President Nicolae Ceausescu was flying home from a trip abroad to a nation numbed by grief and devastation.

Four thousand miles away on the north coast of Puerto Rico, Mother Nature was in a kinder mood. Only the strong trade winds, hissing through the foliage of the tall, swaying palms disturbed the tropical calm as a CBS television crew prepared for a tennis match due to be played that Saturday afternoon.

Earthquake

Jimmy Connors *v.* Ilie Nastase at the Cerro Mar Hotel was a one-shot, big-money challenge match devised and promoted by Bill Riordan who in years gone by had run the US Indoor Circuit and managed Connors. Riordan did neither of those things any more but, from time to time, he still came up with deals that offered certain players more money than they could reasonably refuse.

Nastase had been there for a week, practising at various moments with Vitas Gerulaitis, who flew down from New York for some sun and a few laughs, the South African pro, Terry Ryan, and Dumitru Haradau and Gavril Marcu, both members of Romania's Davis Cup squad. It had been just forty-eight hours before that Ilie finally received confirmation that Connors was coming. Earlier press reports, feverishly stoked by the voluble Riordan, had talked of Connors' poor physical condition which, apparently, was endangering his chances of playing the match. It was only later that Nastase discovered Connors had been practising, with no outward signs of discomfort, for ten days in Los Angeles. But that was only the first trick Jimbo layed on his good friend Ilie.

It was just after breakfast, Puerto Rico time, on Saturday, 5 March 1977 that Mircea Oprea, a Romanian-born New Yorker who had recently become Nastase's manager, was paged for an overseas call. It was Eric Drossart, the former Belgian Davis Cup player and long-time friend of the family, calling from Brussels with the first news of the earthquake. Drossart told Oprea, and Dominique Nastase, who was also summoned to the phone, that he had no personal details of the disaster and therefore had no idea whether Ilie's parents were safe or whether his house was still standing. Communication with Bucharest was apparently impossible but he would try to get further information as soon as he could.

Oprea—known as 'Mitch' to everyone in the English-speaking world—and Dominique quickly decided that it would be best to keep the news from Ilie until after the match. There was no point in doing otherwise. The agonizing uncertainty of not knowing whether one's parents are dead or alive would make it virtually impossible for anyone to concentrate on a tennis match, and for a person of Nastase's nervous and emotional disposition it would have been quite out of the question. Better, therefore, to wait for more definite news.

So while Mitch attempted to make contact with the Romanian Embassy in Washington, Dominique tried to organize her husband's remaining hours before the match so as to keep him away from the radio and television and to make sure that the newspapers, which had just arrived at the hotel with front-page headlines of the disaster, were kept out of his sight.

The plan succeeded, despite the quite extraordinary attempts by Jimmy Connors to sabotage it.

15

When both players arrived at the practice courts for a pre-match hit, Connors, to the shocked disbelief of everyone in the Romanian camp, shouted across to Nastase, 'Hey, buddy, you'd better call Bucharest. You might not have a house any more.'

One could be charitable and simply dismiss it as the most tasteless crack of the year. I suppose it is possible that Connors made the remark off the top of his head without stopping to think what kind of emotional havoc it could cause, or even without knowing about the earthquake.

If indeed it was a deliberate, premeditated act of psychological warfare a couple of hours before the two men were due to play a match involving some $650,000 there can hardly have been a more unpleasant example of dirty pool in the history of professional sports.

That it failed was a direct result of the repetitive unoriginality of Connors' humour. Like many great friends, Connors and Nastase had become accustomed to abusing each other in intimate terms. Whenever Ilie kidded him about the American way of life, Jimmy would be quick to make the obvious retort.

'You better watch it, my friend,' he would say, wagging his finger in a gesture known to millions of tennis fans around the world, 'One day you'll go home and find that commie government of yours has seized all your property and you won't have a house any more.'

Erroneously thinking that Connors was merely repeating this well-worn joke, Nastase inadvertently immunized himself from the psychological sling-shot that his good friend had fired at him.

'I had no idea what he really meant,' Nastase said later. 'I cannot believe Jimmy could make jokes about such things.'

Nastase's disbelief is understandable. If Ilie was reckoned to have one real friend on the tour, it was Jimmy Connors. For long periods the two had been inseparable. There had been a time just over a year before when Ilie's marriage was hitting a rough patch that saw Ilie move out of Dominique's room at their London hotel and double up for a few nights with Connors. And just over a year before this bitter confrontation in Puerto Rico, Connors had been a fêted guest of Nastase in Bucharest; meeting his parents and staying at the same house he was now so glibly suggesting might have been destroyed.

So what lay behind this sudden change in attitude by Connors towards Nastase? Jimmy laid it on the line soon afterwards when he remaked that it was difficult to maintain a sufficiently tough winning attitude in big matches if you were constantly playing against a great friend. Certainly an enormous amount of money rested on the outcome of the next match they were definitely scheduled to play just a few weeks later, the final of the WCT Challenge Cup in Las Vegas, plus other possible confrontations in the WCT Dallas Finals, Wimbledon and Forest Hills.

16

Whether Connors had come to that conclusion himself or whether it had been drilled into him by his ambitious mother, it is still difficult to deny the validity of such an argument. In the top echelons of professional sport there is no room for sentiment. Not, at least, while the action is in progress. And it is no use expecting a person of Connors' upbringing to understand the Australian attitude that enabled Roy Emerson and Fred Stolle, to take just one example, to cook each other breakfast as they progressed to their two Wimbledon finals, give not one quarter during the match itself, and still not impair their friendship.

It is for some other biographer to chronicle the life and times of Jimmy Connors and undoubtedly he will find much to praise and admire. The man has proved himself a truly great champion and, during the period he spent with the beautiful Marjorie Wallace in 1976 he showed signs of maturing into an articulate and intelligent spokesman for both himself and his sport.

But Connors' greatest fault has always been his inability to recognize the degrees of acceptability in human behaviour. For someone who spends so much of his waking hours defining to the last centimetre where to find the lines on a tennis-court—the lines that in a very realistic sense govern the success or failure of his life—he has an incredibly poor idea about where to draw the line in attitude, behaviour and emotion as soon as the ball goes out of play.

As his gestures on court indicate, he obviously has no idea where to find the line that divides funny, *risqué* humour from obscenity. As a dedicated individualist, he obviously has no idea of when it becomes necessary, for one's own sake if for nothing else, to join the group. This became clear when he made such a pathetic spectacle of himself at Centenary Wimbledon by refusing to join the parade of former champions on the Centre Court—thus absenting himself from the greatest group of tennis talent ever assembled in one place at one time.

Somehow, too, there has to be a dividing line between a champion's hunger to win and his ability to live with defeat. No one hated to lose more than Rod Laver, yet after half an hour by himself in the locker-room and a couple of beers that evening he was able to put a defeat behind him. Connors has still not learned how to do that. Right from the beginning of his professional career and even before, it was obvious that Jimmy was going to have problems learning how to cope with defeat. I shall not readily forget an incident in the locker-room at the Los Angeles tennis club during the Pacific Southwest Championships in 1970 when Connors, then only an eighteen-year-old college kid, surpassed everyone's expectations by battling his way through to the third round before losing a close match to Clark Graebner. Just after he had showered, I passed by and made some lighthearted comment about how well he had played and how he might even beat the guy next time out. With his mouth pursed in that downward curve and his eyes on fire, he swung round and, in a voice still strangled with emotion, snapped back, 'It's not funny, you know. I lost. That's nothing to laugh about.'

I knew then that we had a kid with a problem. A burning desire to win is a vital part of any prospective champion's make-up but it is also necessary to learn how to live with defeat. Time and experience have taught Jimmy that necessity but he still doesn't handle it as well as his peers. Certainly the desire to win has not diminished and, as was shown in Puerto Rico and later in Las Vegas, the lengths to which he is prepared to go to achieve victory do not stop short of endangering his friendship with Nastase.

For Nastase, the sudden change in Connors' attitude towards him came as a shock. Although he missed the significance of Connors' remark about his home, he found Jimmy distant and belligerent before the match. But even if this upset him, it was not the reason for his defeat. An unnecessary argument with Mitch about some quite unrelated matter undid some of the good that had been achieved in keeping him calm and unaffected by the news from Romania and then, once the match got under way, the sun affected him. This was Nastase's own fault. Although he knew that television coverage would necessitate a 2 pm start, he had been practising in the early morning and late afternoon, thus ignoring the opportunity of acclimatizing himself to the full force of the sun. After winning the first set Ilie started to feel dizzy and soon the strength went from his legs. With his speed reduced, he was easy prey for Connors who took the next three sets with little trouble.

Physical excuses are never a satisfactory way of explaining the outcome of a tennis match. It is quite possible, of course, that Connors would have beaten him anyway. However one cannot ignore the fact that Nastase is one of the few players with a winning record over Connors. Nor is it insignificant that Ilie won convincingly when they met again at Caesar's Palace Hotel five weeks later.

There, it would be fair to say, Connors got his come-uppance. He got the verbal fight with Nastase he had been heading for; lost it, and then proceeded to lose the match. It may have dawned on Jimmy by now that he was employing bad tactics in trying to pick a quarrel with his friend. There had been a time in their relationship when they were really close, when Ilie seemed almost content to let the younger man win. That would not have held true in a match as important as the final of the WCT Challenge Cup, but it is a fact that Connors' hostile behaviour unsheathed a shaft of cold steel in Nastase's game that he had not used against Jimmy before.

Any doubt that the relationship had gone sour had been dispelled by an extraordinary incident that occurred after the Puerto Rico match when both Connors and Nastase were competing in a WCT event in St Louis.

Realizing that Connors, who was making his first appearance for many years in what used to be his home town, might appreciate some extra privacy, WCT trainer Bill Norris had agreed to let Jimmy use his treatment room as a sort of private changing area. One evening Ilie walked in and, ever ready to forgive and forget, crept up on the man he still considered a friend, clasping him from behind in a playful hug. Reacting like someone about to be mugged in a dark alley, Connors broke free and hurled Nastase against the row of steel lockers. As Ilie and Mitch Oprea stared at him in amazement, Connors slumped down on to the bench, his face ashen white. 'From now on there's no more fooling around between us, buddy,' he snarled through clenched teeth.

More surprisingly still, perhaps, even Mrs Connors was not spared Jimmy's bitter mood. When she put her head round the door a few minutes later, her son told her summarily to get out. Apparently Jimmy Connors was at war with the world.

In a negative sense, the management of Caesar's Palace Hotel were the next to feel the brunt of Connors' belligerence. Although they were paying him a handsome sum to act as their touring professional, Connors failed to show up for any of the press conferences or promotional functions that had been arranged prior to the WCT Challenge Cup final.

'We were fortunate that Nastase turned out to be so cooperative,' said Ron Amos who was then the Caesar's Palace publicity director. 'As far as the PR was concerned, Ilie did all Jimmy's work for him.'

Even so, Nastase nearly blew all his good work by failing to turn up on court at the scheduled hour. Actually it was not his fault. He had been told to wait in a room in the hotel from where he was to be led out into the Convention Arena. But someone got their wires crossed and he was not called at the proper time. Connors obviously thought it was another of Nastase's stalling tactics and when the Romanian eventually appeared, the man recognized as the No 1 tennis player in the world was standing at the net, lashing it with his racket and shouting, 'Fuck you, Nastase, fuck you.'

When he invented the game, that was probably not what Major Walter Wingfield had in mind. But through natural and inevitable evolution and the age in which we live, the call to the court is no longer a question of 'Anyone for tennis?' but rather 'Anyone for a fast buck?' That is not meant necessarily as a critical appraisal of those of who have grown rich off the game since tennis went Open in 1968. The person who says he is not interested in making as much money as possible as quickly as possible is either a genuine member of a tiny minority or a huge hypocrite. There are more of the latter. It is really a question of how one goes about it.

Rod Laver, Ken Rosewall and Arthur Ashe managed to become tennis millionaires with enormous dignity. Ilie Nastase and Jimmy Connors arrived at the same seven-figure goal through an ability to both awe and appal the paying public who flocked to see them, not merely for their mesmerizing talent with a racket, but also for their explosive temperaments which could make them both funny and obscene.

On this occasion there was little that could be classed as funny. But if it was a no-holds-barred contest between two great athletes that the crowd was after, then they certainly got their money's worth. The crowd at Caesar's Palace, that is, for the NBC television audience were denied—or spared, depending on your viewpoint—the great verbal showdown that finally exploded between the two men.

Connors won the first set, but by then the high-tension wire that carries the driving will-power of his personality from brain to racket arm had snapped. The electricity was cut. Emotionally the fuse had been blown. He had asked for it. Failing once again to recognize the line over which it is neither prudent nor even safe to tread, he had carried his abusive aggression too far. And it all happened during a commercial break. In the control truck, NBC sports producer Dick Auerbach, who has little old ladies in Idaho to think about, was thankful for that.

Nastase had just won a game with a backhand passing shot to go 2–1 up. As they walked back to their seats by the umpire's chair, Connors said something about 'That fucking backhand.'

'What you mean? You think it was lucky or what?' asked Nastase, unable to ignore his opponent's taunts any longer.

At that Connors leapt out of his chair and confronting Ilie face to face, let rip with a stream of abuse that kept the court-side spectators agog for almost a minute.

Finally, for the first time since it all started back in Puerto Rico, Nasty lived up to his name and went for the jugular.

'Why don't you get your bloody mother down here on court,' he said, looking Connors firmly in the eye. 'You know you can't win anything without her.'

Jimmy reacted as if he had taken a punch in the mouth. Reeling back, he sat down with a thump in his chair and never said another word for the rest of the match.

'After that I knew I had him,' Nastase said later. 'I play really well and he start to make mistakes. I won the last three sets without much problem.'

And so Nastase retained the Challenge Cup he had won from Ashe when it was sponsored by Avis in Hawaii the year before. In doing so Ilie surprised himself as well as all those people who felt he no longer had the nerve to win big money when the chips were down. For even by Las Vegas standards there were a lot of very big chips lying on that court at Caesar's Palace. It was not just a matter of a baying crowd; a nation-wide TV audience; the pride involved in trying to retain a major title or even the

$100,000 that was on the line. There was the emotional trauma of a wrecked friendship to contend with as well and, for a man of Nastase's character, that was not a trifle that could be easily put aside. His relatives and his house had emerged virtually unscathed from the earthquake that had devastated his homeland. Yet the shock of that disaster, accentuated by more pressing personal problems, left scars on his emotional psyche that would take as long to heal as the shattered buildings in Bucharest. Due primarily to the generosity of his spirit, the relationship with Connors was patched up to some extent just before Wimbledon. But it would never be the same again, and he was obviously disappointed when a friendship with his WCT doubles partner, Adriano Panatta, did not blossom into the intimate relationship he craved.

There were problems, too, with the two people in his life on whom he leant for advice and support—his wife, Dominique, and his manager, Mitch Oprea. He loved them both and they, in their different ways, loved him. Yet the wishes of Dominique's large and close-knit family were often at odds with the demands of his career as a professional tennis-player. Oprea, who is never afraid to voice his opinions, was forever pointing this out. Whether Nastase agreed with him or not—he usually greeted Mitch's outbursts on the subject with silence—it did little for his peace of mind. Although they co-existed amicably enough for the sake of appearance, Ilie knew full well that Dominique and Mitch were poles apart in attitude and upbringing and this, too, was a source of continual concern. Even his own relationship with Mitch was far from peaceful. There were frequent flare-ups then, often just before or even during a match.

People who only see Nastase on court would, perhaps, expect his life off-court to be the same mixture of artistic brilliance and nervous rage. But, by choice, he would not have it that way. He is by nature a happy, fun-loving character who likes to relax despite an abnormal quota of restless energy. But the life-style of a working super-star has never allowed him such ordinary pleasures as finding more than the odd day to spend uninterrupted time with his wife and baby daughter. Obviously this depressed him on occasions and he only signed for World Team Tennis a second time after Dominique had agreed to move out to Los Angeles for the summer. As this meant bringing baby, nanny, sister and brother along too, the apartment offered them by Los Angeles Strings owner Jerry Buss was not big enough. So Mitch was instructed to find a house in Beverly Hills. At short notice there was no time to be choosy or to haggle about the price. The one he found had just been vacated by John Denver and had included Richard Burton among its previous occupants. It cost $5,000 a month.

'At this stage, it's worth five thou to keep Dominique happy,' said Mitch.

Yet although Ilie tends to be flamboyant with his money, he was not blasé about the fact that he could afford to fly his family from France to California for a month and to spend $5,000 just to put a roof over their heads. He has not forgotten how it used to be.

Take Lugano in 1968, for instance. Ilie had just played the semi-final of this long-established Swiss tournament which in those days was played on the eve of Wimbledon, when he stooped to untie his shoe-laces and couldn't get up. A sharp pain pierced through his lower back.

'I had a kidney stone,' Ilie recalled. 'The pain was awful. I was pissing blood and I couldn't sleep at all when I stopped the night in Budapest on my way home. When I eventually got to Bucharest there was no one at the airport to meet me and the pain was so bad. When I got to hospital I was in a ward with fifty other people for three weeks. I lost eight kilos during that time and didn't play again for five months. I was nobody then and it was rough. Remembering all that helps me appreciate things now.'

He was nobody then—and now he is more than just somebody. The name of Ilie Nastase is known to millions throughout the world who have never seen a ball hit over a net. After Muhammad Ali no athelete creates more headlines or controversy. He almost doubled the attendance whenever he appeared for the LA Strings in the summer of 1977; he taped two television shows in one night at NBC's studios in Burbank—including a guest appearance on 'Laugh-In'; a leading French director was discussing the possibility of making a movie on his life and somebody was writing a book about him.

But why him? There is no single, simple answer to that. However, if you believe it is all written in the stars then take a Cancer child with Leo as its ascendant; give it Scorpio as its nadir and Taurus in mid-heaven; mix in conjunctions like the Sun and Saturn at two degrees and Mars and Venus at ten and what you have, at the dawning of the Age of Aquarius, is a strange and complex human being known as Ilie Nastase.

2

THE BEGINNINGS

Marcel Bernard, Benny Berthet and other members of the French team might remember a little naked boy running around the stands when they played for the Davis Cup in Bucharest in 1948.

As the summers were hot and his house was only fifty yards away in the club grounds, two-year-old Ilie Nastase didn't see the point of wearing clothes when he scampered off to watch the tennis matches. At that age the tennis was of no particular interest to him for he was incapable of sitting still for very long anyway. But it was where all the people were and he enjoyed running about, seeing how many sweets he could collect from the club members he charmed with his big brown eyes and cute smile.

Already he was a skinny kid, his nervous, restless energy giving puppy fat no chance to form on his scrawny body. That, however, was small comfort to Mrs Elena Nastase who, at 7 am on 19 July 1946 had found herself giving birth to an enormous baby that weighed all of 11 lbs.

'Ilie was so big,' she said holding her hands out in front of her stomach to emphasize the point. 'It was my sixth child and each one is supposed to get easier. That was true until Ilie. His birth was the most difficult of all.'

So from the moment he first arrived in the world, his mother knew something a lot of other people were to find out many years later—Ilie Nastase was a whole package of trouble. He was not, however, a particularly bad child. There was a mercurial, quicksilver quality about him which immediately set him apart from his brother and three sisters (another brother had died in infancy) and inevitably for a youngster who was forever on the move he had his fair share of scrapes and spills. Once he fell off a roof flat on to his face. 'My nose was small then, not big like now, but I took all the skin off it and bashed my face pretty badly,' Ilie recalls. 'I'm not sure how I fell but I think maybe one of my sisters pushed me.'

It was most likely to have been Georgetta, the sister closest to him both in age and temperament. They were continually playing and fighting together out in the field behind the house where their parents kept a cow and a goat, amongst other livestock. By the time the kindly Georgetta had finished they also had ten stray dogs which she brought home from time to time after finding them starving on the streets of Bucharest.

23

Nastase

Like his elder brother, Constantin, who suffered a similar fate a few years earlier, Ilie once got too close to the cow and was tossed several feet in the air. It will surprise no one who has seen his catlike balance on a tennis court, to learn that Ilie landed on his feet. Ilie doesn't remember there having been any sheep in that field at the back of the house and is as puzzled as anyone at the oft-repeated assertion, carefully noted in numerous tournament programmes during the early part of his career, that he was a shepherd boy. Virtually his whole childhood was spent in Bucharest.

It was sheer chance that he was brought up in a tennis environment. In digging into Ilie's past quite the most extraordinary fact I discovered was that neither his father nor his mother played any sport at all, let alone tennis. Although Constantin became a good, if comparatively pedestrian, tennis-player, there is no record of any of Ilie's ancestors possessing any special athletic prowess. If evidence was needed to support the theory that genious is born and not bred, then Nastase would seem to provide it.

Gheorghe Nastase, Ilie's father, is now a robust white-haired man in his early seventies whose idea of exercise has always been nothing more taxing than a brisk walk. Even now he walks a lot, and ignoring the threat to an already weakened heart, insists on carrying guests' suitcases upstairs for them when they arrive at the house. He has a liking for beer but a marked preference for whisky, if he can get his hands on it without his wife seeing. A pair of narrow blue eyes suggest a tough streak to his character—a toughness that manifested itself in dogged hard work and a determination to succeed. If his son's mercurial talents enabled him to leap like a greyhound from the trap to international fame, Gheorghe Nastase progressed at a speed more akin to that of the workhorse. It was slow but it was steady and in the end he came a long way.

He started life as a policeman in his home town and then began his career as a guard with Romania's National Bank in Bucharest. Eventually he completed some extra studies and earned promotion to the position of cashier.

'I don't remember my father having much time to relax,' said Ilie. 'He had a big family to feed and he was working very hard all the time. Sometimes he enjoyed himself looking after the garden but he never played games of any kind. I don't think he was interested.'

Given that he was to produce one of the great natural atheletes of the decade, it was a strange coincidence that Mr Nastase should be offered a house by his employers actually situated within the bounds of a tennis-club. Ilie remembers it as a large, comfortable house but it is gone now, having been torn down in the late fifties to make way for a modern gymnasium and changing-room area. Ilie was born in that house, within earshot of the tennis balls being whacked back and forth on the very court that would see him develop his remarkable skills—skills that would eventually make the Progresul Club a centre of Romanian sport as a succession of the world's greatest players came to pit their talents against the local prodigy.

Yet surprisingly, perhaps, tennis was not the first game the young Nastase played. 'I don't know why,' he said. 'Maybe it was because it was all around me—it was too obvious, maybe. I played football first. I liked that better. I was six or seven before I picked up a tennis racket.'

But for a natural facility to recover from injury, which he still retains to this day, Nastase might have ended up a cripple before he had the chance to play any sport with more than a beginner's skill. He was six when he fell over while running in the woods near his home with some friends. A piece of pointed wood, as sharp as a knife, pierced his leg just above the knee and went right through the joint, breaking the skin on the other side. Bleeding and scared, Ilie lay in the grass for ten minutes before an older boy came to his aid and removed the stick from his leg. For several months he couldn't walk properly but now there is no legacy of the injury save for a small scar. When he recovered Ilie found that controlling a moving ball, either with feet or hands, came easily to him. He played soccer, handball, volley-ball and just occasionally tennis. His passion for soccer was such that he had to be persuaded to play the game that would soon become his life, and it was not until he won a small junior tournament at the age of twelve that he started to show a real interest in tennis.

'They gave me a nice cup for winning and I thought maybe tennis is not so bad,' Ilie recalled. 'Then a year later I won a bigger tournament and I got my first good racket, a Slazenger.'

The balls most commonly used for tournaments in Romania at the time were also Slazenger and, by gazing at the picture printed on the cardboard box, young Nastase came to recognise the first international tennis star he ever heard of. His name was Ken Rosewall. But it is not simply because of this early hero-worship that Ilie has always held Rosewall in such high esteem. When he finally got to see the little Australian perform, Nastase was mesmerised.

'For ages I could never beat him when we played,' Ilie told me long after his own name was being mentioned in the same breath as his idol. 'I could never understand how he could hit shots like he does; how he was so quick; how he was always in position. I liked his game so much I wanted to clap when he passed me.'

Almost twenty years after he first saw Rosewall's name on that Slazenger box, Ilie found age had done little to dim Kenny's prowess. In November 1977, in the final of the Gunze International Tournament in Tokyo—the first time incidentally that Nastase had ever been to Japan—Rosewall beat Ilie 7-5 in the third set.

'Incredible,' said Ilie shaking his head when he told me about it on his return to France. 'He's forty-four, thirteen years older than me and still he plays like that. For sure no-one has ever played tennis so well at that age.'

At about the time that Ilie was first becoming aware of Rosewall's existence, he started to find himself in the kind of demand that was later to become an inevitable part of his life. Now so many people want a piece of him, either for financial reasons or simply to bask in the spotlight that is forever shining on him. Back in Bucharest when he was thirteen there were just two people vying for his attention—his soccer coach and Colonel Constantin Chivaru who was responsible for teaching him tennis.

It was an intense and, to a degree, a bitter struggle because both men realised the stakes were high. They knew that Ilie's rare athletic ability would virtually guarantee him success at whichever sport he chose.

Why did tennis win? The fact that he was already starting to achieve individual success in tennis probably helped.

But it was not just ego. A mixture of shyness, insecurity and determination turned him towards tennis. 'It was more difficult to be picked out at soccer,' Ilie explained. 'There were so many of us playing it that the coach had a tough time deciding if one boy was really that much better than the other. So many played well. And I was shy, too, in the company of the others. But in tennis, I play by myself. And I could be myself.'

The fact that his brother Constantin, thirteen years his senior like Rosewall, was already playing in the Romanian Davis Cup team and bringing back enticing stories of trips abroad also excited Ilie's imagination. And, most important of all perhaps, was his relationship with Colonel Chivaru. Now a stout, balding figure with glasses and a ready smile, it is easy to imagine that he presented a comforting uncle image to the highly-strung and basically shy teenager.

'He liked soccer very much and I had a tough time winning him away from the football coach,' Colonel Chivaru told me one evening at Ilie's house in Bucharest. 'But once he made up his mind, we became very close friends. Although he did have this temperamental personality, I never had any real problems with him.'

For some coaches Nastase, with his erratic behaviour and wristy strokes, would have seemed like a bad dream. All that talent but how to harness it? And even if one worked out how, would it be wise to try?

In trying too hard to streamline a style and discipline a temperament, to what extent does one risk crushing the tender seed of genius? A fruit will still ripen in the greenhouse but who can deny that wild strawberries taste better?

'The trouble is that melons are supposed to turn on the vine of their own accord,' observed Mitch Oprea with his customary dry wit. 'Ilie never turned. The vine got twisted.'

26

Faced with a youngster of exceptional talent, any coach has to tread warily and in the end there are always people who will say he erred too far one way or the other. Obviously Colonel Chivaru could have been a stricter disciplinarian with Ilie. But how strict should one be with a pupil who gives you no trouble? For when Colonel Chivaru says he had few problems with Ilie, I am sure he is telling the truth. With someone he trusts and respects, Ilie gives little trouble. The British umpire Bertie Bowron who officiates all over Europe provides a perfect example of someone in authority who has rarely had any major problem with Nastase because Ilie likes and trusts him. Colonel Chivaru obviously falls into the same category.

'I never had to do more about the basics than put the racket in his hand just like you put a pen in the hand of a child you are teaching to write,' said Colonel Chivaru. 'I never had to change his strokes. I like players who use a lot of wrist and are happy players who smile a lot and enjoy it. These are the type of players who will become something special. The will to improve comes from inside them. When Ilie hit a bad shot he instinctively went through the motion to analyse what he had done wrong. Improvement comes very quickly like that.'

The stroke play and the speed and agility needed to play the game at the highest level were fundamentals Ilie barely bothered to learn in the formal sense. They came to him as naturally as walking. But learning how to compete and how to win was something else. That took time—and Tiriac.

Ilie first met Ion Tiriac at the age of thirteen when he went to play in a junior event at the International Championships held in a town called Clüg.

'When I lost, the only way to stay on was to become a ball-boy,' Ilie recalled. 'That way you got your expenses paid. So as I had no money and wanted to watch the matches that was what I did. I ball-boyed the final and I was scared to hell. I was at the net which needs a lot of concentration in case you miss a ball. Tiriac was playing the senior Romanian player of the time Gheorghe Viziru. It was him I was scared of—not Tiriac. He didn't say a word. I think he was battling too hard to talk. I remember he was two sets and 2–5 down against Viziru and came back to win. He never lost again in Romania until I beat him.'

In the years that followed Ilie used to watch Tiriac a lot—and not just at tennis.

'He was a big ice-hockey player, you know,' Ilie reminded me. 'He used to play for the police students' team against the Army Club which was my team. Tiriac never looked for the puck, always for the guy. He got a broken nose, broken jaw, broken everything. Once when we were playing soccer and he was in goal I broke his wrist. But he's strong that Tiriac—Jesus, so strong.'

For a nervous, restless athlete, Nastase has an unusual capacity to sit down and watch other perform. During his teenage years in Bucharest, he used to attend soccer, ice-hockey, tennis and rugby matches. He never tried playing rugby union, a game that is played with greater enthusiasm and skill in Romania than any other continental country apart from France, but he enjoyed watching it and it would have been good to see Nastase on the wing.

Yet for an athlete who excels to such a degree at his chosen sports, Ilie is remarkably deficient in others. He doesn't swim, for instance, never having had the opportunity to learn as a child and lacking the fundamental desire to make the effort now. Only once, in India when he was still quite young on the tour, did he ever get on a horse and he was scared stiff.

'It was like being in a plane up there, so high,' Ilie recalled. 'And the horse was a very nervous, crazy horse. I don't think we were good for each other.'

He preferred to watch the exploits of others on horseback when he went to the movies. It was at the cinema that Ilie gained his first understanding of foreign lands and foreign cultures.

'Mostly the films were French,' he remembers. 'I used to see all the films of Gerard Philippe. It was sad that he died so young. And D'Artagnan—I loved that movie with all the sword-play.'

Quick hands, flexible wrists, an eye for the opening—there is much in common between the art of the swordsman and the volleyer at the net. Nastase noted the similarities but it was some time before he gained sufficient confidence to rush the net himself. In his early years on court, Ilie was content to stay on the base-line in the true tradition of the old clay-court artists and develop his ground strokes. He also needed to develop some muscles but until he had the strength to instil some power into his game, he relied on his other great asset—devastating speed. There is no way of gauging precisely who is the fastest tennis player in the world but it is generally accepted by those who have played against them that Nastase rates right up there alongside Rod Laver, Bjorn Borg, Tom Okker and Vitas Gerulaitis as one of the quickest men ever to walk onto a court.

However happily and naturally Nastase developed under Colonel Chivaru's tutelage, he was never, apparently, taught regular and disciplined training habits. Like a select band of very special athletes—Rosewall is an example amongst tennis players—Nastase does not require long hours of training to keep fit. The danger of boredom; of losing his natural eagerness to play has always been a far greater threat to his chances of success than the possibility of not being able to last through a long match. However, even the most naturally gifted performer needs to spend time practising and refining his craft. And if he is to derive maximum benefit from the effort, he needs to do so in a structured and well-prepared way. Nastase's practice habits are sloppy. That is not to say that he is necessarily an unwilling or a lazy practice player. When the tennis bug finally caught him in his early teens, no one could ever get him off the court.

'I worked hard at my game,' Nastase maintains. 'In those days I must have been like Gottfried. I spent five or six hours on court every day.'

Pancho Gonzales, who like most great players admires greatness in others, has tried to help Nastase on occasions but the pair of them have never spent quite enough time together for Ilie to reap much benefit. Nonetheless Gonzales, who is appalled at Nastase's practice habits, is always goading him about them when they meet, in the hope that the Romanian will listen.

Colonel Chivaru must take some of the blame for the fact that Ilie never developed better lifelong practice habits such as Harry Hopman instilled into his great line of Australian champions. But perhaps it would be unfair to expect someone to be another Hopman.

Some of Ilie's schoolteachers were less successful. From the time he first started going to school at the age of six, the contrasting and conflicting sides of his nature became all too painfully apparent. Here was a basically shy child who was mischievous enough to attract the limelight and even to enjoy the attention he received as a result of his actions. Ilie vividly remembers the pain of that shyness—a trait from which he still suffers to this day. 'People were always picking on me at school because I was so shy I would not look anyone in the eye,' he recalls. 'Not even my mother—I could not even look my mother in the eye.'

Yet after a few years in school Ilie was causing enough chaos to be made to sit in front where the teacher could keep an eye on him.

'I think I had lots of friends in class because I was always the one answering the teacher back and making a noise,' he says. 'I saw my old teacher the other day and she said it was tough for me because I was so sensitive and everyone was picking on me. But I think she was just being nice. I get embarrassed now when I hear about the way I used to behave in school. I must have been bad.'

This shyness and compulsion to attract attention to himself is just one of many aspects of his character that are spotlighted by Astroflash, an international company which produces computerized horoscopes of a person's personality based on the time, date and place at which he or she was born. There are passages worth quoting from the Astroflash document, especially the section dealing with basic character traits, as one tries to fathom what makes as complex a person as Ilie Nastase tick.

For instance, the horoscope begins: 'You are a creature of contrasts with a pronounced double nature. The imaginative part of you turns inward and is capricious, not to say fantasy-minded. The other part of you is spectacularly externally orientated. ... Your abundant sensitivity is not subject to inner feelings alone but expresses itself and applies itself to the outside world as well, thus making it possible for you to realize your ambitions and make your dreams come true.' Amongst the weakness of a person born at the same instant and in the same place as Ilie, Astroflash cites a tendency to appear arrogant through an innate recognition of one's own value and a need to seek admiration.

While considering the position of the Moon, which reigns over our dreams, our intuitions and the manifestations of our unconscious, the horoscope places it in the sign of Pisces in Ilie's chart and says: 'Your unconscious has extreme "psychological plasticity", which means that you are receptive to the outside currents which pass through it. Your soul is made to dilate, to vibrate in unison with all else, to mix with the universe and to become part of it. Like a great river, swollen by its tributaries after heavy rain, your inner self is enriched by sensations and emotions which in successive waves fill it and at times even submerge it. Hence this filling process can also be a loss of inner unity which leaves your personality with a tendency to surrender to indifference and to scatter your talents. This can go as far as leading to chaos, when these contradictory currents, this perpetual flux and reflux, enmesh your being like a piece of flotsam.

'However, these deep-felt urges may also carry you to the shores of opportunity. In this case your unconscious being rejoins a universal consciousness borne on the crest of a wave of humanitarian emotion, charity or altruistic ideals.'

What the Astroflash horoscope confirms in such colourful language is that there are two Nastases—the public entertainer capable of the most extrovert and attention-seeking behaviour that can go as far as to create chaos and resentment, and the private person, shy, sensitive, easily embarrassed—someone who quite genuinely shuns the limelight.

Ilie is not alone in having a double nature. For if Nastase is judged by the world at large almost solely through his public persona, it is no use denying that his on-court performances—be it an exhibition of artistic excellence or boorish obscenity—forms a part of his true personality. Yet it still represents only half the portrait. It is, perhaps, the more important half in that it is his 'public' side that affects and concerns the people who pay to see him perform, and who therefore, through their acceptance or rejection of what he offers, ultimately hold the key to his success.

However, there is also the Nastase who refuses to go to certain places in Bucharest for fear of the fuss his presence would cause; who deliberately picks a chair facing away from the entrance of a restaurant so that fewer people are likely to recognize him, and who complains bitterly to his manager when another public appearance deprives him of a day alone with his family.

That, too, is part of the man and all of it was evident in the boy growing up in Bucharest.

3

TIRIAC—THE EARLY DAYS

Ilie Nastase's ears were popping. The Russian-built Ilyushin 18 was bouncing round the skies over Bulgaria and the seventeen-year-old Romanian clutching the armrests of his seat was swallowing hard, partly out of anxiety and expectation and partly because someone had told him that was the best way to unblock the eardrums. It was the first time Ilie had been in an aeroplane.

'I remember the pressure in the cabin was really bad in those old planes,' said Nastase. 'But I didn't mind. I was just so happy to be going to Sofia. It was my first time abroad and it was such a big thing for me.'

A couple of days later, Ilie experienced another first—a quick, sharp lesson from Ion Tiriac in the art of grabbing your opportunities.

Nastase was playing one of the older Bulgarian players in the first round of the tournament. Early in the third set Ilie won the points to go 30–0 up when the umpire suddenly called 'Game, Nastase.' Confused, Ilie stood there not knowing quite what he should do. Tiriac did not leave him in much doubt for long. 'Change, stupid, change,' he hissed from the stand.

The Bulgars may have been kind enough to introduce Christianity to Romania back in the 7th century but Tiriac was not going to transport Christian ethics back to Bulgaria—not if it meant passing up the chance of grabbing a game in a tennis match. One must, after all, get one's priorities straight. For Tiriac, winning, by any means and at all costs, gets a pretty high rating. That is not to say he is a man without principle. On the contrary, I have always found him extremely straight and honest to deal with. However, if he can get away with pushing gamesmanship to its limits and then going for the jugular on court he will do so. He was brought up in a tough world where those who stood around saying 'excuse me' ended up with a broken nose. But off court he is as direct as any man can be. Anybody who says he is not sure what Tiriac thinks about him is either deaf or lying.

Having been elected to the Board of the Association of Tennis Professionals because the players recognized that he speaks his mind and has a very sharp brain, it was inevitable that sooner or later Tiriac would fall out with the other ATP directors.

31

In fact it happened during the American Airlines Tennis Games in Tucson one year. The lawsuit between Jimmy Connors and the ATP was in full swing and, somewhat hastily, Arthur Ashe publicly accused Tiriac of having given some confidential information to one of Bill Riordan's lawyers—Riordan being the driving force behind the lawsuit. Tiriac was rightly indignant that Ashe had so accused him before he had had a chance to defend himself. So that evening, at the ATP Board meeting, Tiriac offered to resign. 'But first,' he told the ATP directors who were agog at the thought of what was to come, 'I am going to explain myself and then tell certain of you here what I think about you.'

He then proceeded to do so. Jack Kramer, Donald Dell, Arthur Ashe and a couple of other members of the Board came under the scrutiny of Tiriac's astute mind and biting tongue. The fact that his English is not perfect was no hindrance. Each point he made hit home and then, with great dignity, he rose saying, 'Thank you, gentlemen. I will now go away and decide whether I wish to remain on the Board and you may decide whether you want me to stay.'

'Gee', exclaimed John Newcombe as Tiriac lumbered off into the night, 'that was great stuff. I never knew Board meetings could be so much fun!'

Tiriac remained on the Board and made a valuable contribution as a kind of devil's advocate for a couple more years. Then at the beginning of 1977 he broke with ATP completely. Again he was devastatingly honest. 'I do not agree with many things the ATP are trying to do,' he told the Board. 'And as I myself will be doing things that will conflict with ATP policy it is best that I leave the Association.'

The 'things' Tiriac wanted to do included setting up big-money exhibition matches against the regular tournaments that the ATP, quite correctly, felt were the life-blood of the professional game. As the coach and inspirational force behind Guillermo Vilas, Tiriac had the opportunity of arranging some juicy deals, and if his motives for leaving the ATP were basically self-serving, no one could accuse him of being devious or dishonest.

As nobody had a greater influence over Nastase during his formative years than Ion Tiriac, this would be an appropriate moment to delve a little deeper into the background and character of the other great personality in Romanian tennis.

Physically Tiriac, or Tiri Baby as he is sometimes called by those who feel confident enough to do so, comes as close to most people's image of Count Dracula as one will find outside captivity. For the weak—or even the quite strong—in heart, he is not a man to bump into down a dark alley. The huge black moustache which began wending its way down each side of a rather small mouth about eight years ago is complimented by a thatch of hair that might be described as Balkan Afro if it did not more closely resemble tightly coiled wire. I will never tire of quoting writer John McPhee's description of Tiriac in his book *Wimbledon—a Celebration,* when he likened him to a 'counter-espionage agent from Outer Mongolia or a used-car salesman from Central Marrakesh'. Tiriac does indeed conjure up weird fantasies of figures pursuing sinister occupations in sinister places. But in fact he had a fairly straightforward start to life. He was born in the town of Brasov, which lies high up in the mountains 150 kms from Bucharest. His father, who died when Ion was ten, worked as a functionary in the mayor's office. Like Nastase he was born in a house that was situated no more than a hundred yards from a football field, a hockey field and a tennis-club. With the opportunities on his front doorstep, sports to Ion Tiriac became second nature.

'I play everything,' he says simply, 'even ping-pong. Actually I played ping-pong before I played tennis so when I started holding a racket I held it like a ping-pong bat.'

Funny: I never really thought of Tiri *holding* a racket in the way that other people do. To me he always seems to clutch it in a massive paw and wield it like some primitive, but very effective, club.

Primitive could be one way of describing Tiriac's attitude towards Brasov High School which finally threw him out because he was always missing classes. His mother, unimpressed by his protestations that he needed more time to practise hockey, tennis, ping-pong and whatever, forced him to go back to school and he eventually concentrated hard enough to make it all the way to the University of Bucharest.

But despite a brain that could have taken him far, it was still as an athlete rather than an academic that he made his mark. First it was as an ice-hockey player. A game well-suited to his pugnacious spirit and physical strength, hockey enabled Tiriac to skate his way to sporting fame with relative ease. He was soon selected for the national team and beginning in 1957 represented Romania in four world championships. By the time he played in his last Olympic Games at Innsbruck in 1964, Tiriac was already heavily into tennis.

Even though at the time he was only playing tennis for half the year, during the Egyptian championships in Cairo in 1961 he beat Neale Fraser, who had won at Wimbledon the year before.

'I knew tennis was a sport I could play much longer than ice hockey and I enjoyed the travel.' Tiriac said. 'I soon realized I would never be world champion because I didn't have the strokes. But I had great legs and could run all day. I knew that they would win me a lot of matches.'

So Tiriac's years at university were divided between ice hockey, tennis and, evidently, a fair amount of pugilistic activity in and out of the ring.

Actually his boxing career was short-lived. 'I had never boxed properly before and this first occasion was supposed to be a test fight,' he explained.

'The guy was supposed to go easy on me. But somehow I hit him too hard
and he goes beserk. We flail away at each other for a while until I decide I
have enough. So suddenly I stop, stand quite still and drop my hands. Then
very slowly I start moving my foot from side to side. The guy looks down
and I hit him. He wakes up a long time later.'

The edges of Tiriac's moustache twitch in pleasure at the memory and
then he shrugs. 'They disqualify me. Say it was unethical behaviour. That
was the end of boxing for me.' It was not, however, the end of his fights,
most of which seemed to stem from a need to uphold the honour of his wife
whom he married in 1961. They separated eight years later.

There was one occasion when a group of guys were fooling around and
one of them pinched his wife's bottom. 'There were about nine of them so I
ride my motor-bike into the middle of them,' said Tiriac. 'I don't think I
kill anyone. At least they all seemed to get up and run away.'

Mrs Tiriac, who was evidently prone to this sort of thing, suffered a
similar fate one day in a store. Having identified her attacker as a guy in a
grey suit, Tiriac goes over and flattens him with a straight right.

'The trouble with my wife, she change her mind a lot,' Tiriac explains.
'After I hit this guy she says "No, not that one, the other one." So I hit
him too. Then the first one gets up and complains he didn't do anything.
"Don't worry. That's for next time," I tell him.'

The macho streak in Tiriac has always been strong. Yet to an extent it
is merely a façade, possibly to cover up some deep-felt sense of insecurity.
For if it would be a slight exaggeration to say that underneath the gruff
and even fearsome exterior Tiriac is just a big cuddly bear, it would,
nonetheless, be a lot nearer the truth than most people would imagine. He
has a kindly, generous nature, of which Nastase was an early beneficiary.
That does not mean to say Tiriac was not tough on the skinny kid he first
noticed one day in the early sixties when Ilie was playing for the Romanian
junior team. 'He was still hung up over soccer at the time,' Tiriac recalled
as we settled down to talk in his room at the Gloucester Hotel in London.
'Sometimes he didn't make the tennis squad because he wasn't good
enough. He was very erratic and by nature very timid. But when I got to
play him a year or so later he took a set off me. I was surprised because I
had controlled Romanian tennis as a player for two years. Really I had no
opposition. But Nastase was so quick and he hit his forehand very late and
low.'

In an effort to fill him out physically Nastase was sent with Tiriac to
an athletics training camp in the mountains.

The camp was populated mostly by boxers, wrestlers and Olympic
gymnasts of various kinds. Lungs pumped air in and out of large,
well-moulded frames; sweat glistened on knotted foreheads and muscles
bulged. The place was built with muscles in mind. Muscles were its *raison*

d'être and Nastase didn't have any. The lack of them did not help his self-confidence in that company and so to hide his embarrassment he made a pest of himself. He ran about all day, cracking jokes, tripping up over great sweaty wrestlers and generally getting under everybody's feet. Occasionally Tiriac, who did not take kindly to infantile behaviour, would swat him and Ilie would retire to a corner in tears. But ten minutes later he would be up to exactly the same tricks again. Then, as today, he was quite irrepressible.

'People talk about disciplining Nastase, fining him or throwing him out of the game for six months, but it is no use,' said Tiriac. 'Either you take Nastase the way he is or you forget him. There is no middle way, believe me.' Tiriac reminded me that there had been one instance when the legendary Harry Hopman did get his hands on Nastase. Yet the liaison was too brief to ascertain whether the tough Aussie coach could actually have had any lasting effect on the way Ilie behaved.

'It was in 1969 when we had to play Britain at Wimbledon so we hired Hopman to help us win on grass,' Tiriac recalled. 'Hopman is one of the few coaches I respect because he has proved he knows what he is talking about. He treated Ilie as a bit of a joke but he made him work like a mad dog all the same. He couldn't make him unbeatable, though. Graham Stilwell played so well that time that he beat both of us. But we won the tie 3–2 so it was OK.'

Apart from the marvellous tennis Stilwell produced against both Nastase and Tiriac, there was a minor incident which also makes that particular tie stick in my memory. I had arrived back in England on the first day of the tie after a trip to the Continent and therefore had not had time to arrange press credentials. But by pure chance I arrived at the main gate of the All England Club at the same time as the Romanian team. I was in the process of explaining my problem to the stern-looking commissionaire when Ilie butted in. 'He's OK,' he said waving his arms about in a distracting fashion. 'He's a writer. He's with us. You let him in.' Before the commissionaire had time to debate the point, Nastase had swept me through. I hardly knew him at all at the time and it struck me as amusing that as an English reporter who had covered Wimbledon for the previous ten years, I should still need the assistance of a young Romanian who could barely speak my language to get into the grounds of the All England Club.

And so where was his shyness then? Where was the shyness of a man who could not look people in the eye but had just volunteered to get involved and even take charge of a potentially awkward situation? Was this the Leo in his nature bursting to the fore? One presumes so.

Yet there was also the timidity. 'Timid' was a word Tiriac used frequently to describe Nastase as we continued our discussion about the first uncertain steps that set Ilie on the road to stardom.

'His style of play was timid to start with, too,' said Tiriac. 'Mostly he would bloop the ball back and use his speed to run down the return. But he was improving all the time. After the Bulgarian trip we took him to Russia for a tournament and he won a match there as well, beating one of the top-ranked Soviets. He was still skinny, though. I remember we couldn't find a shirt small enough for him and he ended up wearing one three sizes too big.'

The tournament was played at Talkin, near the Finnish border, and Ilie with his quick ear for languages remembers that everyone spoke Estonian, including the top Soviet player of the time, Tomas Lejus, an Estonian by birth. Languages had been the only subject Ilie had excelled at in school. He learnt the basics of French and Russian in class and as soon as he started travelling regularly on the circuit, he picked up English and Italian, both of which he now speaks fluently despite grammatical imperfections. In locker-rooms around the world, he switches from Romanian to French, English or Italian, sometimes even in mid-sentence, with the ease of the natural linguist. He can also understand some Spanish.

Whenever Nastase's harshest critics, who tend to view him as a mindless clown, question his intellectual capacity, they frequently brush aside his linguistic talents with the argument that the ability to learn different languages parrot-fashion offers no proof of intelligence. However, Dr Mike Franzblau, an eminent Los Angeles psychiatrist and avid follower of the game, rejects that notion. 'Certainly it is true that a facility with languages does not guarantee a person a high IQ,' says Dr Franzblau. 'But in my experience it does suggest that the brain is capable of following a certain system of logic and that therefore a good linguist is probably fairly intelligent.'

Ilie soon had an opportunity to practise his languages as well as his tennis when he started travelling on the international circuit full-time in 1966. He was nearly twenty then and that, of course, made him a latecomer by today's standards. Even back in the late fifties young Australians like Rod Laver, Bob Mark, Bob Hewitt and later John Newcombe and Tony Roche, had been sent abroad for nine-month trips round the world each year from the age of sixteen or seventeen. So by the time they were twenty they were veteran travellers and seasoned competitors.

Judged by those standards, Nastase had ground to make up. At a comparatively late age he had to learn how to play on surfaces faster than slow European clay—in other words he had to learn how to serve and volley—and he had to accustom himself to the rigours of day-in day-out competition against the best players in the world. The Aussies of his own age, like Newcombe and Roche, had been doing that for three years already and, of course, a decade later, Bjorn Borg had won Wimbledon and the French Open twice by the time he was twenty.

But quite apart from his natural ability which made the technical learning process relatively easy, Nastase was a willing worker and did, in those early days, put in long hours of useful and well-constructed practice. That was largely Tiriac's doing, but Ilie had his own incentives for wanting to improve. 'I wanted to win. That was very important to me,' Nastase admitted to me one day. 'At first I thought I would just be like any other tennis-player in Romania. But then I started to win a few important matches and I recognized the possibilities. In those days before computer rankings winning consistently was the only way to get yourself invited to tournaments. If you lost in the first round one year the chances were pretty good they would not ask you back unless you were a big name. So I started to work hard. And it was OK: I enjoyed it. I spent a long time on court each day, running after balls and practising my volley. It was good.'

Nastase had begun to understand the rules of the strange new jungle he was battling through when he played in the Egyptian Championships at the old Gezira Club, Cairo, in 1966. He played well enough to leave his mark there, beating Jan-Erik Lundquist, the tall, talented Swede, and Marty Reissen, before taking a set off an exasperated Tiriac in the quarter-finals. 'He played me the same way he beat Riessen,' Tiriac recalled. 'Lobbing everything: high, looping balls. I was going berserk.' But at that time, before his forehand developed some real sting and before he learned how to volley, it was the only sure way Nastase could win. So that's how he played. Winning was the thing that mattered most. Like any champion in the making, he had got that one figured out pretty quickly.

The following week, in Alexandria, Nastase overcame the problem of slippery courts by taking off his shoes and beating the Australian Ken Fletcher in his socks. Talking of forehands, Fletcher had one of the best in the business at that time and had been seeded No 3 at Wimbledon only two years before. Even though a couple of cold lagers might just possibly have slipped down Fletcher's throat the previous night, it was still a good win for the young Romanian in his stockinged feet. Having worked out a way to handle the lobs, Riessen beat him in the next round, but after two weeks in Egypt Nastase had done enough to set the tongues wagging on the world circuit. Here, people said, was a player of promise.

His reputation spread quickly. He was selected to play his first Davis Cup tie against France that year and although he lost both singles, he had the luck to catch the eye of the Italian referee, Signor Martini.

Signor Martini, who recalled the incident when he returned to Bucharest eleven years later to referee Romania against Belgium—a tie which took Nastase past the 100-match mark in Davis Cup play—promised to put in a good word for young Ilie when the entry lists were made up for the Italian Championships in Rome. That was the way it worked in those days. A word here; a mention to the right person from a friend; a chance meeting. It was a chaotic way to run a world circuit and inevitably players of talent got left out of tournaments they should have played in, while lesser lights sneaked in because they had remembered to write a nice 'thank you' letter to the tournament director's wife.

Signor Martini, however, was not acting out of kindness. He knew talent when he saw it and, as neither satellite circuits nor the ATP computer ranking system had yet been invented, the only way to ensure that a young player gained the opportunity of proving himself was to back your hunch and recommend that he be put in the draw. Nastase did not let Martini down. He won a couple of rounds the first time he appeared at the Foro Italico and was quickly invited to play in a series of local tournaments round Italy.

By the time the French Championships came round, the Romanian Lawn Tennis Association were anxious that Nastase should have the benefit of Tiriac's company as often as possible. So they asked if Ion would mind partnering Ilie in the doubles at Stade Roland Garros. 'Normally I would have played with Istvan Gulyas,' said Tiriac, referring to the wily Hungarian clay-court wizard who went on winning matches in Europe after the age of 40. 'Honestly, I did not like the idea of playing doubles with Nastase too much. But after we somehow managed to win the first two matches, we developed some kind of understanding and went all the way to the finals where we were badly beaten by Dennis Ralston and Clark Graebner.'

It was an auspicious beginning to a partnership that was to last for the next five years. By the time of the Big Split, they had captured the French crown and won the Italian twice, among numerous other titles.

They became a highly effective team but, almost inevitably, not a popular one to play against. Doubles teams that got mashed to pulp by the greatest combination of that era, Newcombe and Roche, walked off court resigned to the fact that they had just been beaten fair and square in a straightforward manner. There was no point in being bitter about it. Newcombe and Roche, in all probability, had done everything better.

Too frequently, that was not the way teams felt after a defeat at the hands of Tiriac and Nastase. All doubles pairs like to establish a rhythm and that was the hardest thing to do against the unpredictable Romanians. If they didn't actually break the rules—which in some peopole's opinion they did—then they would bend them out of recognition. To coin a British phrase, what they got up to just wasn't cricket. Worse than that, often it didn't much resemble tennis either. They were past masters at the change of pace, switching suddenly from conventional serve and volley aggression to total defense based on the lob. They were quick enough to chase down all but the most cleverly angled smash when positioned near the stop-netting on clay, and even if their opponents did end up winning the point, their arms were hanging off by the end of the game.

Then there was Nastase's favourite ploy, which he still uses in team tennis, of edging close to the centre line and bobbing about at the net while the opponent was getting ready to deliver a second serve. It is, quite simply, an attempt to distract. It would not, of course, be wise to try it on a first serve, because the temptation offered the server of wasting that delivery just to gain the satisfaction of hitting Nastase in the eye would be more than many players could resist.

The relationship between Tiriac and Nastase was cemented during the remainder of 1966 and 1967 when both men toured the world circuit and, interestingly from the point of view of Ilie's ultimate development as a player capable of winning major titles on grass, they spent several weeks in India.

'We played on cow-dung as well, but mostly grass,' said Nastase. 'It was good practice for me. I had never seen grass courts before. They had good players there too. Kodes and Metreveli, as well as Prem Lall and Jaidip Mukerjea who were very tough on their own courts.'

Not just in India but throughout Europe and, when he finally got accepted for the Riordan circuit, in the United States as well, Ilie was led around the world by his faithful father-figure, Tiriac. 'We shared rooms together, we ate together, I watched all his matches,' Tiriac recalled. 'I was tough with him. I tried to bring him out. I accused him of having no personality of his own. The tennis-court was his world but as soon as he stepped off it he became a completely different person, shy, insecure. He did everything I said. Then suddenly he decided to have his own personality. But that comes later in the story.'

There was little doubt that in those early years of 1967 and 1968, Nastase's whole world revolved round Tiriac. Lars Myhrman, the young Swedish official who runs the Bastaad tournament and now represents all European tournament directors on the Pro Council, remembers the first time Ilie played at Bastaad.

'He had just arrived from another small Swedish tournament where he had been playing with Tiriac and Martin Mulligan and he was a very scruffy-looking fellow wearing a tattered red track-suit,' said Myhrman. 'Early in the week we had a party for the players and Ilie came along without Tiriac. For a bit of fun someone phoned up Radio Luxembourg and asked them to play a song for Ilie. I think it was his birthday or something. And I will always remember his reaction when the tune came up because the first thing he said was "I hope Tiriac hears this".'

The need for recognition as well as acceptance by his peers later became one of the most obvious traits of Nastase's character. But in these early years on the circuit it was almost exclusively Tiriac's attention he sought. And sometimes he got more of Ion's attention—one might even say devotion—than he could reasonably have expected or even wanted.

'One year I got arrested for Nastase in Hampton, Virginia,' growled Tiriac with his marvellously understated sense of the dramatic. 'He was fooling around at the stadium with an usher who happened to be the wife of a local policeman. Nothing serious, really, just chatting her up and arsing around while she was on duty at one of the entrances to the court. I happen to come by just as Nastase skips off and the cop appears. He's only a little guy but he pulls out his gun, sticks it in my ribs with his finger on the trigger and pushes me against the wall.

'He slaps a pair of handcuffs on me and twists them until my wrists start to bleed, and he forces me outside into his patrol car. People see what is happening and tell Ilie who threatens to pull out of the tournament unless I am released. A senior police officer pleads with the little cop to let me go but it is his arrest and under Virginian law only a judge can order someone's release once he has been formally arrested. I guess I had been formally arrested although no one seemed to know what for.'

After much ado ' about what was—by Nastase's standards at least—almost nothing, Tiriac, the epitome of 'the savage bull who doth bear the yoke', was finally released, snorting and complaining, after tournament officials had soothed the policeman's wounded pride and had persuaded him to bend Virginian law.

On another occasion at Viareggio in Italy, Tiriac took it upon himself to go to Nastase's aide in a rare locker-room brawl and found it an equally fruitless exercise. The incident occurred a day after the normally placid Yugoslav, Zeljko Franulovic, had walked off court at 6 all in the third set when Nastase's antics finally wore his patience to the bone. Franulovic and his compatriot, Boro Jovanovic, were discussing the match within earshot of Ilie. Understanding enough Croatian to know what they were talking about, Nastase swore at them and Zeljko, still seething over what had happened, reacted by slapping the Romanian around the ear.

'This I don't like,' exlained Tiriac, 'so I grab Zeljko round the throat and am ready to clean the locker-room with him. But other players grab my arms and pull me away. Two days later I walk in to change for practice and I find Ilie and Zeljko laughing and fooling around together. So I say, "What is all this? Two days ago I nearly kill Zeljko for you and now you joke with him." '

Tiriac spreads his arms wide and shakes his curly head. 'But that is typical Nastase. He's always like that. His mood changes so quickly. You can never tell exactly what it is in his mind that switches so fast—nerves, tension. One minute he's funny then suddenly he's angry. It has now become a chronic problem.'

By the time Nastase and Tiriac had welded themselves into a combination strong enough to take Romania to the final of the Davis Cup, against the United States in 1969, Ilie was growing rapidly in self-confidence, both as a person and as a player. Inevitably, as success started to pile upon success and the newspaper headlines kept reminding him of how great he was, Ilie began to view Tiriac's domineering, if protective, presence as a threat to his freedom and individuality. Was he not a better player than Tiriac? Was he not the one everyone wanted to watch?

'As I said, he decided to have his own personality at last,' said Tiriac. 'Like a bird who discovers how to walk, then to fly and he's gone. Suddenly I could not control him any more. Soon I was telling him things I did *not* want him to do, knowing that he would do the opposite to what I told him. It was impossible.'

The trouble that had been simmering below the surface for about a year finally broke out into the open in the spring of 1972 at the French Open. 'He had lost in the first round of the singles after being seeded and we had to play doubles against the Belgians, Mignot and Holmbergen,' Tiriac explained. 'It was very cold that evening and Ilie didn't want to play. I know how he felt. It is tough to get yourself up for a match like that. But, shit, we were good then and were favourites to take the title. But Ilie comes out and plays with one hand in his pocket. I'm jumping all over the court trying to make up for him but we lose and I say, "OK, that's it. It's finished".'

According to Tiriac he left the door open for Nastase to resume the partnership at the West German Open in Hamburg later that summer. But Ilie said he wasn't playing doubles so Tiriac eventually got into the draw at the last minute, as a substitute for the injured Wilhelm Bungert who was to have partnered Bob Hewitt. When he was called to the referee's office to be given this news, Tiriac saw Nastase's name in the draw with Jan Kodes. 'We ended up playing each other in the final. Hewitt had just played the final of the singles and was really tired and we lost in five sets. Nastase was leaping about, playing like crazy.' Tiriac paused to light another cigarette and then fell silent for a few seconds. Even then, five years later, the memory was still tinged with resentment.

'I don't think he tried to trick me—at least not in an evil way,' Tiriac continued thoughtfully. 'I think he was just too timid to tell me he was going to play with Kodes. But that was just the first of many things. Little things, perhaps, but at the time I could not accept them. I could not accept that Nastase would do things against me. I felt he owed me more than that. Now I am more mature and I realize it was normal under the circumstances. It had to happen.'

The fact that Ilie and Dominique became engaged during the summer of 1972 did not make matters any easier for Tiriac. But if there was any jealousy on his part, he never allowed Dominique to see it. 'He has always been very pleasant and courteous with me,' she says. But by the end of the year Tiriac and Nastase were no longer speaking. The crack of two mighty egos colliding had reverberated round the tennis world and now there was nothing but silence. Not even in the annals of Hollywood, where movie stars have been known to turn the air blue with frigidity while co-existing on a film set, has a relationship been iced over with quite such glacial totality. When it is said that not a word passed between them for four years that is literally the truth.

They passed each other in hotel lobbies and airport lounges; changed on opposite sides of the same locker-rooms; and, quite incredibly, twice played Davis Cup doubles together, against Spain and Italy.

'It was not necessary for us to speak,' said Tiriac coldly. 'We could close our eyes and play the game.'

Playing wordlessly from instinct and memory, they won both those doubles in five sets. But though they might have been a team on court in the strictest sense of the term, there was certainly nothing that remotely resembled team spirit in the Romanian camp and, after the débâcle in Bucharest against the United States—a disaster which just preceded the final split between them—Nastase and Tiriac never again managed to take their country to the final of the Davis Cup.

Everyone in Romanian tennis was embarrassed by the feud and both men had their supporters. Vague attempts were made to bring them together but Tiriac was too proud to make a move and Nastase, having let the thing go too far, had boxed himself into a corner.

He didn't know how to get out of it gracefully and worse still, he didn't need to. He was a super star; one of the four or five best players in the world and earning a fortune. Who needed Tiriac?

'If he didn't need me, he needed someone,' insisted Tiriac. 'Nastase always should have someone to take care of him. No one is going to argue that he is not the most gifted player in the world but he needs to organize his tennis better. He needs someone to work with him, to encourage him. But, of course, only someone he respects.'

And so the silence continued and at times it was deafening. The height of absurdity was reached during the US Open in 1975 when Mikette, the beautiful Austrian girl Tiriac had fallen for when they met at a party in Paris the previous year, was invited by designer Oleg Cassini to stay at his Gramercy Park house in Manhattan. The third-floor bedroom is not particularly large but that did not deter Tiriac who, at Oleg's insistence, moved in as soon as he arrived for the Championships. Eyes atwinkle but pretending to be quite ignorant of the social *faux pas* he was about to commit, Cassini then invited Ilie and Nikki to stay and installed them in the more spacious room on the second floor. Like most New York brownstones, the Cassini house is large, in the sense that there are a lot of rooms but as they are all stacked on top of one another, it is impossible not to bump into other occupants either going up or coming down the stairs. On a dark night it is also possible to bump into suits of armour, coats of arms and pennants that seemed to have survived from the Crusades and other bits of medieval memorabilia. Meeting Tiriac on the stairs in that house would have been enought to make Richard the Lionheart pause. But it did nothing to break the ice between the two feuding Romanians.

One evening, as chance would have it, both couples arrived back from dinner at precisely the same moment. Ilie, of course, had forgotten his keys. So as Nikki and Mikette smiled weakly at each other, Tiriac opened the door and Ilie strode in, looking neither to right nor left. The quartet then trudged up the stairs in silence, past the first-floor bedroom where the cunning Cassini lay sprawled on his four-poster bed watching TV, and retired to their separate rooms.

Breakfast-time was an even greater test of the pair's stubbornness. While Oleg, as suave as a silver fox even when attired in flowing bathrobe, answered the phone, yelled at the housekeeper and ordered more coffee, Nikki and Mikette nattered away like old friends and Tiriac spoke to Nikki and Ilie spoke to Mikette. But the two players never exchanged so much as a glance. For one another, they simply did not exist.

'It was bizarre,' Mikette told me. 'The atmosphere was very strange indeed. But actually I think Nikki and I helped to bring them together again because we got on so well. Nikki is such an open, lovely person it is impossible not to like her.'

So appropriately, perhaps, it required a dazzling blonde and a beautiful brunette to force the first crack in the wall of silence and animosity that stood between their men. But it was not until Wimbledon 1976—nine months later—that Mitch Oprea finally coaxed them back into verbal contact by acting as liaison-man when Tiriac was looking for a player to fill in for an exhibition match he was arranging. Trying to make it look the most natural thing in the world, Mitch casually began talking to both of them as they dressed on opposite sides of the men's changing room at the All England Club. Suddenly they were talking to each other and although both were too proud to acknowledge that anything of moment had occurred, one could almost see the ice starting to melt. 'Even now he has his life, I have my life,' Tiriac is quick to point out. 'I make a deal for him now and again. It's business. With Nastase you can do so much. He has charisma and deep down he's a great guy. Very reliable. If he says he'll fly to Virginia Beach for an exhibition match in three weeks time, he'll be there. Maybe for the money; maybe for personal reasons. But he'll do it. He's never let me down.'

And so a strange and complex relationship continues. It can never be the same as it was before—nor should it be—but there is a mutual respect there now and that will prove a more durable bond than hero-worship.

4

DOMINIQUE

Ever since the days of long, white flannels and boaters, male tennis-players have exuded an aura of subdued and slightly sophisticated sex appeal. It wasn't merely a fascination with his forehand that drew Marlene Dietrich in the thirties to the Los Angeles Tennis Club to watch Fred Perry—rumour has it that they became good friends—and when shorts became the fashion, the allure was only heightened. There is a whole generation of solidly married English ladies, now nearing middle age, who would confess to having had their female instincts awakened by the sight of Ashley Cooper's legs or the dazzling smile of a blond Adonis called Lew Hoad. For the modern generation, the phenomenon manifested itself in the teeny-bopper adulation that hit Bjorn Borg at Wimbledon a few years ago and then, for no apparent reason, transferred itself to Ilie Nastase in 1977.

'I don't know why they like me,' said Ilie with his deadpan humour after hordes of squealing schoolgirls had nearly caused a riot when he played a match out on court 14 during Centenary Wimbledon, 'I am thirty-one, married and very ugly.'

The fact that he was married at all would, one might have thought, been sufficient to dampen the teenagers' ardour but Ilie, as the world knows, is not married to just anyone. Among a group of wives who must rate favourably in the beauty stakes alongside any women married to men of a single profession be they athletes, film stars or oil sheikhs, Dominique Nastase stands out as something special.

An eye-popping, head-turning brunette with liquid, brown eyes and a large, sensuous mouth, Dominique, or Nikki as she is known to her husband and friends, has the kind of slim, willowy figure that fashion houses—not to mention a large majority of the world's male population—dream about. She has an impish, almost giggly sense of humour; a will of iron and an over-protective nature that tends to make her unnecessarily suspicious of things she does not properly understand. She also has a smile that would light up the Arc de Triomphe. Quite understandably, Ilie Nastase fell for all of that and despite the numerous girls he jokingly called 'my fiancée' before his marriage and the variety of women he has been known to ogle at parties since, Nikki is the only person with whom he has ever been in love.

45

He has his sister-in-law, Nathalie, to thank for that. If she had not fallen for him with the same kind of schoolgirl's crush that seems to affect so many of his teenage fans to this day, it is quite possible Ilie and Dominique would never have met.

Nathalie Grazia was fourteen when she decided that a tennis-player called Ilie Nastase was to be her idol. The youngest daughter of a wealthy Franco–Belgian banking family, Nathalie was overjoyed when she saw that Nastase was among the players entered for a tournament in Brussels in 1970. Her enthusiasm was so infectious that her sister, Dominique, who had never watched, let alone played, a game of tennis in her life, was persuaded to accompany Nathalie to the matches.

'Actually I was with my fiancé that first year,' Dominique said. She was curled up one April afternoon in an armchair of the Nastases' new and expensively renovated farmhouse in the village of La Basoche, just south of Paris. Seven years had elapsed since she first set eyes on the man she would marry and inevitably things seemed strange to her as she looked back, with hindsight and experience.

'My fiancé was Belgian, six months older than me and very handsome. He was the very first boy I ever went out with and I was engaged to him for two years. Can you believe what a stupid girl I was?' She laughed gently and flicked the long dark hair out of her eyes. 'But, of course, I did not know any better. My parents were very strict and I did not go out with a boy at all until I was eighteen. Really—not even out to a dance or to dinner. In fact I never thought about boys much when I was at school. I had a girl-friend who was interested in the same subjects as me, like history, chemistry, biology and languages, and we just worked very hard and that was it. But by the time I was eighteen I had had enough of school and was working very badly. I refused to go on to university. I just wanted to start living a little. So I got engaged immediately. Really dumb, I was.'

By all accounts, Dominique was a lively, tomboyish little girl who, as a six- or seven-year-old, got involved in all the games played by her older brothers, Daniel, Bernard and Jean.

'I had a great time playing Indians, climbing trees and getting tied up as the poor innocent victim,' she recalled. 'But even that wasn't as much fun as my first convent school. I think that was the best time of my life. I had lots of friends and no responsibility and the nuns were very nice. I just remember laughing all the time.'

Although she says she is no longer a practising Catholic, a large crucifix hangs over the marriage bed at La Basoche. 'I don't know. Perhaps my second convent put me off religion just a little bit. The nuns did not seem like proper nuns to me because they wore ordinary clothes and maybe they did not act so much like nuns either. But the crucifix is there because I think one must believe in something.'

Dominique

Dominique admits to being a well-behaved child mainly because of her fear of authority. 'I remember being very afraid of anyone who had control over me like my parents, the nuns or policemen. I think I have got over that a bit now.'

Again she smiles confidently. You do not survive five years with Ilie Nastase without learning how to cope with people in authority.

But all those kinds of problems were far from her mind when she went to her first tennis tournament on her fiancé's arm, in Brussels in 1970. She remembers being introduced to Arthur Ashe, Bob Carmichael, Tom Okker, Andres Gimeno and a few of the other players. She also watched one of Ilie's matches and said hello to him briefly.

'Nothing happened,' she said. 'It wasn't love at first sight or anything. If it hadn't been for Nathalie, Ilie probably wouldn't have crossed my mind until I went to the tennis again the following year. But with Nathalie cutting articles about him out of the tennis magazines and keeping a scrap-book of his pictures, it was a little difficult to forget him completely.'

When Dominique did return to the tennis in 1971, she no longer had a fiancé and the first person she ran into was Bob Carmichael, a veteran Australian pro who has been adding his own brand of individuality and dry humour to the circuit for about as long as anyone can remember. Nicknamed 'Nailbags' because he began life as a carpenter in Melbourne, Carmichael has copper-coloured hair, a well-chiselled Aussie face and large freckled forearms. In a deep baritone voice that is sometimes barely audible, 'Nailbags' will complain about his lot in life whenever a linesman, an umpire or a girl, fails to follow his line of logic. Having hauled himself up through the echelons of professional tennis to a point where he became good enough to reach the quarter-finals at Wimbledon and worry the best players in the world, Carmichael numbers persistency and a relentless pursuit of his goal among his strongest qualities. And they do not just apply on the tennis-court. Dominique Grazia was not the first girl to discover that.

When 'Nailbags' asked for a date that evening, Dominique somehow avoided the issue and left the club never expecting to hear from him again. 'It was nothing against him,' explained Dominique. 'Bob is a nice guy although I did hear he had a reputation as a bit of a playboy. But he is not quite my type. Perhaps if he had dark hair and Latin looks … Anyway I was very surprised when he called that evening, having somehow found my telephone number. Finally I agreed to go out just because I felt like dancing. We went to a discothèque called Fashion which was about the only place to go in Brussels in those days. A lot of the tennis-players were there, including Ion Tiriac who looked very scary in the half-light with his big black moustache. Someone told me Ilie was there, too, but I never

47

actually saw him. He was probably busy with some birds in a corner somewhere.'

Again that might have been the end of it but for Nathalie, whose persistence matched even Carmichael's. Later that summer she persuaded her mother to take her to New York so that they could watch the US Open at Forest Hills.

'It seemed like such a good chance to see New York—I had never been to the States at that time—so I said I would go along, too,' said Dominique. 'I was not thinking about the tennis.'

But Nathalie was. By the second day of the championships Mrs Grazia and both her daughters were wending their way round the outside courts at the West Side tennis club, looking for a doubles match featuring Bob Hewitt and Frew McMillan and Ion Tiriac and Ilie Nastase. 'Ilie had already lost in the singles and as Nathalie was determined to see him play, we had to find this doubles match,' explained Dominique. 'Eventually we discovered it was on the Grandstand Court just near the main stadium. But there were not so many people at Forest Hills during the early rounds of a tournament in those days and I think the whole crowd totalled about half a dozen for this match. Because of Nathalie all three of us cheered like crazy for Ilie and Ion and Hewitt got really mad. We made so much noise Ilie thought we must be Romanians!'

Dominique found herself being dragged back to the Grandstand Court later in the day for a mixed doubles in which Nastase was partnering Rosie Casals. As soon as the match ended, a Romanian friend of Nastase's came over to Dominique with proof that Ilie had been watching something other than the ball that afternoon. It came in the form of a request that she wait for a few minutes because Ilie wanted to talk to her.

Mrs Grazia and Nathalie had wandered off by the time Ilie had towelled down and Dominique was alone when he found her waiting patiently between a couple of courts on a hot September evening. 'We talked for about half an hour,' said Dominique. 'But it was not too easy because my English was terrible at the time and I could not understand Ilie's French too well. But that did not stop him asking me out to dinner.'

Mrs Grazia, a cultured woman of great charm and ease of manner, deftly saved her daughter from being carried off into the New York night by what she considered to be a wild Romanian youth. When she and Nathalie returned, she simply suggested that all four of them have dinner together. Ilie, passing the first test, readily agreed, and fifteen-year-old Nathalie blushed with happiness at the thought of spending a whole evening so close to her idol. She didn't know what she had started.

The following night Dominique and Ilie dined alone and ended up at the Hippopotamus, one of Manhattan's leading East Side discothèques, with several other players, dancing till the early hours.

Dominique

Even though he had been a bit of a late starter himself, Ilie had known enough girls by the time he was twenty-four to make a quick and accurate evaluation of Dominique Grazia. She was special, and before the week was out he had fallen madly in love with her. That was fine with everyone except Rosie Casals—and her reasons were purely professional. She and Ilie had reached the semi-final of the mixed doubles and had an excellent chance of taking the title.

Ilie, however, had another partner in mind and she couldn't even hit a ball over a net. The Grazias had to return to Brussels midway through the second week of Forest Hills and Ilie, in his mad impulsive way, wanted to go with them. The fact that he had to be in Los Angeles for the Pacific Southwest ten days later did not deter him in the least. Why let an ocean stand between you and the woman you love? Or a mixed doubles match for that matter. Rosie didn't quite see it that way and the little San Franciscan said so in language that would have coloured the cheeks of the sailors in Sausalito. But Ilie went.

Checking into the Hilton in Brussels, he had most of his meals at the Grazias' house and stayed just three days. Then he flew back to Los Angeles. 'It was such a nice romance,' said Dominique. She was laughing when she said it but she couldn't quite hide the sincerity behind her words.

By the time the Stockholm Open came round in November, just two months after their first proper meeting, Ilie was already calling Dominique his fiancée. But this time he meant it. I took engagement pictures of them in the snow outside the Kunglihallen and they appeared to be crazy about each other.

But whereas Ilie skims through life on the surface of his emotions, Dominique, for all her spontaneous vivacity, tends to keep at least one foot planted firmly in reality.

'I knew it was getting serious but I wanted time to think,' she said. 'After breaking off my engagement to the Belgian boy, I had only been free for a year and that is not long when you are twenty-one and have led a very sheltered life.'

So reluctantly Ilie agreed that they should go their own ways for a time. Ilie spent Christmas at home in Bucharest and in the New Year, while he continued his nomadic life on the international circuit, Dominique decided to improve her English by going to live in Cambridge with her brother Jean.

Dominique enjoyed Cambridge but by the time she returned home in the spring of 1972 she knew that the separation had gone on long enough. 'It had been my idea in the first place so I thought I had better do something about ending it before it was too late,' she said.

On reading in the newspaper that Ilie had lost in the first round of the

49

French Open to Adriano Panatta, she decided to send him a telegram that would, if it did nothing else, test his sense of humour.

'Bravo for your brilliant defeat,' it read. The response was immediate. Within twenty-four hours she was in Paris. It was the first time they had seen each other in five months and the mood of that lovely city in the spring—a timeless tonic for those in love—only heightened the pleasure of their reunion.

Dominique had to go to Sorrento with the family during Wimbledon but her mind never strayed far from the restless, riveting and strangely vulnerable athlete who had now, more than ever, become the centre of her life. 'I felt Ilie needed me and by that time I knew I wanted him,' she explained. 'So when we went to Düsseldorf together for a Davis Cup match a week later I asked him to marry me.'

In a gesture so demure and feminine that it was almost oriental, Nikki giggled, her hand masking her mouth. 'Ilie hasn't told you about how I asked him to marry me?' she went on, a gleam coming into her eye that finally hinted at the strength of personality required for a strictly brought-up girl to buck convention and reverse one of the most hallowed traditions in western society. 'We were in the back of a large Mercedes, being driven to a television station just outside Düsseldorf where Ilie was to be interviewed. We were talking about the future and I suddenly thought I had better ask him if he wanted to marry me because he had asked me five or six times before and I had always said "no". I started to get nervous and thought "maybe he won't ask me any more".'

Given the way Ilie felt about her, it was probably a groundless fear but in any case it was never put to the test. By the time they reached their destination Ilie had a real fiancée at last.

Dominique's reappearance in his life just after his first-round defeat in Paris marked the beginning of a twelve-month period that established Nastase as the No 1 player in the world, not merely because of his talent which had been obvious for some time but also as a result of his ability to win big titles, which previously had been open to doubt.

From June 1972 until June the following year Nastase reached the final of Wimbledon and won the US Open at Forest Hills—both grass-court tournaments—retained his Master's title on Mateflex indoors in Barcelona, and won both the Italian and French Open titles on clay. In between he won numerous lesser events, and people in the game, not least those who had to face him across the net, started to wonder who would ever beat him.

Of course as more and more talent came flooding into the game in the early seventies, substantially raising the standard of opposition all players had to face from the first round on, there were many who could, and did, beat Nastase. But none as frequently as Nastase beat himself.

In the course of discussing a slightly different aspect of Ilie's problems with the knowledgeable and sharp-witted *Boston Globe* columnist Bud Collins, I asked Bud if he agreed with some critics who maintain that Nastase, because of his antics and general on-court behaviour, is bad for tennis.

'The first question is not whether Nastase is bad for the game,' Collins replied, 'but whether Nastase is bad for Nastase.'

Certainly it would be difficult to argue that his seemingly uncontrollable temperament has not wrecked his game on innumerable occasions, more often than not completely destroying his chances of victory.

But if Ilie has been bad for himself—and in recent years that has been increasingly the case—then, in that first year of their relationship, Dominique was good for him. He enjoyed the peace of mind that comes from a stable relationship, which for someone who has never experienced it before, offers such a satisfying contrast to the fleeting excitement of the casual sexual encounter.

Ever since Tiriac had got him laid with the traditional Parisian whore, Ilie had expended much of his excess energy on chasing—and catching—girls. For a virile young man on the loose there is nothing that creates quite the same peak of acute anticipation as the possibility of 'scoring' that night with a new girl. But when the opportunities provided by a star's status and an itinerary of constant travel turn that possibility into probability, the urge remains but the satisfaction wanes. The chase becomes a ritual—distracting, demanding and for any athlete let alone one of Ilie's temperament ultimately disastrous. Trying to decide which of half-a-dozen pretty girls ogling you from the stands will provide the most thrills in bed is hardly conducive to concentrating on a top-spin forehand. And concentration, whether on forehands, backhands, girls or anything else, has never been Ilie's strong point.

But as soon as Dominique became a permanent presence in his life, the need to search for social distraction was eliminated. He was in love with her and in love with his profession. On court and off, he was fulfilled—at least until the pressures started to mount.

Reaching the top and staying there are two different things and for a performer of natural, artistic talent the latter is always harder. Ilie enjoys the fun and the by-play of tennis too much to endure the daily grind of beating off hungry pretenders to his throne. Caught in a dilemma as insoluble and somewhat similar to that of Ole Man River, he was often a-bored of winning but a-feared of losing. And when the ugly face of defeat would loom behind the clown's mask, happiness would turn to anger, a playful gesture to bitter confrontation. Then even Dominique could not help.

'At the beginning I thought it was a very attractive life,' Dominique

51

said as we continued our talk one evening at La Basoche. 'Then you start to realize that it can be hard, too. Of course it can be fun and exciting but there are some very bad days. 1973, generally, was a very good year. Ilie got tired sometimes because he was playing so much and the ATP boycott at Wimbledon when everybody was blaming him for playing made me so mad, but on the whole it was a great period. I quickly learned to enjoy watching tennis and at first I wanted him to win—I was always so nervous wanting him to win. But now I am only nervous in case he does something wrong. Winning or losing is no longer as important as getting him through a match without a big fight.

'But that is a special problem one has with Ilie. At least I have the advantage of being with a good player. Some wives are not so lucky as me. We have the highs to go with the lows but I don't know what the other wives do when their husbands are losing in the first and second rounds nearly every week. That must be really terrible.'

Certainly one requires a strong constitution to handle the rigours of a touring pro's wife, no matter how successful your husband might be.

But it was some time before Dominique had to face the reality of the bad days. In 1972 and through most of 1973 it was, literally and figuratively, honeymoon time. On 7 December 1972 Ilie and the girl he liked to call Nikki were married in a civil ceremony in Brussels. Seven days later they were married again in traditional style at the little village church at La Basoche.

'That was just to make sure,' Dominique laughed. Actually a third ceremony was planned in Bucharest so that they could get the benediction of the Pope. But there were complications about the legality of another church wedding which arose over the differences between the Roman Catholic and Greek Orthodox Churches, and eventually the idea was scrapped.

Obviously marriage to the beautiful Dominique did wonders for Ilie's confidence and morale. In the six years that had passed since he had first emerged from the backwater of Bucharest as a shy, uncertain tennis-player he had established himself as an increasingly affluent international star and husband of one of the most desirable young women in Europe.

He had just bought himself a villa in Bucharest where his parents would be able to live in the manner to which he was rapidly becoming accustomed, and for himself and his bride there was a luxury apartment in Brussels. Soon work would start on renovating the farmhouse he had bought from the Rothschilds at La Basoche—the house that would become his permanent home.

But all this side of his life just happened—little of it was planned by the maestro himself. Dominique did most of the long-range thinking while Ilie raced round the world hitting tennis-balls, each year in more cities than most people visit in a lifetime. The man who would soon earn a million dollars in prize-money alone was not even aware how much money he had married.

'I knew Nikki's parents were rich, sure,' he told me. 'But I never realized the Grazias owned half the village at La Basoche and most of the land around it. Bloody hell, man, that's a lot of land, so near to Paris and everything!'

But, like so many before him, Ilie soon discovered that money, even when it comes by the bucketful, does not guarantee an easy life. A luxurious life, perhaps. But not an easy one; not one free of anguish and anger and exhaustion. Especially not if your name is Ilie Nastase.

It might have been easier for him had he been playing in the happy-go-lucky days of tennis shamateurism when the standards were lower, the rules looser, and the game's star performers able to demand their own under-the-table prices before they walked on court. In the years before Open Tennis arrived in 1968 it had been possible for Roy Emerson to drink beer till 5 am and then rely on his superb physical condition to see him through the early rounds of a tournament, or for the legendary Whitney Reed—the nearest thing the fifties and sixties had to a Nastase in terms of talent and eccentricity—to play cards all night and still befuddle the opposition next day.

But by the time the seventies dawned the game's administrators—the ILTF and the ATP, separately at first and then together under the aegis of the Pro Council—were trying to put their unruly house in order. None too soon, as professional tennis blossomed overnight into a multi-million-dollar sport, rules, rankings and regulations necessary for the good of the game as a whole were instigated—rules that, in general, were good for the majority of players. But not necessarily for the special minority. And most certainly not for Ilie Nastase.

Like a magnificent wild stallion suddenly corralled, Nastase bucked and reared as the noose tightened round his free-flowing mane and a battle was joined that would never see a victor.

Inevitably Dominique, as the person closest to Ilie, soon started to show the scars of that battle, emotionally and in a minor way, physically, too. 'My hands are cold and sweaty,' she told San Franciscan tennis writer Susie Trees, who has become a close friend in recent years. They were watching Ilie in one of his tantrums at Wimbledon. 'Can you see how red my thumb is from biting it all the time?' It was raw.

On other occasions, I have seen her hands shake as she wrestles with the fear that grips her every time her husband brings the wrath of the crowd and the rage of officialdom down on his head. Frequently Dominique will get up and leave in the middle of a match when the tension becomes too much. 'I feel everything he feels out there,' she says. 'I understand so well what he goes through. I die when I see him play sometimes. That is why I cannot travel with him all the time now. He would drive me crazy. Maybe I am a little crazy already.'

While Dominique was pregnant and after Nathalie was born, in March 1975, she did spend weeks away from the circuit and often weeks away from Ilie. Rumours that the marriage was in trouble started to circulate and finally Nigel Dempster, ace gossip columnist of the *Daily Mail*, put it up in banner headlines for the world to see.

The first hint of trouble came during the Dewar Cup in London late in 1975. Ilie and Jimmy Connors were as thick as thieves at the time, clowning their way round the circuit, enjoying their reputation as a couple of outlaws who were the fastest guns in town. That was the year they put on bow ties and bowler hats and took a bottle of champagne on court with them to play Wojtek Fibak and Karl Meiler in the doubles final. It was supposed to be a joke but like most of their jokes it was carried too far. Dominique, who has never been particularly fond of Connors, found some of their off-court antics pretty humourless as well and rather than face her disapproval after a night on the town, Ilie ended up spending a couple of nights in Jimmy's spare bed.

Ilie spent much of the rest of that year in Sweden, first for the Stockholm Open; then for the Commercial Union Masters which was also played in Stockholm in 1975; and finally in his temporary role as coach and sparring partner to the Swedish Davis Cup team which was due to play the final against Czechoslovakia in the third week of December.

Everything was fine during the first few weeks when Dominique was with him, but when she left Ilie did not seem to care how many blondes he was seen around with. Stockholm, after all, is not the best city in which to leave a restless husband. But nothing serious came of it. Wives of superstars who concern themselves with every girl who passes in the night when their husbnds are far away soon end up with valium as a companion. However, by the time Ilie went off to Hawaii in the spring to begin his first season with World Team Tennis, the Nastases' lack of togetherness had become too obvious to survive the circuit gossip. Using the baby as a perfectly valid excuse, Dominique had refused to move the household to Honolulu for three months so the separations, already extensive because of his tournament travelling schedule earlier in the year, grew longer. Hating Team Tennis, missing the traditional championships in Rome and Paris that had become so much a part of his yearly routine, and worried about his marriage, Ilie succumbed to the inevitable temptation and sought solace elsewhere.

'It was my fault,' he admitted readily when we talked about his relationship with Nikki over lunch in Bucharest a year later. 'I was away so much that something was bound to go wrong sooner or later.'

Dominique

When Ilie's social activities in Hawaii appeared in the press, Dominique could no longer pretend the problem was inconsequential. Soon reporters were phoning La Basoche and one asked Dominique directly for her reaction to reports that her husband was going out with an Air France stewardess. 'Nikki phoned me in Honolulu to find out what was happening and I told her "Not Air France in Hawaii, dummy".' Ilie smiled but the expression on his face suggested that the conversation linking a French village and a Hawaian island had gone a lot deeper than a few wisecracks. 'Actually she was a Norwegian girl who flew with Pan Am,' he went on. 'She was very beautiful but I was never emotionally involved with her.'

He broke off to order lunch. We were eating on the terrace of a restaurant in Baneasa Park, basking in the warm spring sunshine as we watched lovers drift by in little rowing-boats on the lake. A man eating at the table directly behind Ilie tilted his chair backwards and pointedly tried to eavesdrop on our conversation. He was being too obvious for even the silliest secret agent and Ilie, who doesn't need to worry about such things in Bucharest, turned his back and ignored him.

'I think Nikki is very heroic,' he went on, taking frequent sips of mineral water. 'For five years now she has put up with me and that's a long time. Really I don't know how anyone could stand me for more than three months. I am so crazy—changing moods and ideas all the time. Nikki is a very calm person compared with me and that is a big help. It is a good contrast. Also she has a good education which makes her self-sufficient to an extent. She doesn't have to sit around waiting for me to finish practising or playing or whatever.'

The fish arrived with a request from the waiter for an autograph. Nastase signed and then continued. 'Nikki's family are a big help, too, because they are all very close and look after each other. It seems that most brothers and sisters fight all the time but not the Grazias. They have a very strong family feeling. Their whole philosophy is based on the need to build and save for the next generation.' Ilie picked at a bone and pulled a face. 'Jesus, when I spend a couple of thousand dollars on a new stereo set or something they say "You have a daughter now—you should think of her future". Hell, I can't be like that, it's just not my nature. But I'm not saying it's bad. You should plan a little but with this crazy life I lead it is so difficult to look ahead and know what is going to happen next.'

Predicting what the future holds in store for any marriage in this day and age is a dangerous business but Ilie and Dominique at least have one thing going for them. They are still in love with one another. There is, in fact, little wrong with their marriage that a little bit of privacy wouldn't cure. When they are alone and relaxed, they are like a couple of teenagers, playful, affectionate, romantic. It doesn't seem to matter that they enjoy different things. Before Ilie gets up in the morning—he'll sleep till 10.30 by choice although he's good at getting up early when he has to—Nikki plays her favourite records of Puccini or Verdi. After breakfast Ilie changes the tempo to Presley and pop. But in the evening they both watch television together for hours. Away from home, Dominique and Ilie will seek out the best restaurants in whichever town they happen to be that week, although after a hard match Ilie will frequently order room service and eat dinner in front of the TV. When he is playing, his diet seldom varies from the basic steak and salad with a couple of glasses of red wine.

Out on the town, both enjoy discothèques but whereas Nikki loves to dance, strangely for a man who moves so well on a tennis-court, Ilie rarely strays from his seat. More than any lack of rhythm, it is a basic self-consciousness that keeps him off the dance-floor. He doesn't think he is a particularly good dancer and is therefore shy about it.

He is not necessarily reticent, however, about expressing his interest in a pretty girl—outrageously if he is alone, or in a more subdued fashion if Nikki is with him. Like a great many hot-blooded men, Nastase was fascinated by Bianca Jagger when she attended the French Championships practically every day in 1977. After watching her swirl and gyrate round the dance-floor in a flame-red dress one evening at Castel's Ilie quickly got himself invited over to her table by Jacques Renevand, the former French Davis Cup player who is manager of the best discothèque in Paris. Dominique was there that night, dancing with her brother Bernard and a couple of other friends in their party, not bothering to follow Ilie over to Bianca's table. She is much too cool a lady for that.

At about 3 am Dominique finally made a move. 'If Ilie has finished gazing at his lady love, we had better go,' she said with a grin that masked any hint of concern. 'He's got a doubles match tomorrow and you never know what time they'll schedule it for.'

The fact that they left arm-in-arm without the hint of a row could so easily have been overlooked by some eager gossip columnist searching for a juicy item. In that rarified and very sophisticated world there is a constant undercurrent of attraction between the Beautiful People. Often the reason is that they are, quite simply, beautiful. It is said that there is no smoke without fire but a fire can smoulder without ever bursting into flame.

No flame ever engulfed the brief, smouldering attraction Ilie felt for Bianca and the same was true when he ran into Claudia Cardinale at Castel's a few weeks later, when he had left Dominique and the family in Los Angeles to return to Paris for a Davis Cup tie against France. With Nikki 6,000 miles away, there was every opportunity to let the fire run out of control. But by the time Ilie, Mitch Oprea, Claudia and the two friends who were escorting her had moved on to Le Privé, another elegant discothéque across town, Nastase was feeling the effect of having tried to drown the memories of a badly played match against François Jauffret which lost Romania the tie. Basically a non-drinker, it doesn't take very much to get him happy on the rare occasions he does decide to hit the bottle. A couple of drinks at Le Privé were enough to overcome Ilie's inhibitions about dancing and it was while they were entwined in each other's arms during a slow number, that he thought of whispering sinful suggestions into her ear about slipping off into the night. But then he remembered all the drink he had consumed and glanced across the room at the two well-built French actors who seemed to be in charge of Claudia for the evening and forgot it. A little while later Miss Cardinale left with her friends and Ilie took his headache to bed.

'That's typical,' said Mitch disgustedly when we were discussing nights on the town with Ilie one day. 'I don't give a damn whether he ends up with a girl or not but we spend so much time talking about it and keeping our options open and all that bullshit that in the end it's a sure thing that neither of us is going to get laid.'

Mitch is right. For the most part, Ilie talks hot and heavy but when it gets down to the nitty-gritty, he tends to fade, realizing that the only person he really wants to be in bed with is Madame Nastase.

The publicity; the stardom; the star-fuckers; the opportunities; the travel; the loneliness; the hangers-on egging him on—all this puts so much pressure on a relationship that the newsworthy angle should not be that a marriage is in trouble but that it survives. It would be tragic if the marriage of Ilie and Dominique did not survive because, in their strangely different ways, they have much to give each other and, as I have said, they are in love. What the marriage needs most of all is space, peace and understanding. For as long as Ilie continues to charge round the world at his present demented speed that is going to be difficult to achieve. But relatives and close friends on both sides could help by taking a pace back; by not crowding in with reminders of family obligations or pleas for assistance or unnecessary advice and by letting them live, wherever and whenever, as normally as possible.

What is 'normal'? The word means something different for all of us. Ilie and Dominique know what is normal for them and they should be allowed to get on with it as best they can. If they try to give too much of themselves to those around them, they will end up having nothing to give each other. It would be sad if that were allowed to happen.

5

THE MONEY MEN

Apart from Ion Tiriac and Dominique, no one has been closer to Ilie during his professional career than Mitch Oprea, an interesting, complex man who drifted into the role of managing Nastase by virtue of his availability, Romanian heritage, and willingness to tidy up the mass of problems the tempestuous star left in his wake.

But Oprea was only the last in a line of people who had tried to handle Ilie's affairs. First there was Bill Riordan. This big-time entrepreneur from the little town of Salisbury, Maryland, is one of sport's great opportunists. As controversial a character as tennis has produced over the last decade, Riordan possesses a natural knack of taking a tiny strand of truth and weaving it into a colourful tapestry of exaggeration.

His attempts to con the tennis world into believing that his Independent Players Association was a thriving concern with over two hundred members was a good example of his ability to create headlines and propaganda out of virtually nothing. It was certainly true that an organization calling itself the IPA did exist. It ran an indoor circuit in the States during the winter months; maintained offices in Salisbury and employed a secretary and legal counsel. The only thing it was a bit short on was players. A lot of the young college kids who benefited from Riordan's erratic generosity were members of the IPA. But whenever I asked Bill for his official list of members he would maintain that the list was not for publication.

When asked if he was running a secret society, he would answer by saying that he did not want his youngsters to be pressured and threatened by the Association of Tennis Professionals which was, and still is, the only authentic international association for male players in the world.

When the ATP and the game's old amateur governing body, the International Tennis Federation, joined forces to form the Men's International Professional Tennis Council, which now effectively governs the professional end of the game, Riordan quickly started banging on the door demanding admission. It was not a clever move. Riordan had finally allowed his ego to smother his common sense. When the Pro Council invited him to present his case at a formal meeting, he was able to produce only four names of men who were bona fide members of the IPA—his own, two lawyers from Salisbury and Jimmy Connors. That, the Pro Council decided, did not constitute a proper players' association.

But all that was relatively harmless compared with the Riordan-instigated lawsuit Connors brought against the ATP, Jack Kramer, Donald Dell and the then President of the Association, Arthur Ashe. The reasons for the suit being filed in the first place stemmed from some real and some quite imaginary grievances Connors had as a result of being virtually the only top player in the world who had not joined the ATP.

Apart from guaranteeing Riordan continual doses of eagerly-sought publicity—his lopsided grin was never far from Connors' side whenever his client came within camera range off-court—it also guaranteed that everyone sucked into this unnecessary affair would end up spending vast sums in legal fees. In fact, by the time the case was settled out of court—the ATP terminated the whole thing by agreeing to pay the fees of Connors' lawyers —Ashe's Association had been shelling out approximately $30,000 a month to its own lawyers for well over a year. Barely three years old at the time, the ATP could ill afford that kind of drain on its resources and a lot of plans that would have been of great benefit to the game and the players in general had to be shelved while the case went on.

There are those who maintain that Riordan's better qualities outweigh the other side of his activities. I am not one of them. Apart from the lawsuit, which gave professional tennis an image it did not need at that stage of its development, Riordan's whole attitude and style of speech would have been much better suited to boxing. His cheap publicity stunts and constant need to plaster the press with his comments, cast an unhappy atmosphere of bitterness and division over pro tennis—especially in America—during 1974 and 1975.

Later, when Connors, the player he had flaunted so proudly in front of the world, broke with him and—true to the way he had been taught—sued his old mentor, Riordan complained that Jimmy had no class. And it was Bill Riordan who first brought Ilie Nastase to America. I do not suggest that too much should be read into that fact. Riordan, after all, cannot be held responsible for the darker side of Ilie's character nor for the solid schooling he received from Tiriac in the art of cunning gamesmanship. But Riordan was the big man, the Boss if you like, when Ilie first came to the States as an impressionable, inexperienced twenty-year-old and even if Bill did not teach him how to misbehave—there were times when he actually tried to discipline him—the style and atmosphere of the Riordan circuit inevitably rubbed off. If Ilie had begun his career in the States under the personal tutelage of Lamar Hunt, for instance, one presumes he would have been given a slightly different idea of what was and what was not acceptable behaviour. But, like a great many other young players, Nastase reaped the benefit of Riordan's fertile imagination and dynamism. Back in the middle sixties Riordan was an active member of the United States Lawn Tennis Association—an organization which in those days was peopled by nice, moderately intelligent and not very perceptive gentlemen,

The dear old US LTA was paddling around in a different league. Having made Riordan director of the official US LTA indoor circuit, they soon found that they no longer had much say in the way it was run. It was difficult to lodge too many complaints about that because the circuit was an undeniable success in an era when pro tennis was still a backwater sport. But the extent to which the Association had lost control was evident after a few years, when both players and press all automatically referred to it as 'The Riordan circuit'.

Riordan was not, of course, beyond using his official position to establish some useful connections with other national assocations in Eastern Europe. Each. year he arranged for the best young players from the Eastern bloc countries to play his circuit and the opportunities this afforded such promising talent as Jan Kodes and Jan Kukal from Czechoslovakia; Zeljko Franulovic and Nikki Spear from Yugoslavia; and the Hungarians, Peter Szoke and Szabolcs Baranyi, satisfied Riordan's genuine altruistic instincts. But the benefits to the circuit director himself were equally great. The presence of so many different nationalities from strange-sounding places added colour and interest to the tour as it moved through such unsophisticated cities as Hampton, Virginia, and Omaha, Nebraska, and, more important still, Riordan did not have to pay these inexperienced foreigners so much money. The situation changed when Open Tennis established regular prize-money payments but, prior to that, each individual 'amateur' negotiated his own deal with the tournament or circuit director and a lot of the guys were becoming astute businessmen.

Instead of having to fill out his draw with middle-ranked Americans and Australians who added little to the variety of the event and who would demand upwards of $150 per week plus hospitality, Riordan could get a half a dozen eastern Europeans for expenses and a bit of pocket money. It was good business from Riordan's point of view but when the mood took him he could be generous too, occasionally pressing a hundred-dollar bill into a player's hand after a particularly exciting match.

Riordan quickly realized what kind of an attraction the young Romanian could become and treated him accordingly. But there was more to it than simply making a lot of money out of Ilie. Riordan developed a real affection for this engaging, open-hearted clown whose broken English and old-world manners delighted guests when he stayed at the Riordans' house in Salisbury. Inevitably, Riordan was soon putting his sharp business mind to work on Ilie's behalf and as soon as he had fixed a couple of deals, he was announcing to the world that he was Nastase's manager. At that stage Ilie barely understood what a manager was. Certainly he did not understand the idea of exclusivity and as he found it almost impossible to say 'no' whenever anyone tried to help him—a fault that still lingers with him today—Riordan was not the only person acting on Ilie's behalf.

But among all the others who tried there was the only one who counted. Gene Scott had first got to know Ilie as a player, and when he began looking after the interest of a few other foreign players such as Manuel Santana and Pierre Barthes he started working Nastase into his promotional deals.

It would be difficult to imagine two people who presented a greater contrast in style and appearance than Scott and Riordan. By virtue of his Yale background, Long Island manner, boyish goodlooks and outstanding ability as an athlete, Scott is the prototype of Erich Segal's Preppy in *Love Story*. Had he only been able to act as well, Ryan O'Neal would never have got a sniff at the part.

A lawyer by training and a promoter, consultant, agent and writer by profession, Scott was good enough to reach the semi-finals at Forest Hills in 1967, losing to the eventual champion, John Newcombe, and he is still a player of note. But although he has taught himself how to be tough, he lacks the gut-fighting instincts of a Riordan. With his name, contacts and ability, Gene could have grappled for a much larger share of the managerial pie that was there for the taking in the late sixties.

But there were aspects of the business he simply did not enjoy and while Riordan made all the noise and most of the money, Scott became content to fade into the role of adviser and friend. If he felt it had better long-term prospects, he was right. He is still Ilie's friend while neither Riordan nor the next man on the scene, Mark McCormack, is any longer his agent.

As Nastase's name grew and the possibilities of exploiting his unique personality and enormous talent became all too readily apparent, it was inevitable that McCormack's expanding organization, the International Management Corporation, would snap him up. If ever a marriage was doomed from the start, this was it. Nobody could be less suited to fitting into the American corporate image than Ilie Nastase. It will surprise no one to learn that until quite recently he treated formal contracts, legal documents, and binding signatures with carefree disdain. What might come as a greater shock to those who know him only through his on-court reputation is that his word, given face to face to someone he knows and respects, is his bond. Needless to say, that was not the way in which the McCormack organization was prepared to do business. It might have worked had IMC's individual agents been able to handle Nastase on a purely individual basis. Both the jovial, extrovert Bud Stanner, who has an excellent working relationship with another IMC client, John Newcombe, and David Armstrong, a likeable and intelligent young lawyer, enjoyed Ilie as a person and strove hard to make the relationship work. But although Stanner and Armstrong may be fine agents they are not free agents. They work for the Corporation and, true to the American business ethic, the Corporation puts profitmaking first, second and third on its list of priorities. That is fine in as much as business managers are hired to make their clients money.

However, when one is dealing with the delicate psyches and finely tuned bodies of artists and athletes, there are other things that have to be taken into consideration. The IMC balance sheet may look very healthy when it includes a 30 per cent agent's fee for a big-money exhibition match arranged for a client called Bjorn Borg. But the balance sheet does not reveal what it cost Borg, then an overworked and inexperienced eighteen-year-old, to make all that lovely lolly for himself and his managers. On this particular occasion Borg was completing a tournament in Teheran one week before he was due to play in the Stockholm Open—an event which was obviously of great personal importance to him. In the seven days that intervened, IMC had Bjorn fly from Teheran to New York and then down to Hilton Head Island, South Carolina, to play against three of the best players in the world within hours of stepping off the plane.

Before he had the faintest chance of overcoming a crucifying dose of jet lag, Borg was back on a plane for another journey across the Atlantic to Stockholm where he arrived in absolutely no condition to give his best in front of his home crowd. Not surprisingly, his weary body gave up early in the tournament when he pulled a muscle in his leg, and in the circumstances, it was a miracle he got as far as the semi-final. The hyper-critical Swedish press paid scant regard to what Borg had allowed himself to be put through in the preceding ten days and, largely as a result of this experience, Bjorn has rarely been able to handle the special pressures of playing in Sweden since. Was this worth a few thousand dollars in the IMC profit column?

Nastase never paid quite so drastic a price for McCormack's benefit although his travel schedule has been hardly less hectic in recent years. Generally he has proved himself a little less malleable to IMC's profit-making schemes. And that, of course, did not suit the Corporation.

The breaking-point in the Nastase–McCormack relationship came over a deal IMC tried to set up in the Philippines. The original idea was to have Nastase, Rod Laver, Bjorn Borg and possibly Jimmy Connors play a four-man event in Manila in October 1976. Big money was involved for everybody and Ilie's guarantee was set at $65,000. When the McCormack people first spoke to Ilie and Mitch Oprea, who was already acting as unofficial go-between for the Romanian, Nastase agreed to play and signed a contract to do so—specifically for the October date.

Then the date was changed to Janauary 1977. Already weary after a long year's travel, Ilie decided he was no longer interested. Even for that sum of money, a round-the-world haul to Manila was more than he felt he could handle so near the start of another arduous WCT circuit which was due to begin in the States a week after the rescheduled Manila date.

In late October Nastase and Oprea met Stanner and Armstrong at Hilton Head Island, South Carolina. The IMC agents were told that Ilie was no longer interested and that they should find a substitute. That, of course, is never easy. Superstars are a scarce and elusive commodity in pro tennis and anyway promoters in a place like Manila tend to want Nastase above all others.

Concerned that without Ilie the whole deal, which was complicated enough anyway, might fall through, Stanner talked of an even bigger guarantee. Normally IMC takes up to 30 per cent of exhibition or 'special event' money it raises for its clients but Stanner did not need to be told that, when your major talent plays hard to get, a smaller percentage of a big package starts looking better than no package at all.

But still Ilie said no. It wasn't a question of the money. He just didn't want the aggravation of all that extra travel. By the time he spoke to Stanner at Hilton Head, he had already been approached by Pancho Gonzales to play an exhibition match in North Miami on 7 January—a date that would conflict with the Manila event. The money in Miami was $7,500—a poor substitute for $65,000 plus. But Ilie has always admired Gonzales and, as he had to be in Philadelphia for the US Indoors just a couple of weeks later, it made much more sense geographically.

Shortly after the Hilton Head meeting, IMC were informed that Nastase had committed himself to Gonzales. Yet apparently the McCormack people still hoped to change his mind because neither Laver nor Borg were told that Nastase had categorically pulled out.

Nastase returned home to La Basoche in December and as no phone had been installed in his recently renovated house, became difficult to contact. Stanner and Armstrong maintain they made repeated attempts to reach him, without success. However, two days after Christmas Oprea visited the McCormack headquarters in Cleveland to help sort out some of Ilie's taxes. There he found Armstrong still agitating over the possibility of Nastase playing in Manila. So Oprea gave him the number of Ilie's in-laws at La Basoche and he was in Armstrong's office when Ilie finally came on the line. Two months after first having said no, Nastase reiterated that he would not play in the Philippines.

Either the deal did depend entirely on Nastase's participation or it had already fallen through and IMC were merely threshing around for a scapegoat. Whatever the true facts were, Ilie was indeed made the scapegoat. Laver and Borg were told that that the tournament was off because McCormack had been trying to reach Nastase for weeks, and that he had finally come out of hiding and refused to play. Not surprisingly Laver and Borg, who both stood to earn similar sums of money as had been offered to Nastase and who both wanted to play, were not pleased. Laver, in fact, was livid. When I met him in Philadelphia in the third week of January he was as furious about Nastase as I have ever heard him be about anyone, let alone a fellow player. In the bar of the Hilton Inn one evening Laver and John Newcombe, as a couple of old friends and top IMC clients, discussed the possibility of asking McCormack to leave them out of any deal involving Nastase in the future. Such a move would obviously be damaging to Ilie professionally but, having only heard IMC's version of the story, Rod and Newk quite reasonably felt that they should think about safeguarding their own interests.

At the time I knew nothing of the background to the problem. Now the facts as I know them have been laid out here. I have related them in detail because of the serious repercussions the incident could have had—and might still have—on Nastase's reputation for reliability among his fellow professionals. I should, however, make it clear that the story I have related is the version told me by Oprea and Nastase. I went to some pains to get IMC's side to it but without success. I wrote a letter to Stanner, which I handed to him personally on 3 September 1977 at Forest Hills, in which I laid out the facts in abbreviated form and asked for either confirmation or denial.

A few days later I met Armstrong on another subject in the locker-room at the West Side Tennis Club with Allen Fox, a former high-ranking player in the States who is now a business partner of mine. At the end of our meeting, I brought up the subject of my letter to Stanner. Armstrong said he had read it and that, in his opinion, many of the facts were erroneous. He added, however, that he did not wish to dignify the issue with a formal reply. Nor, in conversation, did he specify which facts he considered incorrect. He left me with little option but to draw my own conclusions.

It is possible that the story is not quite as clear-cut as I have related it here but, having carefully weighed what I know of the McCormack organization and what I have come to learn of Nastase's character after following his career for the past ten years, I am satisfied that Oprea's version is essentially correct. No matter what behavioural standards he may abuse on court, it is not in his nature to double-deal off it and, with Oprea at his side, the chances of his inadvertently committing himself to two conflicting events were remote. In any case, he had learned a few tough lessons in the past as a result of the carefree way in which he used to promise his services to anyone who asked. Painfully, he discovered that trying to please all the people all the time—which, instinctively, he would like to do—can lead to a lot of aggravation and not much sleep.

A classic case in point involved promises to play in Jamaica and then also to play an exhibition match in Miami.

Both events were scheduled for the third week of December 1973, immediately after Ilie was due to play in the Commercial Union Masters in Boston. When Richard Russell originally approached him during Forest Hills in September he had agreed to play in Jamaica. Then several weeks later, he also said yes to Gene Scott.

'Shit,' said Ilie when Russell confronted him at the Hynes Auditorium in Boston. 'I forgot.'

After talking it over with Andrew Bloomfield, chairman of the Jamaican Citizens Sports Group that was promoting the Rothmans Spectacular, Russell had wisely decided that it was worth flying to Boston to make sure that Ilie got on the plane.

'I had only had a verbal commitment from him at Forest Hills and had not heard from him since,' said Russell, who, for more than a decade has been the No 1 player in the Caribbean and is now an increasingly influential tennis figure in Jamaica. 'And in any case there were visa problems that needed sorting out between the Jamaican and Romanian Embassies in New York. As it happened, it was fortunate I went. We would never have worked out a solution otherwise.'

The fact that a solution was possible at all was partly due to Russell's flexibility and partly to Ilie's determination not to let either of his friends down. As the Rothmans event was only a sixteen-man draw, there was time to manoeuvre. Luckily, Scott's exhibition was scheduled for the middle of the week so Russell checked the flight times and Ilie readily agreed to play both.

Flying to Kingston on the Monday, he played a young, hard-serving Jamaican called Audley Bell on the Tuesday; flew off next morning to Miami; fulfilled his commitment to Gene on Wednesday night and was back in Kingston in time to play Ove Bengtson in the quarter-final on Thursday evening. Delighting a vociferous crowd who had never seen tennis of this calibre before, Ilie went on to win the tournament, beating Brian Gottfried in the final.

'I thought of going with him to Miami,' admitted Russell. 'But as he had left Nikki here, we reckoned he really did intend to come back! Actually I have never had any reason to doubt his word. I don't care what anyone says, for me Ilie's still one of the nicest guys in the game. Sure, he'd made a mistake agreeing to play for both Gene and myself but no one could have asked him to do more than he did to make up for it. It would have been tough at the best of times but he had just played a really hard week's tennis to win the Masters and a strained arm muscle was giving him a lot of trouble.'

Tiriac, as we have seen, expresses much the same sentiments, as do most people who have dealt with Nastase on a personal basis. Pierre Barthes, the former French No 1 who now runs one of Europe's largest and most successful tennis camps at Cap d'Agde, supports that view.

'If I was running a tournament at the Cap and wanted Ilie to play I would probably have to get his signature in order to persuade French television to cover it,' says Barthes. 'But for me personally I would want nothing more than Ilie's word. That, for me, is enough.'

Even now, Nastase's better organized but still tight scheduling can find him overtaken by events outside his control. But even when given the most reasonable excuse to duck a commitment, he is loath to do so. When the Paris Racing Club staged its first Grand Prix tournament in late September 1977, Mitch arranged for Ilie to fly to Cologne to represent Adidas at a sports fair on the Monday following the final day of the Racing Club tournament. But rain caused frequent delays in the programme and by Sunday afternoon Ilie and Tiriac were only just completing the quarter-finals of the double.

Adidas had already arranged to lay on a private plane for Nastase so that he could fly straight from Cologne to Aix-en-Provence where he was due to begin another Colgate Grand Prix tournament on the Wednesday. Now, of course, the situation had become even more complicated. Many players I know—even if they had been receiving as much money as Ilie from Adidas and especially if they hated flying in small aircraft as much as Ilie does—would have cited the basic commitment to complete the tournament and cancelled the trip. But not Ilie.

After asking tournament director, Patrick Dubourg, not to schedule him before 3 pm the following afternoon, he made a dash for the airport, leaving Le Bourget around 8.30 pm. At 11 am on Monday he duly made his scheduled appearance at the trade fair in Cologne, signing autographs and talking to people for over an hour which, for an athlete, is often a more exhausting procedure than playing a match. Then another chase to the airport and, at 2.50 pm, Pierre-André Jau-Jou, the Adidas tennis representative in France, escorted him back through the gates of the Racing Club. Fifteen minutes later Nastase and Tiriac walked on court to play the semi-final of the doubles against Tito Vasquez and Jairo Velasco. Ten minutes after beating the South Americans, Ilie and Ion returned to the court where they eventually lost the final to Christophe Roger-Vasselin and Jacques Thamin, both of whom were using the double-strung rackets that had caused to much fuss throughout the tournament. That night Ilie drove 100 kms back to La Basoche and left for Aix-en-Provence the next day.

Whether or not that kind of itinerary is good for Nastase's tennis is quite another question. But at the very least it suggests a man who is prepared to go to any lengths to fulfil a commitment. Certainly Ilie did not deserve the unfair and damaging publicity he received when he formally broke with the McCormack organization at the beginning of 1977.

In a surprising lapse of taste for so experienced and sophisticated a public figure, McCormack gave the *Daily Express* gossip columnist, William Hickey, enough information for the paper to run an extremely unpleasant lead story about Ilie right in the middle of Wimbledon when all tennis-players are hot news items in England.

Under the banner headline 'Agent Mark delivers a Nasty shock' the article began, 'Ilie Nastase has been sacked by Mark McCormack, the Ohio lawyer who has guided him throughout his money-making career.

'The sacrifice is a huge one. Mr McCormack loses his 30 per cent slice of Nastase's earnings which run into millions. "Lets put it this way," says tough-talking Mr McCormack, 46. "We'd ask him to do something and he wouldn't do it. Our corporate credibility came into doubt with our customers. We therefore decided we couldn't handle him any more. He's on his own now." '

Just in case one had missed the slant of the piece, Hickey continued, '*Happily* [my italics], he [McCormack] will continue to coin his percentage for contracts negotiated for Nasty before the split.'

If McCormack wanted to give the impression of bad little Ilie being kicked out in the cold so that he could no longer tarnish IMC's lily-white reputation, he did a magnificent job. It would not have been as easy, however, if the Hickey desk had given their arch-rival, Nigel Dempster—an avid and accurate chronicler of the tennis scene—less to laugh about by checking their facts.

Firstly, McCormack could hardly be described as having 'guided him throughout his money-making career' when Ilie had been making good money for seven years and IMC had only handled him for three. Secondly, as Mitch Oprea had been acting as his full-time manager for at least six months, it was ridiculous for McCormack to suggest that he was on his own. But most misleading of all was the insinuation that the split had been entirely the wish of McCormack. While Oprea had been quite happy to let IMC arrange certain suitable exhibitions for Ilie for a straight percentage and no strings attached, he was far from content to allow them to continue handling Ilie's taxes and investments.

'They were charging $10,000 for that service,' said Oprea. 'So I decided that from 1977 on they would no longer handle Ilie's money.'

If there was any 'sacking', it seems, at the very least, to have been mutual.

It was bad enough that such a damaging piece had appeared in England during Wimbledon when virtually everyone of any importance in the tennis world was in London to read it. But, of course, it was quickly picked up by other publications round the world and a condensed version of the same story was printed in the mass-circulation American magazine, *Parade*, as well as one of the game's leading magazines, *Tennis*. Considering all the money IMC had made out of him, Nastase deserved better than to be publicly condemned by people who had been hired to promote, rather than to destroy, his career.

That is not to say IMC had had an easy ride with Nastase. They would have been fools had they expected such a volatile and temperamental character to provide them with a quiet life. Nor can they absolve themselves entirely from blame for some of the problems Ilie created. Many of these could have been avoided had they paid as much attention to the fluctuating graphs of their client's playing career as they did to the opportunities an exploding, dollar-laden sport was constantly providing for its top performers to sign lucrative contracts.

Nastase's first, disastrous flirtation with the new World Team Tennis league was a good example of the way in which IMC pushed him towards something he was not ready for. After a series of unhappy experiences and precious little success in the major tournaments in 1975, Nastase's confidence was at a low ebb by the autumn of that year. Although it was absurd to think that, at the age of twenty-nine, he was past his peak, he had become a ripe target for anyone who could offer him a big contract that did not require him to go on winning major titles in order to earn money. World Team Tennis offered just such an opportunity, but even then Ilie shied away from it. He didn't like the concept of one-set matches and no advantage games and the idea of the crowd being *encouraged* to scream at players filled him with horror. Crowds screamed at him quite enough already without being invited to do so.

But the McCormack people talked to him about security for the future; the chance of opening up a new career that only required his services for three and a half months a year—the WTT season runs from May to the end of August with a three-week break for Wimbledon—and the fact that the money being offered him was excellent considering his form that year. That in itself was nonsense. The $125,000 that the Hawaii Leis were offering was good money, to be sure, but it was not enough from a League that was crying out for superstars to stimulate action at the box office. Given that WTT were trying to attract the average American sports fan rather than the tennis connoisseur, no one could have been better for them than Nastase. But $125,000 was the maximum IMC could extract from them and that was the sum for which Ilie signed. It was a poorly negotiated, poorly thought-out deal, that was only moderately good for Ilie financially and extremely bad for his morale and confidence. For a star of his stature to have signed for WTT at that stage of his career for that kind of money was tantamount to running for cover. It was admission on Ilie's own part that he didn't think that he could win big any more. It was a real downer.

But, as I have said, they caught him at a vulnerable moment. He hadn't been winning much; there was no one around to whom he could turn for really expert advice and he was scared. So when Stanner finally tracked him down in Scandinavia—it was the time when Ilie was coaching the Swedish Davis Cup team—he reluctantly scribbled his name on the contract sheet. The signing took place in a hurry at Helsinki Airport just after Ilie had played in a small tournament in Finland, so that his team could get some proper match practice before playing Czechoslovakia in the final.

Airports are not the best places to sign documents that can alter the course of one's life but IMC were afraid that Ilie might change his mind—with good reason—and the 10 per cent they were to collect from the deal would look nice in that profit column. But if Ilie, depressed and confused at the time, signed in a hurry, he regretted it almost as fast. Only ten days later he was receiving the Masters Trophy for the fourth time in five years, having just given Bjorn Borg a lesson in the arts and skills of the game during the course of a mesmerizingly one-sided 6–2, 6–2, 6–1 victory. The match had lasted just sixty-five minutes on a medium-paced Supreme Court that had been laid over the Kunglihallen's fast tiles, and if ever Nastase had looked like a true master of his craft, this was it. From the pit of despair, he had climbed back among the stars and he was bubbling over with happiness as we drove to the airport in the Saab that had been loaned to him for the duration of his stay in Sweden that winter. But even during that moment of euphoria, there was a dark cloud on his horizon.

Talking to himself almost as much as to me, he suddenly blurted out, 'Oh, why do I sign for Team Tennis? I was so stupid. But, you know, I thought I could never win a big title again. I thought I better take the money. Now I don't need it. Now I know I can win again, everything's OK.'

But it wasn't. When the time came for him to leave for Hawaii five months later, the whole idea filled him with dread. Spending three and a half months on a Pacific Island for $125,000 might seem like an extremely pleasant idea to most of us, but from Ilie's point of view it just wasn't so great. For a start he was missing the French and Italian championships, two tournaments he had won in the past and which he enjoyed more than any other. Then there was Honolulu which, for all its sunshine, palm-trees and pretty girls, is not everybody's idea of heaven. Not, at least, unless you have a passion for plastic and concrete and over-sized American matrons revealing too much flesh on over-crowded beaches. And then there was the travel. No one had dwelt much on the travel aspects of the World Team Tennis when they had been persuading him to sign, but the weeks spent on the road, playing in as many as five different cities in seven days, are bad enough for teams based on the mainland. But every time the Hawaii Leis had to play an away match, it was five hours in a plane before they even hit Los Angeles.

And then, of course, for Ilie personally there was the biggest problem of all—his marriage. With Dominique staying at home in France, he knew their relationship was in danger and quite apart from missing his wife, he was missing his baby daughter.

When after a few weeks all these problems crowded in on him from all sides, Ilie followed the dictates of his heart and his emotions and quit. Concocting some story about the Romanian Government demanding his return, which fooled no one, he got on a plane and flew home to Paris. He arrived there in time to catch the last few days of the French Championships and appeared at Stade Roland Garros, a forlorn and slightly sad figure, watching Borg, the man he had crushed so completely six months before, carry off the title for the second consecutive year.

'It was bad what I do,' he told me. 'But I tell you if I had stayed any longer, I would have done something really crazy. Those crowds—you can't believe how bad they are. The names they call me before I even walk on court, it's unbelievable.'

Nastase had, of course, been reaping the whirlwind. But there was still no excuse for his breaking a contractual agreement and leaving his team without its No 1 player. For that he was, quite rightly, sued. Later WTT dropped the suit when IMC worked out a compromise deal in which Ilie agreed to return to Hawaii for the second half of the season for less money.

But if Nastase cannot escape being condemned for his action, no one who knew him well and who understood the pressures he was going through, could pretend to be surprised by it. From the moment he signed at Helsinki Airport to the moment he set off for Honolulu, it was the safest bet in tennis that somewhere along the rocky road he would have to travel with WTT, Ilie would blow his gasket. It was not something that required an excessive degree of perception to work out. Do you send an opium addict to work in a poppy field? How long would you expect an arsonist to survive in a match factory? How many times ... one could paraphrase Bob Dylan but the answer would never be blowing in the wind. The answer was staring McCormack and the rest of us in the face. Sending Nastase off to play Team Tennis in 1975 was the same as lighting the fuse on a stick of dynamite. When it duly exploded and IMC were left to pick up the debris, there weren't too many places to lay the blame. Nastase, obviously, could not escape carrying his share of it and it was a sizeable share. He had, after all, signed the bit of paper and he had been around long enough to know what kind of responsibility that entailed. But managers and agents are supposed to have some understanding and sensitivity when it comes to deciding what is good for their client and what is not. And for their total failure to realize what they were getting Ilie into, IMC have to be held culpable.

A year later when under Oprea's guidance, Nastase signed with WTT for the second half of the season only, the circumstances were radically different in many significant aspects. Under the sensible leadership of the new Commissioner Butch Buchholz—who coincidentally had been the Hawaii Leis coach in 1975—the League matured to the extent that crowds were no longer encouraged to stamp and yell during points and abuse visiting players. That didn't exactly put WTT spectators on a par with the Centre Court crowd at Wimbledon but it helped.

In addition Nastase was joining the Los Angeles franchise which, apart from the geographical improvement, put him under the ownership of Jerry Buss who is probably the most understanding and best respected of all the WTT bosses. And this time the contract made sense financially, too. From 1978, when he was due to play the full WTT season, Nastase was guaranteed a quarter of a million dollars a year for five years with an option in his favour to pull out after two. In other words, the money amounted to double the sum IMC had negotiated for him. But perhaps most important of all were the personal arrangements Ilie had made with his own family. Dominique had agreed to move with Nathalie to Los Angeles for the summer. And that made all the difference in the world.

The difference in his attitude towards playing for WTT the second year as opposed to the paranoia induced by his Hawaiian experience was, in fact, as marked as the difference in his attitude towards a cold, impersonal legal contract thrust upon him by a business corporation and a solemn promise given a friend.

As we have seen, he would break his back to honour the latter while the former would feel the full brunt of his innate distrust and deep-seated antagonism towards overbearing authority. Ask him nicely and there is always a good chance he will follow. Try shackling him by blocking off his escape routes with legal barriers and all you will have caught is a wild-eyed package of trouble.

For better or for worse, that is Ilie Nastase.

Mircea Oprea understood all that and more about Nastase when he started becoming involved in Ilie's business affairs. Mitch had first been introduced to the new wonder-boy of Romanian sport in 1965 by his close friend, Silviu Stanculescu, one of the country's leading actors. But it was not until 1972, when Oprea was bumming around the periphery of the tennis world, mostly on the Riordan circuit, that he started to know Ilie properly.

After more than thirty years of using his brawn and his brain to battle against life's odds, his luck had temporarily run dry. He was broke and out of work. Typically, Ilie came to his rescue and lent him some money. Later, it became a matter of pride for Mitch to take on assignments for Nastase for virtually no financial return. Now that their business relationship is formalized, Oprea takes a straight percentage of any deals he fixes for Ilie, albeit a smaller percentage than IMC.

To understand the important relationship that Ilie now has with Mitch Oprea—a relationship based on a common background and characters that are really too similar for either man's good—one should trace Oprea's unusual history. For a start there is no record of his birth. The only document concerning his arrival in this world can best be described as a non-birth certificate in that it states in Croatian—presumably for the benefit of the Yugoslav authorities—that he was *not* born in Yugoslavia.

'Legally, I don't exist,' sayd Mitch with his sardonic smile.

Quite apart from the wars that have tended to alter them with bewildering regularity over the past few centuries, national borders in the Balkans have never been particularly easy to pin-point. A multitude of races and creeds, all speaking numerous languages, have spilled across artificial boundaries traced by kings, princes, politicians and other despots, often for highly artificial purposes. As all this has created sufficient confusion to start new wars and overthrow governments, it is not surprising that a by-product of this geographical chaos should include an error or two concerning the precise location of the birth of a schoolteacher's son.

In fact, Mircea Oprea *was* born in Yugoslavia in as much as the town of Vrsac is reputed to be thirty miles inside the Yugoslav border. However, Mitch's parents are Romanian and at the time were sufficiently nationalistic to take a trip down the road to ensure that their son was baptized in Romania.

'But, really, it was all pretty confusing,' admits Oprea. 'The first fifty miles of railway track heading out of our town passed through five other towns whose inhabitants all spoke different languages. Every time the train stopped you had to remember which language to say "Good Morning" in.'

Mitch's first childhood memories are of the Second World War which engulfed that unhappy part of the world long before Romania, already under the Nazi yoke, formally declared war on the Soviet Union on 22 June, 1941.

The soil is very dark and rich around Vrsac and when the rains came in winter, the black mud outside the Opreas' house was constantly churned by the procession of Jewish and political prisoners being led away to concentration camps in the north. Later the windows used to rattle as German convoys passed through in the night and occasionally shots would ring out. Before his parents could stop him, Mitch would run from the house to find a hostage lying in a pool of blood.

'Usually it would be someone I knew,' said Mitch. 'Someone I called "Uncle". In our town, everyone we knew who was grown up was called "Uncle".'

By 1945 the survivors from the concentration camps started returning and Mitch remembers being warned not to give them food.'In their emaciated state, too much food would have killed them,' Mitch explained. 'But they were crazy with hunger.'

Having watched Communism clamp its iron fist on their country in the immediate post-war years, the Opreas decided to make a move while it was still possible. Initially, however, there was nowhere for them to go except to a refugee camp in Trieste. Mitch, already a strapping teenager, quickly put his athletic skills to use and won a place on the camp soccer team that was sent on a tour of Europe to play against British Army sides to aid the Dutch flood disaster. The travel provided a welcome change from life in the camp.

'We weren't prisoners, of course, but sometimes you would never have known it the way the camp guards behaved,' said Mitch. "I remember one big Bulgarian—the guards all seemed to be Bulgarians—who had been particularly obnoxious over something and a few of us beat the shit out of him. I remember enjoying it, too. I really laid into the bastard.'

Oprea considers himself lucky to have got out after two years when his parents found a means of getting to Venezuela, where they still live, with Mitch himself going to the States.

'One more year of that place and I would have developed a sub-human attitude towards life,' Mitch continued. 'It's the refugee camp syndrome. There's no way you can escape it. Although I can't condone it, I quite understand the Palestinians' mentality. Some of them have grown up in camps like ours and have known nothing else for thirty-five years. It doesn't make you a good human being.'

In 1957 Oprea started coaching soccer at the University of Michigan and it was there that he had his first contact with tennis. Barry MacKay, who was then just beginning a Davis Cup career that would bring him an impressive 22–9 singles record for the United States, was studying at Michigan at the same time and it was partly through knowing Barry, and also through watching pros like Lew Hoad and Pancho Gonzales when the tour passed through the Detroit area, that Mitch became interested in the game. But although he eventually learned to play a robust game of tennis, soccer remained Oprea's sport. For seven years, until he went to Columbia University in 1965, he played for a steelworkers' union team called the St Andrews Scots. But as the game started to grow in popularity, pro offers came in from Seattle and Los Angeles and the team eventually broke up.

At Columbia, Oprea switched the accent from brawn to brain. Soccer took a back seat while he earned degrees in economics and political geography and, a little more than a year after arriving in New York he was teaching political economy at New York University. Of the numerous colleges within New York City's university system, few are as conservative as Queen's College, at least as far as the administration is concerned. In the turbulent sixties students of a conservative bent were thin on the ground which was one reason why Mitch became rather more popular with his students than his superiors. For all his family's dislike of Communism, Mitch is no conservative. Perhaps he could best be described as a left-wing socialist who believes in free enterprise. There are more of those around today than one might imagine.

The New York University authorities were not, however, interested in making such fine distinctions—not when they were trying to keep the whole system from falling apart in the face of student lock-ins, walk-outs, strikes and outbreaks of violence. For it did not escape their notice that Mitch never seemed to suffer from the little indignities perpetrated on other professors—such as having his office ransacked and his books burned. They could hardly have been surprised. Unlike most of the teachers, Mitch tended to sympathize with the students' radical views and often kept his classes amused with his biting, anti-establishment wit. In the circumstances it was, perhaps, inevitable that Oprea would eventually get the sack—on the grounds of being a Communist. Mitch thought that was pretty funny but seven years' teaching in New York does little to bolster one's bank balance and being broke is a less amusing aspect of the American dream.

But, apart from the assistance he received from Nastase, Mitch also began to make use of his other contacts. Having obtained his American citizenship, he had been able to return to Romania in the sixties and had quickly established links with people in the academic and business world. So when his teaching career came to an abrupt end, he drifted into a consultancy role in New York, both on behalf of Romanian interests and also in the more lucrative field of North African oil.

So his name was already familiar to the Romanian Embassy in Washington when the antics of a certain well-known Romanian tennis-player started to cause ructions in the world of international diplomacy. With due deference to Basil the Wolf, Mihnea the Mean and Stephen the Great, all eminent enough fellows in their time, only the partially mythical Count Dracula from the annals of Romanian history could claim as much world-wide fame as was now being enjoyed by Ilie Nastase.

Whether the Romanian Government enjoyed it, however, was another question. They liked Ilie all right but were often less keen on the publicity he created and they became openly concerned when his continual rows with the tennis establishment took on legal overtones. The Embassy staff did not want to get directly involved so they turned to Oprea as a logical middle-man. Fluent in English; familiar with the habits and thinking of lawyers and other establishment figures in America, and yet still able to put Ilie at ease by talking to him in Romanian like a Romanian—these qualities, when added to a certain independence from both sides, made him a unique candidate for the role.

'I started by just clearing up a few of the problems from time to time,' Mitch explains. 'Initially that meant finding a really good lawyer who could stop Ilie being thrown out of the game. So I got Fred Sherman, a really sharp New York attorney I knew, to come in and act for Ilie on various occasions. He's not a sports lawyer, which might be an advantage in a way. His firm represents the General Tire Company and he does a lot of labour stuff which touches on similar ground to tennis when you are defending a player against the sport's administrators. Anyway we managed to keep Ilie in the game and the Romanians reasonably content.'

But Ilie's troubles did not diminish, and, with his relationship with IMC becoming increasingly less satisfactory, Mitch, by circumstances rather than design, found himself following Nastase from place to place in what had become a full-time role of aide, confidant and trouble-shooter.

'When it was becoming obvious the McCormack thing was not working Ilie asked me to take over all his affairs, at least as far as seeing that everything was properly taken care of,' Mitch explained. 'As far as I am concerned that means getting experts to do the legal work and the taxes, etc. Obviously there are areas in which I am competent to handle his affairs and areas in which I am not. But I have enough contacts always to be able to reach people who are competent in a certain field. It is a complex job looking after someone like Ilie. A lot of money is involved and a lot of people want chunks of it. But now that we are no longer tied to anyone in the managerial sense Ilie is a free agent to do special deals with anyone he chooses—Dell, even McCormack. But apart from the two big contracts he has with World Championship Tennis and World Team Tennis which tie him up for seven months a year, he can take his choice of where he plays and what he plays and, just as important, when not to play at all.'

Oprea is right. It is a complex job, and frankly, I can't think of anyone who would be the absolutely ideal person to do it. But, primarily because of his Romanian heritage and American training, Mitch has unique qualities which are of great benefit to Nastase. As I have intimated, however, it is not always an easy relationship. Often they get on each other's nerves; the Romanian tempers flare and Oprea, in particular, makes some pretty scathing remarks at times. But basically he has Ilie's interests at heart and that is more than you could say for some of the others who have gone before. But then there is the problem of Oprea's relationship with the Grazia family and that in the long run may prove to be the biggest problem of all. Sorting out a clash of egos and life-styles is never easy.

Ilie, meanwhile, soldiers on, trying to keep his act together, and letting much of the turmoil his mere existence causes wash over him. But I suspect he notices a great deal more than people might imagine.

6

THE TRIUMPHANT YEARS

Baranquilla is a windy, dusty Colombian town on the Caribbean coast that does not readily spring to mind when one thinks of the world's tennis centres. But for many years it was a traditional stop on a circuit that used to wend its way around the Caribbean and in 1969 it happened to become a milestone in the rapidly developing career of Ilie Nastase. Winners of the tournament used to receive emeralds by way of compensation for their efforts; but it was not the lure of precious stones that motivated Nastase in an ultimately successful bid to land his first international title of real significance.

'I was starting to earn a little money by then,' Ilie remembers. 'But I wasn't worried about the money. What concerned me was that nobody thought I could win. A lot of players were making fun of me because I played well but usually lost in the second or third rounds. I wanted to show them they were wrong. I was hungry just to win an important tournament.'

As we shall see, Ilie's preoccupation with the way in which other people view his talents has always acted as the keenest spur to his performance on court. When he is being belittled, he becomes determined to prove his critics wrong. When he is acclaimed by people he believes genuinely wish him well, he tries desperately to justify their support. He needs not only to be loved but to return that love through the satisfaction he knows his own success can give. But above all he needs the approval and respect of his peers. These are the factors that underlie Nastase's hunger for victory and it leads one to wonder what motivates the all-consuming drive for success in other champions.

Jimmy Connors wins for himself. For his mother, perhaps, too, but basically for himself because that is his nature and that is how he has been trained.

Guillermo Vilas is more generous in his recognition of those like Ion Tiriac who have helped him achieve success, but he is also basically winning for himself, to feed the hunger and pride of his own ego.

Bjorn Borg is almost entirely self-motivated, having developed at a very early age a singular pursuit of excellence. But, in a similar way to Vilas, he seems more aware now of the pleasure his success gives to those who support him.

Raul Ramirez wins to satisfy his pride and justify the extraordinary degree of self-confidence he has exuded throughout his career. For a rich man's son who never needed to fight for life's comforts, he has maintained a remarkable level of dedication to the demands imposed on a winner.

For Adriano Panatta there is the aesthetic satisfaction of playing the game in the classical manner, coupled on occasions with a street-fighter's gut desire to kill off the opposition. But it is not a desire that manifests itself very often, being almost totally submerged a lot of the time by a generous spirit and the more potent lure of good food, rare wine and the all-embracing luxury of having his family about him on a yacht.

For Arthur Ashe it is an intellectual exercise that must be planned with logic and skill. One can hear Ashe pondering the problem. 'What do I need to be recognized as No. 1 in the world?' he might have mused in 1975. 'To win WCT and then to win Wimbledon. Now to win Wimbledon in all probability I am going to have to beat Connors. Now to beat Connors I am going to have to keep a hold of myself; push medium-paced balls up the middle and dink short stuff low to his forehand.' Having achieved all that, Ashe felt he had succeeded for a multitude of people, not least himself.

The great Australian champions like Rod Laver, Roy Emerson and John Newcombe, win because they think losing is something that should always happen to the other guy. If not exactly a disease, losing, or worse still, anyone suffering from a loser's mentality, should be avoided at all costs. Any deeper intellectual or psychological reasons for the need to win should be swiftly drowned in a glass of beer.

But for both positive and negative reasons, Nastase wins for others. That does not mean he is selfless in his search for victory nor that he lacks an ego. But either through a basic insecurity or a need to constantly relate to others, Nastase is never alone out there, winning for himself in the manner of a Borg or a Connors. Usually there is some external motivation which drives him on.

In Baranquilla, it was the snickering of his fellow players that spurred his ambition and provided the incentive to hone his natural talents into a solid, cohesive force. As usual the wind blew as fiercely as Jan Kodes fought when they met in the final, but nothing distracted Ilie. He wanted to win and he did.

A year later he claimed an even more impressive title when he won the US Indoors at Salisbury, Maryland, and then under a burning Roman sun in May 1970, the full flower of his genius blossomed as he glided over the red clay of the Foro Italico to win the Italian Championship. Again the luckless player facing him in the final was his old rival Kodes.

'I was so confident then,' recalled Ilie with a trace of nostalgia. 'I felt strong, like I could do anything. I practised four, maybe five hours every day. I was so hungry to play and to win.'

With Tiriac's help, he had already taken Romania to the Davis Cup Challenge Round in 1969 and was destined to do so again in 1971—the last year in which the Challenge Round system was used. Since then the holders have been made to play through the early rounds like any other seeded team.

But creditable though his Davis Cup achievements had been, it was his breakthrough in Rome that lifted Nastase one notch higher towards a goal that was becoming increasingly accessible to him—the topmost rung on the world tennis ladder. But even so he did not achieve it quite as quickly as some people expected. He was, after all, nearly twenty-four when he won in Rome for the first time and most athletes of exceptional natural ability have reached their peak by twenty-five, if not long before. He might have got there a little sooner had not Kodes, for the first and almost the last time in their long rivalry, thwarted Ilie's ambitions in a match of major significance. Kodes did beat him in the WCT Finals in Dallas in 1974 but it was in the final of the French Open in 1971, a tournament that Nastase fully expected to win, that Jan stopped him dead in his tracks.

In 1970, when he beat Franulovic in the title match, and again the following year when Nastase became his victim, Kodes owned Stade Roland Garros. There have been some great champions since then, players like Borg and Vilas who will be remembered as greater all-round champions than Kodes. But nothing they have produced on that Centre Court so far has surpassed the fearsome dominance Kodes established during his title-winning years. He might have lost more sets than Ilie did when he won it in 1973, or Vilas during his blitzkrieg triumph in 1977, but the gleam of deadly determination in the Czech's eye and the bone-crushing power of his ground strokes, bore down on each opponent's confidence, and, one by one, eventually blasted them all to smithereens. More like Connors than the big top-spin clay court players of the modern generation, Kodes, at that moment of his prime, had developed the ability to hit power-packed drives to within an inch of either corner of the court, time after time after time. When necessary he could volley, too, but it was this unrelenting pressure from his ground strokes that wore his opponents to a frazzle. Even a player of Nastase's exceptional speed was continually forced back on his heels or caught a fraction of a second late on the shot as he tried to handle deep, heavy balls that exploded off the red clay.

The contrast between the two men was as marked as anything you will ever see on a tennis-court. Kodes is a serious man who plays serious tennis and every gesture he makes on court bespeaks seriously the effort he is expending. While Nastase slides, glides and flip-flops about, providing a living illustration of what Chekhov defined as grace—the ability to complete one definite action while making the least possible number of distinct movements—Kodes, who in some ways is a character better suited to brooding Chekhovian drama, jerks through each set movement of his serve; the skin drawn so tightly across his face and every muscle of his body wound up to such a point of tension that you feel sure something will snap.

Nothing has, but although the old intensity of effort still shows itself on occasions, Kodes has never again quite reached the level of whipcord precision with which he momentarily arrested Nastase's rise to the top in 1971. Not, at least, on clay. Obviously he played well to win Wimbledon in 1973 despite the absence of eighty-six members of the ATP, but to my mind his only comparable performance on grass was the magnificent five-set final he lost to Newcombe in the US Open at Forest Hills that same year. The margins that divide the quick and the dead in pro tennis today being what they are, Kodes has slipped imperceptibly from being a champion and runner-up in major tournaments to a consistent quarter-finalist and occasional semi-finalist. To a slightly less degree, Nastase has done the same thing. With Kodes it is the body that has slackened through the constant demands that have been made on it. With Nastase it has been the mind.

By the end of 1971, Ilie had forgotten the setback to his ambitions that he had suffered at Stade Roland Garros. Returning to Paris for the last Masters sponsored by Pepsi-Cola, Nastase locked horns with Stan Smith to begin a personal rivalry that was to become the focal point of his career throughout his triumphant title-winning years.

Either by chance or some good organization on the part of Pepsi's tennis expert, Alex Leon, that year's Masters, held at Stade Coubertin on the outskirts of the city, was played for the first and only time on a French carpet called Matesoft. Faster than the Supreme surface which is now so popular with the players, Matesoft, with its true bounce and good footing, produced some of the best spectator tennis I have seen. Nastase, who was then as quick as any player that has ever played the game, loved it.

Even against a mighty serve and volley expert like Smith, Ilie's catlike reflexes and sprinter's speed over five yards enabled him to use much of the American's power to his own advantage. The tennis the pair of them conjured up was mesmerizing to watch, and when Ilie emerged a hair's breadth winner in the third set, he had taken the first step down a road that was to lead to greater fame and riches, not to mention notoriety, than he could possibly have imagined. It was not that by this time anyone doubted Nastase would become one of the game's great players—that was a foregone conclusion—but rather that few of us could envisage the speed with which the tennis explosion, which had just started to take hold in America, would propel its top performers into the limelight and shower them with dollars.

But again, it was not the financial return that concerned Ilie that cold December evening in Paris. Of far greater importance to him was the question I remember a reporter putting to him in the locker-room just after the match.

'Do you think this victory makes you the No. 1 player in the world?' the reporter asked.

'Not yet,' Ilie replied quietly. He knew then that it was within his grasp. Winning the Masters had put the seal on a year that had seen him start to collect important titles with the regularity of a true champion. In the spring he had won at Nice and Monte Carlo; the Swedish Open title at Bastaad followed after Wimbledon and then, most satisfying of all, he had won the Embassy Championship at Wembley over Rod Laver. That had been a classic encounter. Laver, possibly the greatest of all post-war players—some would say the greatest of all time—had produced some of his best tennis and Nastase, to his great glee, discovered that he could match the maestro blow for blow, stroke for stroke. It was one of those matches that could have gone either way, but Ilie's nerve held in the crunch and he won it in the final set tie-break.

Now he had a new and increasingly prestigious title to his credit. He was The Master. In Tokyo twelve months before Stan Smith had claimed the first ever Masters title a few hours before having to fly back across the Pacific to report to base camp. Ilie hadn't qualified for Tokyo, having finished 1970 no higher than twelfth on the Grand Prix points table. But there had never been much doubt that he would make the eight-man field in Paris and, in fact, he finished second behind Smith with 172 points compared with the 187 Stan had collected during the course of the year's Grand Prix events.

For the next two years the Masters and the Grand Prix belonged to Ilie Nastase. He turned them into his playthings as well as his source of income. Refuting all arguments that he could not win big and win consistently, he not only retained his Masters title in Barcelona in 1972 and Boston in 1973 but, in both these years, he finished top of the points table as well—a feat only Guillermo Vilas has been able to equal since the inception of the Grand Prix format.

Until his disastrous flirtation with World Team Tennis knocked him out of the running for Masters qualification in 1976—statistically he could have played enough tournaments to make it but emotionally he was never ready for the challenge—Nastase's record in the Masters was phenomenal. Since his initial success in Paris in 1971, he had never failed to reach the final and had, in fact, won the title four times in five attempts. His only lapse came when Vilas defied all the odds by beating him in the 1974 final in Melbourne on grass—a surface the Argentinian barely knew how to play on at the time. But in 1972 and 1973, winning the Masters became just a reaffirmation of what had gone before; a nice big dollop of icing on an already fruity cake.

In the twelve-month period between July 1972 and June 1973, Ilie reached the Wimbledon final; beat Ashe to win the US Open at Forest Hills, and then won the French and Italian titles back-to-back—the two sets he lost to Paolo Bertolucci in the semi-final in Rome being the only ones he dropped in either event. Add the Barcelona Masters and a top place finish in the Grand Prix points table into that time-scale and at the end of it, when someone next asked him if he felt he was the No. 1 player in the world, there was only one answer.

The Wimbledon final of 1972 does not easily fade from the memory. But so as to ensure that the details are not forgotten it is best that I simply reprint the story I wrote for *World Tennis* magazine just hours after the match as I flew the Atlantic on my way to cover the Republican Convention in Miami. I remember describing the inevitable renomination of Richard Nixon as a tasteless charade. Compared with what Smith and Nastase had offered by way of a spectacle it was also numbingly dull. But, unfortunately, there was no one around to take Nixon into a fifth set. At Wimbledon, there was Ilie Nastase—and he nearly made it on the final ballot. This was how it happened:

'In the end it all came down to Stan Smith and Ilie Nastase. All that had gone before through two cold, dull weeks was but a preparation for the eventual meeting between these two players of intriguingly contrasting styles and temperaments.

'After Saturday's rain, the All England Club opened its gates to player and public alike for the first time ever on Sunday, and the offering from Smith and Nastase in the cathedral of tennis was worth the pilgrimage. The statistics themselves are interesting enough but they tell only half the story. Smith, becoming the first American since Chuck McKinley in 1963 to win the Wimbledon crown, beat Nastase 4–6, 6–3, 6–3, 4–6, 7–5 in two hours forty-five minutes.

'But more than mere figures, it was the drama and excitement and sheer skill displayed on that famous Centre Court which made this one of the great finals in the eighty-six-year history of the Championships. It was a final of the mind, for if ever there was proof that tennis is a mental game this was it. Smith's character triumphed over Nastase's skill—it was as simple as that.

'Having given himself no chance of success despite his No 2 seeding at the outset, the Romanian had played relaxed, carefree tennis throughout the preceding rounds and had never allowed his volcanic temperament to betray him. "I play like in practice," he said. "I hit shots you only hit when you don't care." By the time he found himself in the final, Nastase cared. This much became obvious by the sixth game of the first set. Nastase was comfortably level at 3–all and more than holding his own. He had hit an ace—something super-server Smith was not able to do until the fifth set—he had held service to love in the fourth game; he had picked up incredible half-volleys off slashing Smith service returns and leapt acrobatically to angle away superbly timed smashes.

'There were two things wrong with Nasty's game: his crosscourt forehand and his heavy lapses of concentration. When trying the heavy topspin roller, the maestro was finding that it was either going high or floating out wide. He decided to go mainly for the forehand down the line, and in the crucial stages of the fifth set Smith protected the down-the-line and saved the match. On court, Nastase decided that his problem was the strings. With the rest of his game tuned to such perfection, this seemed unlikely. But logic and Ilie Nastase have always had a distant relationship. As far as Nasty was concerned it was the strings and after every missed forehand he thumped them with the palm of his hand, plucked at them with his fingers and, finally, in a fit of agonized desperation, turned to his great friend Michele Brunetti and called out in Italian for help. But Brunetti, an Italian lawyer from Ancona who had refereed an India-Romania Davis Cup Zone Final the year before, knew like the rest of us that only Nastase could help Nastase. The imploring, desperate monologue from Nastase in the pit of the arena to Brunetti sitting in the front row of the players' enclosure, soon took on all the overtones of a Shakesperian tragedy. Smith, at the other end, kept glancing up briefly, breathing deeply and concentrating on solving his own problems. He had plenty of them. In fact if Nastase had stopped worrying about his own forehand and taken a good look at Stan's backhand in that first set, he might have derived a great deal of encouragement from it. By my count, the Californian missed eleven backhands—six of them on the volley—in the first ten games of the match and several of them were on crucial points. His service, too, was a pale shadow of its normal self. Seemingly reluctant to let rip in the cold, damp weather, Smith was serving at three-quarters pace through most of the first set and even so his first serve seldom found its mark.

'Smith was in trouble in the fifth game when the Romanian held three break points against him and again in the ninth when Nastase reached break point five times before finally clinching the breakthrough when Smith netted a low forehand volley off a dinked service return. Nastase served out for the set, looking happy for the first time as he did so (on his first set point he tried a crazy, non-percentage drop shot when Stan was way out of court). He broke Smith to love in the first game of the second when Stan double-faulted. But just when Ilie should have consolidated his lead, he played an absent-minded sort of game, double-faulting for 0–40 and losing his serve on the next point. Encouraged, Smith started attacking his opponent's serve and, after service had been broken in three consecutive games mid-way through the set, emerged leading 4–2.

'Glaring at the offending weapon after another forehand error, Nastase changed rackets at last, but the initiative he had gained with the old one had already passed from him and Smith was now in control. He was beginning to look like the real Stan Smith—sure and positive on his volleys, lunging left and right to smother the net with his gargantuan reach and even sprinkling this natural power game with a few judicious lobs and drop shots. He took the next two sets without difficulty even though his service was not all that he might have wished and then got an early break in the fourth. But the match was not over. Nasty broke back and levelled for 4–all. This was the incredibly brilliant Nasty, gliding about court with a speed that defied the eye. He broke Smith with the loss of only one point and served out for the set in the next game.

'The packed Centre Court stirred and hummed in anticipation of the final showdown, knowing that the match could now go either way. Nastase had stopped worrying about the light string job in his rackets, about a let call from the netcordsman (Nasty had glared at him for the next ten points) and an "out" call from a sidelinesman (this had resulted in furious Romanian glares for three games). The match was almost won in the fifth game. Smith advanced to 40–love on service and seemed in no danger until Ilie conjured up a spiralling lob out of nowhere that landed smack on Smith's baseline for 40–15. Suddenly it was deuce; then followed seven advantage points, four to Smith and three to Nastase. On one of these the Romanian hit a forehand long. The racket again took a thumping from its master and in the stands Brunetti received a brooding stare. Then Nastase was back at advantage point for the third time. Smith knew that a break would be fatal. Taking extra, calming seconds over his preparation for the serve, the American let one go, deep and strong, and Nastase couldn't handle it. Two points later Smith popped over a little drop shot that was worthy of his opponent's touch and the danger had passed.

'A lucky drop shot, this time off the wood, saved Stan from what would have been a love–40 situation in the ninth game (Stan had gambled that Nasty's forehand would go down the line). Nastase seemed to be fighting a rearguard battle as Smith began pounding back service returns with mounting confidence. The Romanian saved two match points at 5–4 and had Smith brooded about being so close to the title, only to be denied, he could have played a loose point or two and been out of the combat. He got another match point at 6–5 and then, on the fourth, all Nasty's skill crumbled in ruins as he reached for an easy high backhand sitter and dumped the ball in the net.

'Throughout the Championships Smith had believed in himself. Nastase had not. Maybe now this brilliant Romanian, truly one of the great players of the age, will realize that his very special talents can survive and even thrive on grass as well as other more familiar surfaces.'

He may not have realized it even then but thrive on it he did—and in short order.

With the turbulent tennis world temporarily at peace, the 1972 US Open at Forest Hills provided the first opportunity of the year to measure the skills and temperaments of the world's best players in one place and at one time. It was to be the ultimate test. As it was Nastase who passed that test in what remains one of the outstanding achievements of his career, I intend to quote again at length from a description of the Championships that I wrote at the time for *World Tennis*.

It might be interesting for the reader to note in the introduction to the piece which follows that the players were already agitating for the grass to be removed from the West Side Tennis Club as well as for an end to the 'sudden death' nine-point tie-breaker. It was not the first year I had wholeheartedly supported their sentiments in print but both issues were still controversial enough for the *World Tennis* editors to deem it necessary to put a footnote at the bottom of the page, pointing out that the paragraph in question 'bespoke the right of WT staff writers to state their own opinions'.

Actually it was the players' opinions that counted and by the end of Forest Hills that year the players had devised a method of making their opinions felt. At a meeting attended by forty-two players in the US Open Club next to the Stadium Court, the Association of Tennis Professionals was officially brought into existence. Ilie joined and then spent much of the rest of his career wishing he hadn't ... but that is another story. Change at Forest Hills did not come immediately but by 1975 both the grass and the nine-point tie-breaker had gone. With hindsight, it's nice to look back on battles won. But in the first days of a typically hot but untypically pleasant September 1972, Ilie Nastase's battles were still to come. This, through the eyes of your reporter, is how he triumphed:

US Open, 1972. Extracts from World Tennis

'Ilie Nastase of Romania, an electrifying, multi-talented performer prowling the world's sporting stage, took the US Open title—and a cheque for $25,000—by scores of 3–6, 6–3, 6–7, 6–4, 6–3. Although Ashe had by far the more difficult road to the final—he had to beat three seeds including the favourite, Stan Smith, while only Bob Hewitt, placed sixteenth, survived to meet Nastase—the Romanian's achievement in winning a major grass-court title was considerable. 'Nasty', a clay-court player by upbringing and inclination, now joins Manuel Santana and Rafe Osuna as the only touch artists since World War Two to pit their more delicate skills against the blood-and-thunder brigade at Forest Hills and emerge unscathed.

'A case can now be made for regarding this incredibly gifted athlete as the No 1 player in the world. With Rod Laver out of form and troubled by a back injury, Ken Rosewall finding it difficult to maintain over extended periods the peak of precision on which his game depends and Stan Smith still highly vulnerable on clay, Nastase stands alone as a player capable of beating anyone on any surface under any conditions. Only the dark stirrings of his unfathomable temperament remain open to criticism and if Ashe, with his customary candour, was correct in telling the crowd as he accepted his runner-up cheque that Ilie would become even better if he improved his court manners, it is also true that those childish outbursts no longer lose him matches.[1]

'The US Open of 1972 was a great tournament. With peace restored to the tennis world, there was hardly a player of note who was missing, save for the luckless Tony Roche, who underwent his second elbow operation in ten months at Lenox Hill Hospital the day before the Championships began. The weather was almost too good to believe. The skies were rarely anything but blue; after the first two days it was never too hot and even a hurricane, which the meteorologists had programmed to hit New York in the middle of the semi-finals, had the courtesy to die somewhere off the Carolinas. Encouraged by all this, the crowds flocked in as never before. 130,000 crammed the West Side Tennis Club over the twelve days play, breaking the record set in 1970 by more than 7,000.[2]

'The tournament should have been the most comprehensive test of skill this modern generation of players had ever faced. But it wasn't. In any test of skill it is essential that the element of luck be reduced to minimal—or at least manageable—proportions. At Forest Hills, the state of the grass which the normally reserved Britisher Mark Cox described bitterly as a "joke", and the tournament's insistence on using the nine-point tie-breaker, put Lady Luck in the driver's seat.

'Tom Okker echoed the sentiments of the vast majority of players when he said: "The nine-point tie-breaker is pure lottery. And when you use it on courts that give you one bad bounce every three balls hit, it's Russian roulette."

'The hopeless state of the courts was not the fault of the groundsman. The grass is simply beyond chemical assistance or tender, loving care. It isn't fit for tennis and if the West Side is interested in holding the US Open next year, it will have to go. Conversely, the continued use of the sudden

1 Oh, really?
2 If 130,000 felt 'crammed' imagine what it was like in 1977 with over 200,000 spectators.

death tie-breaker format *was* the fault of the tournament committee. They refused to listen to the well-documented protests of the players a year ago, presumably because it was felt that the public preferred the nine-point finish. Yet when the crowd on finals days was asked to indicate by volume of applause whether it preferred the nine-point or the twelve-point system (as used at Wimbledon and on the WCT tour) the twelve-point won easily. Death to sudden death.[1]

Early Rounds 'Two British left-handers played critical matches in the second round. The success of one and the failure of another had a vital bearing on the outcome of the Championships. Roger Taylor narrowly failed to beat Nastase, the ultimate winner, while Mark Cox eliminated Ken Rosewall, the No 2 seed who, had he survived, would have posed the biggest threat to Nastase in the lower half of the draw.

'Before a large crowd on the Grandstand Court, Nastase was coasting to victory when he led Taylor by two sets to love and a break in the first game of the third. Perhaps "Nasty" thought it was all too easy. He should have known better. Taylor had beaten Rod Laver when he was favourite at Wimbledon and had upset "Nasty" in the first round of the Stockholm Open last winter. Nastase double-faulted for 15–40 in the second game of the third set and then dropped serve with a careless volley. It was just the kind of lapse Taylor had been hoping for. At four points to three in the tie-breaker, Taylor chipped back a service return and bravely chose the narrowest of angles as he went cross court off the backhand with another short chip. That gave him the set and he quickly roared through the fourth, breaking Nastase's serve twice with more excellent returns to win it 6–2.

'At 4–all in the fifth set, Taylor had his man against the ropes and let him escape. He was not to get another chance. A forehand service return down the line gave him 0–30 on Nastase's serve and, after the Romanian pulled back to 30–all, Roger unleashed a great topspin cross-court pass off the forehand to reach break point. One point and he would be serving for the match. But the Englishman's backhand, so much better than it used to be but still vulnerable in the crunch, let him down once again although an uneven bounce as he went for the shot was probably equally to blame.

---

1 In the nine-point tie-break the first player to score five points would win. Player A would serve two balls; then player B would serve two; then player A two more and finally, if the issue was still unresolved, player B would serve the remaining three points—a considerable advantage on bad grass. In the so-called twelve-point tie-break, the first player to win seven points wins, providing he has a margin of at least two points. The tie-break continues for as long as neither player can gain a two point lead. Therefore one can have a series of alternating 'match-point, set-point' situations which, in my opinion, is far more exciting than the finality of 'sudden death'.

Nastase was back at deuce and it turned out to be his nearest brush with disaster until Ashe led him 4–2 in the fourth set in the final. Holding serve two points later, Nastase took the match into the deciding tie-breaker. He won it by five points to one. It sounds decisive and in a way it was. Of the six points played, Nastase served four of them and Taylor two. Taylor made a single error with a forehand volley on one of his serves and that, according to the crazy logic of sudden death, was sufficient to lose him a match that had been exquisitely balanced in almost total equality at 6–all in the fifth set. Strange justice.

'But Nastase was not the only one creating excitement as the tournament moved into the holiday weekend. The Labour Day crowd were rewarded with some of the best tennis of the tournament and it came from an unlikely source. The thought of John Newcombe *v*. Fred Stolle no longer quickens the pulse as it might have done in 1966 when Stolle won the tournament unseeded and Newcombe was on the threshold of his title-winning years. One expected Fred to strike a few hefty blows at inconclusive moments and bow gracefully out of the tournament. But when he won the first set tie-breaker by five points to one, reporters' typewriters momentarily stopped clattering. As it is quite impossible to get any realistic idea of what is happening out on court from the vantage point offered by that glass-enclosed apology for a press box, I accepted Peter Duchin's invitation to sit in his box, which was ideally situated just behind the base-line. From there it was possible to appreciate the brand of tennis Stolle and Newcombe were playing.

'For a period during the second and third sets, Fred was playing the chalk. There was a streak of six points where practically every serve he hit, every ball he volleyed, every passing shot he went for, landed smack on the line. The chalk flew, the crowd roared and Newcombe, shaking his head in disbelief, gave his old rival a long, lingering stare. "You've got to be kidding," said the look. This was all Stolle's yesterdays rolled into one and for long stretches of the match he could do nothing wrong. Those lanky legs that resemble broken matchsticks more than ever now were bending obediently for the low balls and getting him high off the ground for the overheads. Newcombe wasn't playing badly and, apart from the inevitable miscue when a shot hit a scarred piece of turf, these two great pros presented the serve and volley game at its brilliant best.

'In his only bad moment of the match, Stolle gave Newcombe the third set by serving three double faults in the twelfth game. His rhythm returned long before the fourth went into the tie-break, however, and he won it five points to three after a superb backhand service return down the line had taken him to match point. "Fred thinks its 1966 again," said one of the Aussies. Nastase, who was going to have to play Stolle in the quarters, didn't much care what year it was just so long as Stolle's volley would grow old quickly. On the evidence of the Newcombe match that seemed a dubious proposition.

'If luck had not been playing such a vital part in the proceedings—who could say if Alex Olmedo really deserved to beat Zan Guerry with a score like 6–3, 7–6, 6–7, 7–6 with the nine-point tie-break in operation?—it would have been possible to draw more decisive conclusions from the compostion of the last sixteen. But with the bad grass and so many close matches, it was not logical to state categorically that, in every case, the best man won. One can only say there were indications that the Americans have begun to establish a numerical dominance over their Australian rivals. Eight United States players reached the last sixteen as against three Australians and an unlikely trio they were, too: Rod Laver, Fred Stolle and John Cooper. South Africa had a surprisingly strong representation in Cliff Drysdale, Bob Hewitt and Frew McMillan and the list was completed by a Spaniard, Andres Gimeno and a Romanian, Ilie Nastase.

The quarter-finals 'It had been eighteen months since the two superstars of American tennis, Stan Smith and Arthur Ashe, had faced each other across a net. There was a great deal at stake for both men but once they got on court only Ashe looked as if he realized it. The pressure, the physical exertion and the mental strain came crashing down on Stan's blond head, sapping him of his strength and desire to win. He played well in concentrated if somewhat desperate bursts of energy and, to the casual observer, there seemed nothing especially wrong with his game. But Ashe knew. "Stan was mentally gone," Arthur said at the press conference afterwards. "He wasn't out there today. He's been playing too much tennis."

'In vivid contrast Ashe was in great shape. He had excellent control over his serve and volley, and if both players served a high proportion of double faults, that was almost inevitable between two players who had a healthy respect for each other's ability to demolish a short second serve. They were pushing the length and direction of that second delivery to its limits and inevitably they sometimes pushed too far. Ashe had said earlier that the man returning better would win on courts like these. Not since he annihilated the field in the Stockholm Open last November had Ashe played with such zest and confidence, especially on the return of serve. Here once again was one of the world's most exciting stroke makers in full cry and the Stadium Court crowd gasped whenever he drew back his Head racket to unleash another blistering drive.

'Smith hung on until he netted a backhand service return on the ninth point of the first set tie-break; after that the die was cast. Smith eventually double-faulted on the first match point to give Ashe a 7–6, 7–5, 6–4 victory.

Nastase

'On the Grandstand Court, Tom Gorman and Roscoe Tanner were bludgeoning each other with power serves of incredible consistency. In the end, one break early in the fifth set was enough to decide the issue in Gorman's favour but not before young Roscoe, who only dropped serve once during the course of a 7–6, 5–7, 7–6, 6–7, 6–4 defeat, gave notice of greater things to come.

'After losing the first set, Cliff Richey hustled and bustled his way past Frew McMillan while Nastase finally got it into Stolle's head that this really wasn't 1966. Fred, who had never played Ilie before, found the Romanian's speed and deftness of touch more than a foil for his serve and volley game. The Aussie is not an easy man to impress but he was impressed by Nastase. "He's got an exceptional amount of ability," Fred allowed over a beer at the locker-room bar after the match. That made the defeat sufferable. Losing to a player of exceptional ability is, in Fred's book, a great deal better than losing to a hacker. The latter hacks Fred off.

The semi-finals 'There was little Cliff Richey could do to prevent Arthur Ashe from reaching the final. Arthur had too much power and penetration on a fast surface against a player who is not heavily endowed with either. Cliff, as usual, battled and chased and lunged and killed himself trying to get into the match but Ashe was doing brutal things to his second serve. When Richey's last hope—the ninth point of the third set tie-break—went against him after a thrilling rally, it was all over 6–1, 6–4, 7–6.

'As at Wimbledon, Gorman had his chances against Nastase but the American has yet to find a way of putting Ilie on the canvas and keeping him there. Tom won the first set 6–4 and, at four points to three in the second (the first of two set-points for a two set to love lead), he drove a fine forehand cross-court. With those amazing reflexes of his, Nastase flung himself at the ball and just touched it back over the net for an irretrievable stop volley. Like Stolle before him, Gorman couldn't believe it. "I let myself worry about losing that point for too long," Gorman admitted. Soon his whole game had fallen apart. He looked as if he didn't know what was happening during the last two sets which Nastase won 6–2, 6–1.

The final 'The anatomy of a final is tied closely to the regularity or irregularity of both players' heartbeat. This was a match of nerves and emotion, of great highs and bad lows. Fortune genuflected to whichever master was best able to keep a firm grip on his racket.

'The contrast in personalities was total. Nastase, with the black mane and wild eye, wore his emotions like medals on his chest, dazzling and jangling in the bright sun. Ashe, the epitome of cool, showed nothing. Erect and correct, sombre and silent, he appeared outwardly not to care. Inwardly all was in turmoil.

90

'In the first game of the match Ashe double-faulted twice and dropped serve. In the second game Nastase was foot-faulted on a first serve for straying across the centre-line mark. On the previous point he, too, had double-faulted and he, too, dropped serve. Nastase was 0–40 on serve in the fourth game and climbed out of it with a leaping smash after Ashe had served six break points. But Arthur got him in the eighth game and served out for the set 6–3.

'Nastase levelled at a set-all, 6–3, but temperament flared as a bad bounce and a doubtful call ruined the rhythm of the artist's brushwork. Nastase walked up to the umpire's chair at the change-over, airing his despair to anyone who would listen. "I lose point—I can't concentrate," he complained. The words were unnecessary. The gestures were saying it all.

'By the time the tie-breaker arrived, Nasty was in bad mental shape. After another doubtful call he threw a towel at a linesman, then hit a ball at him. Boos and shouts of "Play tennis" erupted from the vast wall of faces. It was 3–1 to Ashe in the tie-break and Arthur, calm and together, played brilliantly to win 5–1 and so lead by two sets to one.

'In the third game of the fourth set, Nastase netted a backhand volley to lose his service to love. In the next game Ashe served an ace. It was going to be Ashe. The crowd sensed victory. Ashe led 4–2. Then suddenly, out of nowhere and for no apparent reason other than the tension and the pressure building up inside, he was in trouble. Maybe, at the moment he needed to concentrate most, he allowed his mind to wander. The creeping shadow reflecting the huge horseshoe stadium at Forest Hills was reaching the perimeter of the court itself and as the sun dipped away to the west over the tall towers of Manhattan, so, too, did Ashe's hold on the match loosen and fade. Nastase, whose psyche may be better equipped to survive the mysteries of the twilight zone, suddenly threw off the mantle of defeat and let his genius run riot in the shadows.

'Ashe's service started to waver and very soon his suspect forehand volley followed suit. Nastase leapt hungrily at the second delivery and top-spun passing shots down the line. Ashe pulled back from 0–40 down but Ilie rolled another heavily spun ball past his outstretched racket and a point later it was 4–all. Two games later the American blew a high forehand volley and it was set to Nastase 6–4. Hope flickered briefly for the home crowd when Ashe broke serve in the first game of the fifth but immediately he dropped his own. The rhythm was gone. Nastase, alert and alive as never before in this match, opened the flood-gates and, as the great river of his talent flowed from him, Ashe was engulfed. A break in the sixth game gave the Romanian a 4–2 lead and three games later he was leaping and dancing and tearing his hair as all that pent up emotion burst like compressed steam. He had earned his moment of delirium. He is a great player.'

Five years later that moment was still lodged vividly in Ilie's mind. 'It was unbelievable,' he told me. 'I never thought I could win a major tournament on grass—not even after I had got to the final at Wimbledon. I was still not really sure what I was doing on that stuff. Everyone said my volley could not hold up under pressure on grass but I guess I was lucky. That second set-point Gorman had to go two sets up in the semis—you know, the one after I hit the stop volley? I hit a second serve and Tom runs round on to his forehand and puts it in the net. If that had gone over, who knows? Two sets down against Gorman on grass is tough. He was a big player then. He got to the semis at the French Championships, Wimbledon and Forest Hills. He had to be unlucky not to get to a big final.'

Then Ilie told me something I had never known about his match with Ashe and the unlikely switch of fortunes in the fourth set.

'I was never really confident I could win the title although by the time I beat Gorman I was pretty hot,' he continued. 'I was very nervous at the beginning of the final and when Arthur got that 4–2 lead in the fourth I thought it was all over. The crowd were down on me because I complain about line calls and I thought, screw them. But there was this one guy in the crowd who kept yelling for me. He wanted me to win so badly I could see him suffering every time I lose a game. So I think maybe I better try and win for him. Maybe he had put a lot of money on me or something. Anyway it helped me because it gave me new reason to fight. I never knew his name although I had seen him around the locker-room and I think we played backgammon together once. Funny how he may have changed my life and I don't even know the guy.'

One voice in a crowd. An anonymous American making himself heard above the screams of 14,000 compatriots and changing the course of tennis history. Far-fetched? Possibly, but, as I have said, Ilie is like that. Logically one would have expected Dominique, then his lovely, wide-eyed fiancée, to act as the spur to his flagging ambitions but maybe she was already too close to him. It had to be somebody else, a cry from the unknown. There is no safe conclusion to be drawn from analysing this trait in Nastase's character. But it seems, as one who has watched him over the years, that the almost childlike need to perform *for* someone—anyone—is a very powerful force in his make-up.

Apart from the agony of losing to Stan Smith in front of his home crowd when the United States played Romania in the Davis Cup in Bucharest—of which more later—Nastase's year continued as if the tennis circuit was just a pathway to heaven. As Ashe had suggested to the crowd after the Forest Hills final, Ilie's court manners left something to be desired, but for the most part he managed to stay away from any real trouble and simply enjoyed himself. Since his triumph in the US Open, his reputation had spread far beyond the confines of tennis and its followers.

He was now recognized throughout the sporting world as an athlete of rare ability and the possessor of a personality that would ensure his box-office appeal for years to come.

'Superstar,' wrote Linda Timms in *World Tennis* later that year, 'is the most overworked hyperbole in the 1972 vocabulary. But one cannot deny its applicability to Ilie Nastase.'

Linda Timms, a demure Englishwoman who is not given to lacing her tight prose with superfluous superlatives, was writing about the finals of the Dewar Cup which, for many years, brightened London's October scene by bringing many of the world's leading players to perform amidst the Victorian splendour of the Royal Albert Hall. But Miss Timms obviously felt that no praise would be superfluous if directed at Nastase's performance that year.

Of Ilie's semi-final she wrote: 'He beat Jimmy Connors 6–3, 6–4 after being 3–1 down in the first set. From that moment his play was so varied, so brilliant and so fascinating that no comparison with the great names of the past seemed exaggerated. The beauty of his game for the spectator is that he relies neither on raw power nor on dogged accuracy but on speed, delicacy and that rarest of combinations, flair with precision.

'Connors, and then Gorman, who performed creditably but scarcely threateningly in the final, were merely straight men. And on receiving the Dewar Cup and the cheque, Nastase, predictably and to the delight of the crowd, could not resist the theatrical gesture of kissing Lady Elizabeth Dewar's hand. It all made one think of the musical, *Applause*. Superstar really is the only word.'

Stan Smith had lost in the early rounds of that tournament to Onny Parun and so Ilie had to wait for the Commercial Union Masters in Barcelona to exact his revenge for the humiliation in Bucharest.

Played at the Palau Blau Grana, a compact indoor stadium situated just across the Avenida Generalisimo Franco from the Real Club de Barcelona, the traditional site for top tennis in the city, the first Masters organised by Geoff Mullis on behalf of the new Grand Prix sponsors, Commercial Union, turned out to be an event for night-owls and insomniacs. The Spanish tend to keep late hours as a matter of habit but even they were beginning to look a little bleary-eyed when each evening's programme stretched into the wee small hours of two and three in the morning.

But no one, perhaps, had a right to look more bleary-eyed than Ilie and that, I must confess, might have been my fault. It was the night—or rather the morning—of the semi-finals and a group of us had just got back to the Hotel Presidente at the usual hour of around 3.15 a.m. Much earlier in the evening Nastase had given his young friend Connors another lesson in the finer arts of the game—such as drop-shots and top-spin lobs which he sent whirring over the American's head from the most impossible angles—and had retired to bed at some relatively civilized hour to prepare for the ordeal of facing arch-rival No 1, Stan Smith.

As Stan had played murderously authoritative tennis to crush Jan Kodes 6–0, 6–1 in the last of the round robin matches, he was considered a good bet to defeat his Davis Cup colleague, Tom Gorman. If you want to get as Irish as Gorman about it, you could say it both did and didn't work out that way. Yes, Smith did make it through to the final and no, he didn't beat Gorman. The explanation lay deep in the twisted, torn and much abused lumbar region of Tom's back.

Gorman has suffered from a chronic back problem throughout his career and he has come to recognize just how bad each attack is going to be through painful experience. At 4–3 on serve in the fourth set with Gorman leading by two sets to one, Tom went for a forehand passing shot and felt his left foot grip the plastic Mateflex court and stay firm as his body twisted. He felt the pain and, over the next two or three minutes, the whole lower region of his back stiffened up to the extent that he could not bend half-way to the ground. There is never a good time to get injured but the gremlins could not have been in a meaner mood than to strike at Gorman then. For much of the previous three sets, Gorman had been playing the most daring, the most aggressive and quite the most effective tennis of his career. Smith was simply being outplayed and, ironically, lacking Gorman's natural agility, could do little to counter the stream of acrobatic winners that were flashing off Tom's racket.

But even when Gorman was so suddenly and so cruelly deprived of his agility, a bemused Smith, who did not realize for a couple of games what had happened, could not capitalize on it. Stan actually thought Gorman was trying to psych him when he stayed back on his serve and proceeded to hold it with ease to lead 5–4. In fact he stayed back because, had he gone to the net, he wouldn't have been able to bend for a volley. On Smith's serve in the next game, Gorman, knowing that all was lost, slashed wildly at his returns and, of course, they all went in. At 7–6, 6–7, 7–5, 5–4 and 30–40 on Stan's serve, Gorman had reached the match-point that could have taken him into the Masters final and yet he knew it was a point he must not win.

'I know my back well enough to realize I could not have played the final the next day,' Gorman said afterwards. 'I knew I was going to have trouble getting out of bed, let alone on to a tennis-court, and as it would have been quite unfair to the crowd and the sponsors to deprive them of a final, there seemed to be only one thing to do.'

So before Smith had a chance to serve at match-point, Tom Gorman walked up to the net and shook hands. It was one of the better gestures pro tennis has witnessed in the past few years but then Gorman is one of the games's better people.

However the Irish imp that lurks not so far behind those twinkling eyes does nothing to control his mischievous spirit and after we had got back to the hotel, following endless press conferences and post mortems, Tom was looking for ways of making the best of a bad job and having some fun. Connors, Tom and I, and a couple of other people, were sipping wine and munching a couple of sandwiches the hotel had miraculously produced when I retold the famous story of Fred Stolle phoning Roy Emerson at 2.30 a.m. from Bud Collins' party in Boston during the US National Doubles. 'Just wanted to know if you were having a good kip, fella,' said Fred cheerily. Emmo, who was trying to get his first good night's rest in three weeks so that at least one half of the Emerson-Stolle partnership would be able to stand up the next day, was not particularly amused. Gorman, however, thought it was pretty funny. As the train of thought developed it didn't take long for some bright spark to wonder if Ilie, who was sleeping on the floor below would be interested to know who he had to play tomorrow.

'Of course he would,' exclaimed Gorman with a wicked look in his eye. 'Let's go tell him.'

So we trooped off downstairs and banged on Nastase's door until a sleep-laden apparition appeared in shorty pyjamas.

'Just thought you'd like to know we play tomorrow,' said Gorman who, in critical moments such as this, is the master of the straight face. Stan Smith, who had come out of his room when he heard the scuffle of feet past his door, was hanging over the staircase railings, peering down on the scene and trying to stifle his mirth.

'Hey, be quiet, you bloody bastards,' Ilie mumbled, too drugged with sleep to know whether to be amused or angry. 'I've got Nikki in here and you'll wake her.' Then, before he turned to disappear back into the darkened room, a quizzical expression came oiver his face. 'What, you sure we play tomorrow—you mean you beat Godzilla?'

'Killed him,' said Gorman airily as Connors cupped his hands over his mouth and shuffled back out of Ilie's sight so that his laughter wouldn't give the game away.

It was only when Nastase woke a few hours later that he discovered he had to play Smith, the man he always referred to as Godzilla. Although Stan is the gentlest of men, the name gave a fair impression of the figure he cut on court with that towering 6ft 4in. frame and arms that seemed to go on forever, especially when an opponent was trying to pass him at the net.

But I always suspected that Ilie was revealing a little too much of the anxiety he felt about playing Smith when he referred to him as Godzilla. During that period of their intense rivalry in 1971 and 1972 when Smith was regarded by many to be the No 1 player in the world, Nastase seemed to be haunted by the image of this blond giant who always emerged at the psychological moment to make that final hurdle all the tougher.

Had Smith got him psyched? Ilie will not admit that now. 'No, I was never dominated by his personality,' Ilie replied hotly when I put the question to him. 'Shit, he can't beat me just by looking at me. Every great player has his year and Stan was so confident then. He seemed to think he could win every time he walked on court. Sure, he beat me at Wimbledon and in the Davis Cup but I beat him all the time in the Masters. Our matches were always very close, always good matches to watch.'

It was true Ilie dominated Stan in the Masters. For the second consecutive year, Nastase came out on top in Barcelona, despite that lack of sleep and despite a gutsy fightback in the third and fourth sets by Smith after the Romanian had toyed with him in the first two. But the year had been a long one for the reigning Wimbledon champion and, whereas for Nastase tennis is the most natural of pastimes, for Smith it is hard work. Always he has had to expend vast amounts of energy both in practice and match play to maintain the standard he demands of himself and as a result fatigue became as big an enemy as the man across the net after a long run on the circuit.

And so it proved in Barcelona. With Ilie still fresh and fast as the match moved into the fifth set, Smith was struggling to maintain the power on his serve and a single break was sufficient to ensure that Nastase remained the Master.

By the time 1973 dawned Ilie was also a husband. Although the official honeymoon had taken place in Acapulco, it just seemed to go on and on as Ilie swept through the early months of the year with Dominique at his side, winning titles at will.

On the Riordan Circuit, he beat Connors to win the Midlands International at Omaha, Nebraska, and repeated that success by beating Jimmy again to take the Equity Funding title in Washington D.C. Connors had beaten him once in between, in the final at Hampton, Virginia, and had not been around when Nastase beat Paul Gerken to take the Canadian International at Calgary. With most of the other big names competing on the WCT Circuit, these were not major achievements but, as any player will tell you, the mere act of winning week after week is the best tonic your confidence can get. As soon as winning becomes a habit, a player holds a psychological advantage over most of his opponents. I have lost count of the number of times I have seen a middle-ranked player produce far better tennis on the day than a more illustrious opponent; seen him battle his way into a substantial and well-merited lead and then blow it because he suddenly remembered that the guy across the net was called Borg, Smith or

Okker. As soon as someone starts playing the man rather than his shots, the player with the big reputation will always win.

With his own reputation now firmly established, Nastase cemented it still further in the minds of his rivals every time he won a tournament—any tournament. Nobody was making fun of him any more. Ilie Nastase was a winner.

Returning to Europe, he proceeded to rub in that fact week after week as he picked up still more titles at the Rothmans Indoor in London and then all round the Mediterranean—Monte Carlo, Barcelona, Madrid, Florence. Back on the shifting shingle of European clay where he could glide and slide into his shots with effortless grace, Ilie was starting to look invincible. And when the big tests came in Paris and Rome, he just about proved it.

It was a wet year at Stade Roland Garros. For much of the second week, crowds huddled under the dripping chestnut-trees and players fidgeted over cards in the steamy restaurant. As the programme fell further and further behind, it required a player of calm self-confidence to handle the delays and interruptions. But after he had got most of the idiocy out of his system by trying to make a fool of Roger Taylor—tactics which almost cost him the third set which Roger finally lost in the tie-break by 9 points to 7—Ilie moved imperiously towards his title.

He was fortunate in that a lot of potentially dangerous rivals—Smith, Okker, Panatta and Kodes—fell before they could reach him, but if every champion needs a little luck to win a major title Nastase tends to need less than most when he is attending to business.

Having put his back together again with a six-week session of massage, exercise and steam-baths at home in Seattle, the persistent Tom Gorman emerged as the sole American survivor among three Europeans in the semi-finals. Stan Smith's bid to extend his great run of success over the previous eighteen months came to an end when Tom Okker, a man of speed, skill and experience, recovered from losing his service in the first game of the fifth set and proceeded to destroy Smith's own faltering delivery with top-spin returns.

By the second weekend the sun had reappeared to decorate the one remaining match of note—in fact the best match of the tournament. The score of 6–3, 5–7, 6–3, 6–4 which put Panatta into the semi-final at Okker's expense tells little of the scintillating standard of tennis these two attractive players produced. It was a delightful duel, full of touch and guile, power and placement, speed and quick-witted inteligence. Brilliant use of the dropshot and his consistently accurate service—mostly to Okker's backhand—were the factors which helped Panatta dominate. But there was no shot which offered a better illustration of the Italian's maturing skills than that which won him the third set. Forced to take a deep Okker return late and behind him, he still managed to connect perfectly with a cross-court forehand passing shot that hummed low over the net. There was a spell when the Dutchman's fantastic turn of speed enabled him to run on to many of Panatta's delicately placed dropshots but although Tom led 3–1 in the fourth set, Adriano surged back powerfully to sieze victory.

It was a costly success for the effort seemed to have drained the Italian's resources when he met Nikki Pilic in the first of two disappointing semi-finals. To give credit where it is due, much of the reason for the one-sided affair lay in Pilic's superbly commanding performance. Swinging into that low-trajectory, left-handed serve Nikki exploded aces all over the place and loped into the net to pummel away volleys with relentless precision. The Yugoslav, who had waited a long time to do proper justice to his talents, can seldom have played better and Panatta was rushed out of it in straight sets.

It was the same story with Nastase and Gorman. The American, fearful of giving Ilie the pace he enjoys, deserted his net-rushing tactics of the previous rounds and stayed back, trying to vary the pace of his ground strokes. But he was too tight at the start to get his timing synchronized properly and with Nastase a model of calm concentration, he found himself being outmanoeuvred by his wily opponent. The score was 6–3, 6–4, 6–1 and that says it all.

On the Tuesday, two days behind schedule, Nastase and Pilic contested the final. By that time the Italians were tearing their hair out down in Rome where the Italian Championships—which followed the French in those days—had been trying to get started since the previous Saturday. But once the match in Paris got under way, Ilie made sure no more flights would be missed. Pilic broke serve to lead 2–0 in the first set and that was as much as he was allowed. Incredibly, it was not until the eighth game of the second set that he managed to hold serve again, although in the meantime he had taken Ilie's once more. It was a momentary and inconsequential lapse on the Romanian's part. Displaying his full range of adroit and nimble stroke play, Nastase carved up his opponent in a match that produced none of the fireworks that might have been expected from these two volatile performers.

It was the third all-Eastern European final in four years and even more one-sided than that in which Kodes had beaten another Yugoslav, Franulovic, in 1970. By winning 6–3, 6–3, 6–0 Nastase boosted his rapidly growing bank balance by $16,000—a lot more in real terms then than it is today—and, more importantly, furthered his reputation as the game's most consummate artist.

As they boarded the plane for Rome together, neither Nastase nor Pilic could have been aware that they were setting out on very different journeys. Pilic was already at the centre of the storm which was brewing over his suspension by the Yugoslav LTA for refusing to play for the Davis Cup. At meetings in Paris, the ILTF had upheld that suspension and were now trying to get the Italians to agree that the worldwide suspension which had consequently come into effect, should begin immediately. But not for the last time that turbulent summer, ILTF President Allan Heyman discovered that someone had called his bluff. Dr. Gianfranco Cameli, the bright, progressive Secretary General of the Italian Federation, was not interested in what the ILTF did or did not want to do with Nikki Pilic. All that mattered to him was that Pilic was the French Open finalist and would therefore add a great deal to the Italian Open by merely walking on court. So Cameli hit the ILTF with the argument that Pilic had been in good standing with the international body when the draw for Rome had been made and therefore any suspension levied against him after that should not be allowed to interfere with the Italian Championships. Cameli won.

So Pilic played in Rome, lost in the second round to Patrice Dominguez, and returned home to Split. There he would have remained for six weeks had not the fledgling ATP decided to make the Pilic affair their *cause célèbre* and boycott Wimbledon in his support.

Having been on opposite sides of the net in Paris, Nastase and Pilic found a much wider gulf dividing them when Nikki arrived in London to bring an injuction against the ILTF in a last-ditch attempt to find an alternative solution to a boycott of Wimbledon. On that issue, Ilie was not simply on the other side of the net, he was in the other camp. Only three ATP members broke ranks and played at Wimbledon that year and Nastase was one of them.

If Nastase had taken more interest in locker-room talk at the Foro Italico he might have realized just how strongly the majority of players felt about the issue. When he canvassed them for their views, ATP President Cliff Drysdale was amazed to discover how militant they were. It was not Nikki Pilic they felt particularly sorry for. Some even doubted that Nikki had played it fair and square with his association over whether or not he had promised to play in the Davis Cup for them. But in the players' minds that was not the issue. In trying to force Pilic to play in the Davis Cup, an amateur body had tried to dictate to a professional athlete on the manner in which he should run his career. That was just one example of an intolerable situation that had been going on throughout the tennis world ever since the advent of Open tennis five years before. The players were going to put up with it no longer. It was not a question of money, as the British press insisted so hysterically as soon as Wimbledon became threatened, and it was almost certainly not Wimbledon itself. It was simply that the game's hierarchy had treated the players like workers for too long. Now the players were acting like workers and contemplating their right to strike. If some of the more militant ATP members adopted an attitude of 'up yours' towards the officials who had treated them in such a snobby, autocratic manner over the years, then the officials had only themselves to blame.

It is possible that much of this passed over Nastase's head in Rome. He was, at the time, very wrapped up in himself and his success. He was, for once, concentrating on his tennis and behaving with a champion's detachment to all that went on around him. Certainly he was playing like a man who had forgotten the meaning of defeat.

By the time he crushed Jan Kodes to reach the semi-finals he had still not lost a set since beginning his assault on the twin peaks of the clay-court game in Paris almost three weeks before. It was Paolo Bertolucci who ruined the possibility of Nastase completing another triumph without the loss of a single set. Then a portly twenty-two-year-old whose aristocratic air suggested that tennis was something he wedged in between languid nights on the Via Veneto, Bertolucci was, and still is, a deceptive performer. When Italy began their successful run in the Davis Cup a few years later the Italian captain, Nikki Pietrangeli, admitted to me that Bertolucci possessed the most natural talent of any of his players. As they included Panatta, Barazzutti and Zugarelli the compliment was considerable.

'But always I feel as if I should strap a miniature tape-recorder to his ear before he goes on court,' said Pietrangeli. 'Then I could record a message which would repeat over and over "Move your arse, move your arse".'

In the semi-finals of the Italian Championships in 1973, for four sets Bertolucci moved his whole short, solid frame to great purpose. A powerful hitter in the style of a Kodes, Paolo possesses a greater flexibility of stroke-play than the Czech, and as darkness started to fall he pulled himself back into the match against Nastase by winning the fourth set 6–3. I am sure Bertolucci did not spend that particular night on the Via Veneto. But he did something wrong, for the next morning Nastase ripped off the fifth set 6–0 before the Italian had got both eyes open.

In the final it is possible that Manolo Orantes never focused at all. As Frank Rostron, then nearing the end of a long and distinguished career with the *Daily Express* wrote, 'It was the worst and most one-sided final in memory with the 6–1, 6–1, 6–1 score in no way misrepresenting a travesty of a match. Had this been a horse-race, the stewards would have ordered an enquiry and caused the Spaniard to be dope-tested.' Little did Rostron know at the time that Kodes would ask for just such a test after an injured François Jauffret beat him in the French Championships the following year. But in fact there was nothing much wrong with Orantes except the after-effects of a gruelling five-set battle with Okker in the semi-finals and an opponent, in Nastase, who never allowed him to find his rhythm and get into the match.

So, for the loss of only two sets, Nastase had won the French and the

Italian titles consecutively—a very special feat. Panatta did it in 1976 and, for sheer stamina, perhaps his was the greater achievement for he was challenged fiercely in both events and twice had to stave off match-points—indeed he needed to save no less than eleven of them against a despairing Kim Warwick in the first round in Rome.

In contrast Nastase ruled supreme. Always a class above his opposition, he seemed not merely to be too clever and too dexterous with a racket but far too formidable an athlete to brook any serious opposition. Not until Nastase himself broke Guillermo Vilas' 56-match-winning streak on clay in 1977 did a player so completely dominate the clay-court game as Ilie in 1973. By the time he triumphed in Rome he had won forty-two out of forty-three matches in Europe since returning from America—a defeat by Panatta in the final at Bournemouth being his only setback.

How could it ever end? Wasn't life a perpetual harvest for a man of such fertile talent? Surely the crop couldn't fail? By the time winter came, Nastase had reaped enough success to ensure his position as the No 1 player in the world for a long time to come. Or so it seemed. Out of thirty-three tournaments played in 1973—an enormous number for a player who is constantly winning—Nastase won seventeen of them, including such prestigious titles as Queen's; the Swiss Open at Gstaad; the Godo Cup at Barcelona; and the Jean Becker Open in Paris. He also, of course, retained his Masters title.

Considering the amount of court-time it required to win as many singles titles, it was a tribute to his enthusiasm for the game as much as to his incredible physical condition that he also managed to pick up thirteen doubles titles. Although he has never been considered a great doubles player in his own right, his obvious flair for the game can make him highly dangerous when teamed with someone who complements his style. 'The fact that he is not a great volleyer means that you cannot class him as a truly great doubles player,' says doubles expert Frew McMillan. 'Also being the artist he is, Ilie will try the non-percentage shot too often. But if he was properly governed I think he could still become a great doubles player, albeit an unorthodox one.'

Nastase's doubles results in 1973 may not have satisfied the purists but they frequently proved extremely dissatisfying to his opponents. Rather like Wojtek Fibak a few years later, Nastase seemed to win with anyone. He won the British Hardcourts, Monte Carlo and Istanbul with Juan Gisbert; Calgary with Mike Estep; Hampton and Charleston with Clark Graebner; Barcelona and Madrid on the autumn circuit with Tom Okker; and, most important of all, Wimbledon with Jimmy Connors. There were others as well and had there been a Grand Prix for doubles in those days, he would probably have equalled Raul Ramirez' 1976 feat of finishing top in both singles and doubles.

A rich harvest indeed. But it was not, as the coloured South African poet Don Mattera once wrote of Arthur Ashe, 'tendered by the rains of tolerance and patience'. Twice at least during the year the morning sky had been streaked with red as he allowed a careless temper to ruin his chances at both Wimbledon and Forest Hills. They were bad omens that Ilie, laden with the fruits of other victories, all too readily ignored.

If one can pinpoint a change in his fortunes; the decision to defy the ATP at Wimbledon was probably the moment when the clouds first started to gather. But, nine months earlier, in the autumn of 1972, Nastase had suffered a major blow to his ego and his reputation during that Davis Cup tie against the United States in Bucharest. It is impossible to say just to what extent it affected the ability to handle pressure in the years that followed. But there seems little doubt that it left a scar.

There has probably never been a Davis Cup final quite like this amazing confrontation which saw Dennis Ralston's team defy all the odds in beating Romania on clay in front of their own wildly partisan crowds, not to mention a few somewhat partisan linesmen.

'The atmosphere was tremendous but hardly conducive to the fair government of a trial of lawn tennis,' wrote David Gray in *The Guardian.*

In fact the atmosphere was too tremendous for Nastase. He not only lost to Smith in the opening singles—an unlikely result given Stan's relative lack of success on that surface—but also played poorly in the doubles.

As Gray wrote, 'Smith gave the United States a better start than they expected. The odds were against him beating Nastase at home on clay, but he upset all the prophets and played the best clay court match of his career. He was relaxed and resolute, maintaining a steady pressure on the national hero and Nastase, overburdened with national expectation, was nervous and distracted. He was brilliant in flashes but the flashes never lasted long and once he had lost the first set, he collapsed. He also had a blistered hand which did not help. The Romanian's instinct for success deserted him. He never served well and when Smith commanded the court with his weighty shots, he wasn't able to change the pace ...'

According to Tiriac, Ilie was ill-prepared for the match. 'I wanted him to come back home with me to practise,' Ion told me. 'But instead he decides to rest after playing some tournament on cement in America and sits around watching TV. Eventually he arrives in Bucharest only six days before the match. So after we practise hard for a bit he gets blisters on his hand. Sure it affected him. He was much too nervous in the doubles but he would never have got blisters if he had prepared properly.'

After Smith had beaten Nastase 11–9, 6–2, 6–3 in the first rubber, Tiriac battled back from the brink of defeat against Tom Gorman to level the tie for Romania. No matter how much one could question Tiriac's disruptive tactics, even Ralston's team were grudgingly forced to admire the way in which the rugged Romanian recovered from trailing by two sets to love and two breaks in the third set to beating Gorman 4–6, 2–6, 6–4, 6–3, 6–2.

In a surprising tie, nothing was more surprising than the doubles. For, while Nastase played well below expectation, Smith's inexperienced partner Erik van Dillen rose above himself to produce a devastating display that contributed fully to the amazing American victory. The score of 6–2, 6–0, 6–3 was barely believable and never before or since have Tiriac and Nastase lost by such a decisive score.

On the Sunday a chill October wind blew ominously for Romania. Surely it was asking too much of Tiriac for him to produce further miracles and conquer the commanding Stan Smith? Well, yes it was, but no-one could accuse Tiriac of not giving it a try. David Gray wrote in *The Guardian*: 'The match with which the United States won the Davis Cup when Smith gave them a 3–1 lead by beating Ion Tiriac, 4–6, 6–2, 6–4, 2–6, 6–0, in two hours fifty-one minutes must have been the noisiest, angriest, the most absorbing and the most passionate contest in the history of the competition.

'It was uninhibited; it contained all the ingredients for superb entertainment (including a great many things that should never happen on a tennis court) and in the end justice was done ... In the last dead rubber Nastase beat Gorman 6–1, 6–2, 5–7, 10–8 and then Peter Davis, son of Dwight Davis who donated the trophy, presented it to Ralston who gave a speech which seemed a masterpiece of diplomatic understatement. Tiriac also made a good speech, reminding all Nastase's critics that if it had not been for the younger Romanian's victories against Russia and Australia, they wouldn't have reached the final at all. That was almost the nicest thing that happened all week.'

For the Americans it had been a tremendous achievement and, if the towering presence of Stan Smith had provided the inspiration, every member of the squad played his part in overturning the odds.

But for Ilie Nastase it was a very different story. 'Romanians make you a hero in twenty-four hours and put you down in two minutes,' Tiriac pointed out and Ilie will not argue with him. He had failed at a crucial moment and it took some time before his fellow-countrymen put him back on the pedestal reserved for their sporting heroes.

Ilie was certainly scarred by the experience. But not broken by it. He continued to play Davis Cup for Romania and now has a record of play in that competition surpassed only by a handful of other players.

7

THE HIGHS AND LOWS

The Queen's Club, London, June 1977. Pancho Gonzales is slumped in one of the big armchairs in the members' lounge. Ilie Nastase is perched on the edge of his seat, twiddling his racket, waiting to play doubles. They are talking about motor-racing, one of Pancho's passions. Nastase says the cars are too small.

'You can't get out if there's an accident,' he says.

'You've gotta think positive—take a mature attitude,' growls Gonzales. 'How old are you now anyway?'

'Almost thirty-one.'

'Hell, some men never mature until they're thirty-two,' says Gonzales, grinning.

'Why do you want me to mature?' asks Ilie. 'Then I'll be boring. Then what'll I do?'

It is no use responding to that question by suggesting that, if he was a little more boring, he would play better tennis. He knows that. What he is less willing to admit and may not even truly understand, is that the swearing and the clowning and all the other intolerable antics he pulls on court are a defence mechanism intended to shield him from the fear of defeat. In a highly individual sport like tennis, that fear is very real and very powerful. Defeat is peering over every player's shoulder and when its cold, clammy hand comes down on your neck, you can wriggle and scream but it will do no good. The defeat and the blame are all yours. The pressure of defeat is heavy in other sports as well but in soccer, cricket, baseball or whatever, there are others with whom to share your misery and a player can always kid himself that it was not his fault. And, indeed, it may not have been. If Arsenal lose 3–5 and Malcolm Macdonald gets a hat-trick, it is unlikely he is going to get blamed or dropped. His job and his reputation are not *necessarily* on the line.

In tennis defeat means minimum prize-money—barely enough to cover expenses for the week if it comes in the first round—no points on the ATP computer and the fear that if the defeat occurs in round one again the following week, that computer ranking will start to plummet. For a top player that means he could soon lose his protected seeding position in tournaments. If he is a middle-ranked player, he could soon find himself having to qualify. Of course it is true that once a player becomes an

104

established superstar then he can go off and make as much if not more money playing exhibition matches. But that merely cushions the fear of defeat—it does not exorcize it. For although it does not always manifest itself under the name of fear, the repugnance of defeat or the sheer bloody-minded refusal to accept it, is what has made a player a superstar in the first place. During twenty years of involvement in the game, I have not known a single top player who does not care about losing. There is a word that all the cynics tend to overlook and it is pride. Without pride no player, however talented, is going to have the extra drive required to break through to the very top. Oh yes, the money is nice, too, and it is a great big incentive when one is starting out. But it is not the money that keeps a player in the world's top ten year after year.

No one enjoys his money more than Tom Okker. But when I have been with Tom after a bad defeat, it is not the loss of a few thousand dollars that is eating him up. 'Christ, I should have beaten that guy,' he will mutter. 'I'm a better player than he is. How could I lose to a bum like that?'

That is not his bank balance talking. That is his pride. And when Ken Rosewall—another man who keeps a canny eye on his finances—misses a backhand down the line by half an inch and throws his racket down in disgust, do you think he's annoyed because it might cost him money? Like hell. He's annoyed because hitting that backhand to absolute perfection is his craft and when he misses, it just burns him inside. It's called pride of performance.

Ilie Nastase has that pride. But it is not a simple, singular pride like Rosewall's. It is mixed with a showman's desire to be noticed, to be acclaimed. By preference he would rather be acclaimed for the feather-weight delicacy of his drop shot or the power of his first serve. But should they not be working with the precision required, then something else will have to do. As Ilie's natural inclination is to have fun, he will clown and hope that the crowd has fun, too. If his opponent doesn't like it, too bad. It's not Ilie's fault that the other guy's not funny. But if no one laughs or worse still actually complains about the distractions being caused, then the lava starts to churn and very soon that volcanic temperament is spitting fire. The dark, vengeful, arrogant side of his nature erupts from deep within him and suddenly the man who stands on centre stage is no longer Ariel, the supernatural sprite, or Trinculo, the hapless clown, but Caliban, a raging, frothing creature full of wicked guile who, indeed, 'knows how to curse'. But if cursing is what it takes to hold the spotlight, then let the tempest rage. At least it won't be boring. At least, thinks Nastase, if I can't make them love me or laugh at me then I'll make them hate me. One way or the other, they'll come back.

Often this escalation of emotion is not a conscious act on Ilie's part and one of the great puzzles in analysing his nature is to try to pin-point the exact moment when—and if—spontaneous joy or rage gives way to premeditated attempts to distract his opponent. But either way it is all part of a sometimes conscious, sometimes unconscious defence mechanism designed to provide alternative escape routes from the all-embracing fear of defeat. This element in Nastase's make-up had been evident from the moment he first appeared on the circuit. If he had been strictly disciplined at the outset, everything might have been different. But the game's officiating body was even laxer then than it was when Nastase became a star and by then it was too late.

By the time he knew he was good, the arrogant streak in his character was too well-formed for him to bow to instructions handed down from anonymous officials he had never seen before. It was partly that arrogance and partly the insecurity from which it sprang that made him turn on umpires who tried to order him about and say, '*Mr* Nastase to you. You call me *Mr* Nastase'.

Always he has been less inclined to fool around with people he knows and respects. And, of course, it is necessary to win his respect. As a player, there are only two ways to do this. Either beat him regularly by virtue of a superior talent or frighten him to death with a superior personality. In a celebrated incident at the Albert Hall, Clark Graebner did the latter.

Before he began to take a slightly more gentle view of the world, Graebner was everybody's idea of a US Army bull sergeant. Tall, strapping, with slick-back hair and horn-rimmed spectacles, Clark often gave the word 'obnoxious' a new meaning through his behaviour on court. But his ability to take a joke against himself was always his saving grace and now, as a successful executive for Pandick Press, one of America's largest paper manufacturing companies, he can look back on the highs and lows of his career with a certain detachment.

'Actually the Nastase incident in London ended up as a big plus for me,' Graebner said when we met at his New York office recently. 'Until then I was always thought of as the testy little soul but suddenly I was the big hero because I had stood up to Nastase. When I got back home, people stopped me in the street in New York to say "Well done". It was great exposure.'

Inevitably the press made a meal out of the story and it was probably overblown. Nonetheless Graebner made his point.

'Nastase was playing extremely well,' Clark recalled. 'He had a break and it was deuce on his serve. He hit a sharply-angled shot and I was running like hell to reach it when suddenly this ballgirl stands up and catches the ball just as I am about to start my swing. I had two choices. Either I could have continued my swing and decapitated the kid or not swung at all. Being a nice guy I didn't swing. The umpire then called "Advantage Nastase" and I thought Now hang on, chum. I don't necessarily think it's my point but I don't think it's Nastase's either. So I complain and the umpire says "Play two" and Ilie goes off the deep end. Really hacked off he was and I didn't think he was being reasonable. After I won the point and the game to level it up, he's still carrying on as we change ends so I say to him, "Listen, you jerk, why are you trying to pull this on me? I wasn't trying to screw you. I couldn't play the ball." But he won't listen and then I get really pissed off. So I march up to him and stare him straight in the eye and say "Listen, you asshole, try and pull any more of your stunts on me and I'll beat your head in." Everybody said I touched him but that's not true. We were standing only inches apart but I never laid a finger on him.'

It was, however, too close for Ilie. He barely got a ball on the strings during the next game which Graebner won to love and walked off at the end of it, mumbling something about being too nervous to play. 'You can't let him just walk off like that,' Graebner complained. But the referee, Captain Mike Gibson, wanted to give Ilie one chance to come back on court and play.

'OK so he's got thirty seconds,' said Graebner who was not unreasonably thinking of the £1,000 difference in prize-money that was at stake.

'But he never did come back,' recalled Clark. 'So I said "See you later, pal" and left Gibson to get the next match on court. There was no real problem between us in the locker-room afterwards. Nastase just looked scared. Actually I like the guy. I don't think much of what he does is malicious. He starts off in a playful sort of way and then doesn't seem to be able to control that switch which takes him from comedian to boor.'

Unfortunately it was a switch that was being flicked with increasingly regularity as the triumphs of 1972 and 1973 faded into the past. In 1974 he still played brilliantly on occasions, winning a total of eight singles titles but the ones that mattered most—the French, the Italian and the Commercial Union Masters—all slipped from his grasp, and as his confidence waned so his insecurities emerged to dominate his personality and behaviour. Not many people stood up to him like Graebner and those who allowed themselves to be dominated by his fame and his talent often found themselves ruthlessly abused. The nickname "Nasty" stuck because he made it stick. Whenever the magic failed to flow, his nerves got the better of him and he ranted and raved, creating the kind of headlines Hollywood press agents dream about. But unlike some stars of the screen, Ilie was often every bit as bad as his publicity. Yet there were moments when he had good reason to be. Sometimes he was the victim of abuse before he had put a foot wrong—the victim of his own reputation. In the minds of the players, the press and all those around him he had become a target for both good and evil. Even when he slipped off the top perch to a position of fifth or sixth best player in the world, he remained the greatest lightning rod for excitement the game possessed.

But, of course, there is no absolute about Nastase. The dark, offensive side of his nature was only a part of his character and, despite the headlines and the notoriety it created it remains, I believe, the smaller part. To a much greater degree, he is a naive and fun-loving type of person who is not particularly well-equipped to handle the responsibilities that tend to be thrust upon any star of a multi-million-dollar professional sport.

So when the Association of Tennis Professionals banded together and presented the amateur establishment with a hard-line ultimatum the week before Wimbledon in 1973—drop the ban on Pilic or we boycott the Championship—Ilie was confused. The ATP was only nine months old at the time and Nastase did not fully comprehend what far-reaching goals it was attempting to achieve for the long-term benefit of the professional player. And the dominant forces in his life did not help him to understand it.

Dominique was innately suspicious of the ATP's tough, brash American leaders like Jack Kramer and Donald Dell and felt that, whatever their motives were, they were not in any way geared to the individual needs of her husband. As attempts were made to make Ilie join the picket-line, Dominique took on an increasingly protective role.

'These people are not your friends,' she told Ilie. 'If you want to play, you should play.'

The British press, which blindly turned its wrath on the ATP, lent powerful support to her argument. As it became increasingly likely that Nastase, along with Roger Taylor, would be one of the few major ATP stars to break ranks and play he was flattered and lionized by tennis writers who had been pretty quick to criticize him in the past. It was seductive stuff, especially for someone as susceptible to public acclaim as Nastase.

And then there was the Romanian Federation. Like all other national tennis federations, Romanian officials were being pressured by ILTF president, Allan Heyman, to keep their players from joining the ATP boycott. Nastase, not yet enjoying the independence he is afforded today, was obviously affected by this but to what extent has never been precisely established. Nastase maintains he received a cable from his federation in Bucharest ordering him to play. But Tiriac who, it should be remembered, was not on speaking terms with Ilie at the time, hinted darkly that it had only been sent because Nastase had asked the President of the Romanian Federation to get him off the hook with the ATP.

Wherever the truth may lie, there is absolutely no doubt that Nastase wanted to play. It was an entirely selfish desire on his part for he didn't much care what the ATP were trying to achieve. Like the British press and consequently the vast majority of the British public, Ilie was trying hard to believe that the whole thing was a game of power politics between Kramer and Dell on one side and Wimbledon and the ILTF on the other. He didn't *want* to believe that playing colleagues like Cliff Drysdale, Arthur Ashe, Stan Smith and Charlie Pasarell, whose respect and acceptance he craved, were totally committed to such a drastic move—which, of course, they were.

So he only listened to the voices that told him what he wanted to hear—that told him to play. As they included his wife, his Federation back home and every newspaper he set eyes on during that fraught and dramatic week of Queen's—a tournament he sailed through blithely despite the distractions—it was not difficult for him to rationalize that he was doing the right thing.

Considering my close involvement with the ATP in later years, it will quite rightly be considered a subjective viewpoint when I maintain that Nastase was wrong. But in this particular instance I am making that statement purely on the grounds of whether or not it was good for Nastase and his career. Obviously I am of the opinion that the ATP boycott of Wimbledon in 1973 was necessary. It was as inevitable as the Packer affair which hit cricket in 1977. Professional athletes will only be taken for a ride for so long, and if the major battle had not been fought for tennis players then, a series of minor and ultimately far more damaging skirmishes would have been fought endlessly in the years that followed, causing far more bitterness and division and, more importantly still, delaying the progress that has since been made.

But from Nastase's personal point of view, his decision not to join the boycott was bad for several reasons. First, it is never very clever to alienate oneself so drastically from the people one must live and work with, even if they are competitors.

'It's all very fine for Nastase and Taylor to say they want so badly to play at Wimbledon,' growled Bob Carmichael one night in the bar of the Gloucester Hotel after the boycott decision had been accepted by 95 per cent of ATP members. 'But that's not the point, is it? How dare they think they bloody well want to play more than I do?'

That just about summed up the feeling of the majority of players towards the blacklegs and it made for a very uneasy atmosphere in locker-rooms around the world for many months afterwards.

But that, for a character as irrepressible and basically genial as Nastase, was a passing problem. If players who have been driven to distraction by his antics on court can forgive and forget within a matter of days, it was inevitable that most of his fellow pros would not bear any long-standing grudge against him for his action at Wimbledon.

Of more serious and lasting consequence to Nastase's career was the mutual state of suspicion and distrust that now existed between the

Romanian and the officers of the ATP, the one governing body that was supposed to look after the interests of all the players. One of the main reasons for the ATP's existence was the obvious need for professional tennis to have rules written and enforced for the players by the players. It was no longer tolerable for professional athletes to be governed by an archaic set of rules administered by a bunch of bankers, businessmen, farmers and retired army officers who understood little and often cared less about the special problems facing the touring professional.

Contrary to what the public might think, the rules written by the first two ATP presidents, Cliff Drysdale and Arthur Ashe, in consultation with a wide spectrum of players from all levels of the pro game, has improved immeasurably the administration of the circuit as well as the conduct of the majority of players.

It is sad but true to relate that the casual tennis follower might have less difficulty in accepting that fact had it not been for the headlines involving, if not always created by, the subject of our story. At a conservative guess 75 per cent of the stories that have hit the press in the last four years regarding rows, disputes, fines, and suspensions in professional tennis have revolved around Ilie Natase.

Now that might have been inevitable. If one accepts Tiriac's theory that one has to take Ilie as he is or forget him, then indeed nothing could have been done. Certainly nothing would ever have turned him into a paragon of virtue or forced him into maintaining the standard of court manners exhibited by the likes of Jaime Fillol. But it is just possible that, had someone been able to draw him into the ATP fold, gained his trust and guided him through some of the more obvious pitfalls, Ilie would not have turned into quite the alienated maverick he became. But with Tiriac a dubious influence as far as court behaviour was concerned, and in any case no longer his friend, he had literally no one to whom he could turn for advice or support.

The loneliness of the long-distance tennis traveller is not something that should be lightly dismissed. Strange cities, strange hotels, interminably long hours to fill in between practice and matches and more practice—there are few ways to overcome this other than the cameraderie of one's fellow pros. In this respect the Americans and the Australians have it easier. There are always a lot of both at any tournament and, in their different ways, most of them spend a good deal of time together socially. As nearly all the leading Americans are married, theirs tends to be a more structured social scene of dining in groups of four or six, while the Aussies just lump together in the bar and meander off to eat, dragging the odd wife along with them. The need to get together for a few beers every night is a serious ritual for the Australians and is possibly the only thing that keeps them sane during the six or even nine months many of them spend on the road each year. One season when Rod Laver, then a senior citizen on the tour, elected to play the WCT circuit, he noticed to his horror that there were no Australians in his group—it being the period when the WCT format divided the tour into three separate divisions. So Colin Dibley, one of the most popular of all the Aussies, was persuaded to switch groups so that he could keep Rod company over a couple of beers each night. I'm not sure how many matches Colin won that season but 'Rocket' was never lonely.

For players of other nationalities there is always the grim possibility that they might be the only Spaniard, Italian or Hungarian on the tour. As practically everyone speaks English, with most Europeans speaking several other languages besides, superficial friendships are not difficult to form. Nastase, with his multilingual facility, is certainly never short of someone with whom to exchange jibes, comments and jokes. But that is different from having a close friend to whom you can open your heart and your problems. That is where the loneliness starts to hurt and whenever Dominique was not travelling with him, Ilie felt it keenly.

That was one reason why the friendship with Jimmy Connors quickly became so intense. It was not just that Ilie had found a friend but that their rollicking, devil-may-care attitude to life forced them more and more into the role of outlaws who were forever teasing and occasionally defying the establishment.

Having been raised by his mother and Bill Riordan to be the complete loner, Connors was inevitably anti-ATP, especially in view of Riordan's attempts to get his own player's association off the ground. So although Nastase remained a member of the ATP, his attitude towards the association and some of the individuals who ran it became increasingly antagonistic. Jimmy and he had a lot of harmless fun together and often entertained the crowds at various tournaments with their uproarious and genuinely funny behaviour. But Ilie was the senior half in a partnership that was not heavy on maturity and the stabilizing influence he desperately needed was never there.

He won the doubles with Connors at Wimbledon in the boycott year but his attempt to win a singles crown that should have been his for the taking, considering the standard of opposition, was a disaster. Sneezing with hay fever and playing with an injured thumb, a college kid called Sandy Mayer still managed to produce tennis of sufficient severity and skill to beat Ilie 6–4, 8–6, 6–8, 6–4 in the round of sixteen. Mayer went on to reach the semi-finals and is now established as a fast-court player of high repute. But in 1973 it was a bad loss for Nastase and there was little consolation for him when his old rival Jan Kodes, not an ATP member at the time, went on to win the coveted title over Alex Metreveli of the Soviet Union in a predictably lack-lustre final. When the ATP slapped a $5,000 fine on both Taylor and himself for having defied the ban, Ilie wondered whether all the fuss had been worth it.

Nastase also blew it at the next tournament of major importance when he went down to Rhodesia's Andrew Pattison at Forest Hills after leading by two sets to love. Despite the fact that Pattison is a deceptively skilful player, it was not a match Ilie should have lost after establishing such a long lead. At the time it was rare for him to do so but as the years wore on it became a frustratingly repetitive story.

But as we have seen, his performances at Wimbledon and Forest Hills were the only blemishes on an otherwise outstanding year. In 1974 those blemishes began spreading like a rash and at the end of a confusing twelve months I found myself writing the following review of Ilie's year for the Commercial Union Grand Prix *Annual*: 'I suppose it could have been the carrot juice. Certainly it is as plausible a reason as any other when one tries to attach logic to the unfathomable fortunes of Ilie Nastase. Obviously something happened to him between August and October.

'When he lost to Bill Brown in the first round of the Canadian Open, Nasty's summer of discontent reached its nadir. Such was his morbid state of mind that one wondered if he were not munching deadly nightshade in his hotel room every night. He wanted to give up and crawl away to some dark, secluded place. At the very least he wanted to withdraw from Boston and catch a plane home to Bucharest. Friends persuaded him that such abuse of his commitments would only bring him more trouble and so he stayed, playing a little better without achieving much of note at Longwood and Forest Hills.

'But slowly the atropine seemed to drain out of his system. Before finally returning home, he won a $50,000 Grand Prix event at Cedar Grove, New Jersey, and when he reappeared in Spain in the autumn he was a new man. Serious, relaxed and totally in tune again with his effortless talent, he swept through two of the strongest clay-court fields of the year in Madrid and Barcelona and then carried his winning streak back across the Atlantic to win the ABC Television Classic at Hilton Head Island, South Carolina, beating Rod Laver and Bjorn Borg in the process. In twenty matches, he had always seemed a whole class better than his opposition.

'So maybe it was the carrot juice. "I have this friend in Bucharest who tells me the juice of the carrot is very good to help you concentrate," Ilie explained after he had beaten Manolo Orantes in Barcelona. "So now I have this juice every morning for breakfast and suddenly I concentrate very well. Before, as you know, I concentrate not so good."

'He wags his finger and chuckles as he says it, revealing once again that captivating charm. Searching for a broader explanation for Ilie's revival one turns to Dominique Nastase, four months pregnant with his

112

child and not showing it, still as chic and elegant as ever with her lustrous brown hair, huge brown eyes and tall mannequin's figure.

'She flashes a knowing smile when you mention the carrot juice. "Yes, maybe that helped," she says. "But three weeks rest and plenty of time with his wife helped even more."

'I know a few guys who wouldn't be able to hit a ball if they spent too much time with Dominique but then Nasty isn't your average sort of chap and I suppose he knows how to handle it.

'Of course, no matter how hard any of us try, analysing Ilie Nastase is a thoroughly hopeless pastime. He is kaleidoscopic in his moods; mesmerizing in his unpredictability; scarcely credible in his facility to both please and to annoy. He is not, by any conventional standards, a normal man. But then anyone born in the Balkans, reared by that great grizzly glass-eater, Tiriac, and then clasped to the bosom of the wondrous Dominique, has the right or, at the very least, a damned good reason for being a trifle different.

'Nevertheless his attitude and performance in Spain did suggest that at the age of twenty-eight, Nastase's genius might be maturing. Apart from one outburst during his match aginst Harold Solomon in Madrid, his behaviour in both Spanish Championships was exemplary. Even under trying circumstances in the Barcelona final against Orantes when high winds tore at the loose red clay of the Real Club's Centre Court, blowing grit in his eyes and ruining his accuracy, Nastase buckled down to the task in hand and won the match with the same kind of professional determination that Rod Laver displayed in similar conditions in Tokyo and Houston earlier in the year.

' "I am so confident again now," Ilie told me as we climbed aboard the Air France Caravelle for Paris. "Early this summer I was scared, you know. I didn't know what to do on court. I was tired. Everything seemed so difficult."

'It is a little hard to imagine tennis being difficult for Nastase but anyone who watched him fumble and grope his way through the summer months will know what he means. It is precisely the incredible facility with which Nastase normally wields his racket that makes him one of the most extraordinary talents the game has ever known. I can think of many people I would rather have my money on in a big match but none, in my memory, who have had a great variety of skill; a wider repertoire of shots. Hoad, Laver, Santana—all possessed greater killer shots and all, in their varied styles, could make the ball sit up and bark, but none looked quite so natural doing it as Nastase.

'Despite his superb performances in Paris, Rome and Forest Hills and his consistent triumphs in the Grand Prix Masters, Ilie still has not quite stamped his mark on the game as a consistent Champion of Champions.

'That he has the skill to do so is not in doubt. But does he have the will? The year 1975 will go a long way to answering that question and I have a feeling that the answer will be positive.'

Wrong. I was too optimistic. 1975 was worse. As I mentioned later in that article, Ilie, realizing that he was playing too much, had intended cutting down on his playing schedule. But he didn't. When Rodgers and Hammerstein wrote 'I'm just a girl who can't say no' for their musical, *Oklahoma*, they should have switched genders and waited until Ilie came along. For a guy who was going to play less, Nastase must have spent most of 1975 saying 'yes'. The previous year he had played in twenty-nine tournaments and ended up exhausted. So in 1975 he agreed to play in thirty-one. Good thinking.

But it was not simply the amount of tennis he played but the amount of trouble he got himself into that made 1975 such a traumatic and disappointing year. All through 1974 the temper tantrums had been getting worse as fatigue and loss of form made him less and less tolerant of petty officialdom. Often he was rude and sometimes obscene but only once that year had his bluff been called. That was during the US Clay Court Championships at Indianapolis. At one set up and 5-all in the second against Raul Ramirez in the quarter-final, Nastase began stalling and swearing at a linesman. Veteran umpire Bill Macassin warned Ilie that there would be problems if he did not behave. 'You can't give me any problems, you son of a bitch,' replied Nastase who, to his considerable astonishment, promptly found himself defaulted.

Nastase protested at this sudden, unusual but perfectly reasonable ruling and managed to get his case reviewed. There were, I believe, some officials who felt that Ramirez was not entirely blameless. However, after a six-hour discussion, Macassin's decision was upheld by a committee headed by Stan Malless, then president of the US LTA. Connors, who was behaving like a real friend in those days, publicly rushed to Ilie's defence after he and Nastase had won the doubles together. (Jimmy himself won the singles over Borg, adding credence to his growing superiority over all types of opposition following his victory at Wimbledon a month before.) 'What the people at Indianapolis did to him was scandalous,' Connors told the press. 'They kept him waiting for hours while they discussed his case and then threw him out. I am not surprised that he talked about leaving America. That was no way to treat the greatest player in the world.'

Although it was good to hear Connors talk in such a generous fashion, it was not what Nastase needed to hear. Indianapolis should have been a warning to him. It should have offered him a clear indication of just how far he could go with his stalling, his swearing and his abuse of officials before their patience snapped. But just like Tiriac slapping him around the ear at that training camp in the Carpathian mountains, the disqualification at Indianapolis stung briefly and was then forgotten.

In 1975, however, incidents like that became less easy to forget because they occurred too often. The first explosion came during the American Airlines Tennis Games—a tournament master-minded by the ATP as a fund-raiser for the Association—which was being played that year at Tucson, Arizona.

Nastase, having beaten Rod Laver in the previous round, was facing Ken Rosewall in the semi-final on the medium-fast Laykold cement court. As usual against a man he admired more than any other in the game, he was losing. Ilie had never beaten the little maestro the tennis world knows affectionately as 'Muscles' and when Rosewall led by a set and a break in the second it didn't look as if anything was going to change. But, of course, Nastase ensured that it did.

He had been the recipient of a couple of bad line-calls from a particular line-judge earlier in the match and had moaned about them in his normal manner. But when yet another ball was called out that Ilie felt was in—and, indeed, he could have been right—he walked up to umpire Boyd Moarse and said, 'I quit.' That, at least, was what everyone understood him to have said but, as it transpired, it was not all he said. Nonetheless, at the time, it seemed as if Nastase was pulling one of his great acts of brinkmanship. Sitting down in the chair at the courtside, he argued for several minutes with referee John Fowler who had hurried to the court. At a rough estimation, four or five minutes had passed when ATP Executive Director Jack Kramer turned to me and said, 'You know Ilie. Go and see if you can't get this thing settled one way or the other.'

Although the intervention of ATP officials was criticized in some sections of the press afterwards, the fact that I, as European director of the ATP, should become involved with an incident concerning a European player seemed reasonable at the time if only because the delay was becoming embarrassing.

Rosewall, his head down, was walking round the middle of the court in small circles, trying not to be distracted by it all and Nastase seemed to be off on one of his endless tirades against officialdom. That was how it looked to the 6,000 spectators and nation-wide television audience. One of two things should have happened several minutes before. Either Nastase should have been taken at his word and the match awarded to Rosewall or the referee should have given him fifteen seconds to get back on court under threat of default.

As neither of those two things seemed to be about to happen, I followed Kramer's suggestion. Walking along the front row of seats, I crouched down behind Ilie's chair. Then adopting as friendly and as informal a tone as possible, I butted into the referee's conversation and said to Ilie, 'Listen,

115

this isn't doing anyone any good. Either quit or get back on court and forget about it.'

I do not pretend I was solely responsible for getting him back on court because I think even Ilie realized the stalemate could not go on forever but he did, at any rate, resume playing immediately.

But in many people's minds the most unfortunate aspect of the whole affair was yet to come. Despite his long experience in the game and the knowledge of exactly what Nastase was like to play against, Rosewall had allowed the incident to distract him and when play resumed, his concentration was shot. He missed three easy volleys to drop serve and eventually lost the second set 7–5. Ilie pounced on his frustrated opponent in the third and won it 6–3. The next day Nastase lost to John Alexander whose serve was virtually unplayable with the light Spalding balls that were being used.

By then Nastase had become public enemy No 1 amongst the sports fans of America. Within an hour both the Tucson Racquet Club and the television network headquarters had received over fifty cables from irate viewers, condemning Nastase for his behaviour and for being, among other things a 'Commie bum'; condemning the referee for not defaulting him; and condemning the ATP for interfering.

Most of the Australian and American players were also livid that Rosewall, an idol to many of them, had been the victim of what they considered to be an act of gamesmanship on Nastase's part. At a meeting between Kramer and some members of the ATP Board it was decided that Nastase should be fined a token $500.

Although Ilie was never convinced of the fact, Kramer genuinely wanted to help him. Like so many great champions, Jack hated to see exceptional talent go to waste and during the course of a long private talk he had with Nastase that weekend, he tried to point out the error of Ilie's ways.

Kramer refers to this talk in a letter he wrote to Nastase the following week, a copy of which was sent to me at the ATP Bureau in Paris. In part it read: 'Ilie, the other clippings (enclosed) are being sent to you as I can't help but feel that, had you played straight tennis, allowing nothing to distract you, you most probably would have had your picture in the winner's saddle instead of having the various other pictures which, quite honestly, do not show you to your best advantage.

'I do wish that you would seriously consider my remarks to you on Sunday as there is no doubt in my mind that if you conquer the impulses that seem to destroy your concentration when things occur on court, you can really show the world who has the most talent by compiling the best tennis record.

'Before closing, I want to say, once again, that you have ten days from the time you receive this letter to request a hearing on the Tucson matter ...'

Kramer signed off with this final paragraph: 'Believe me, the ATP still values your being a member and hopes that what has occurred can be forgotten and that you and the ATP can both help tennis in many, many good ways.'

Clearly, this was a wholehearted attempt by Kramer to prevent Nastase from being alienated by the Tucson incident. But it didn't work. To Ilie the size of the fine didn't matter. It was the fact that he had been fined, and therefore condemned, that hurt him. As is so often the case when he stirs up a rumpus that finally gets out of hand, he cannot comprehend why people fail to see his side of the argument. Did Nastase have any kind of any argument to put forward in Tucson? When I spoke to him about it recently I was surprised to find that Kramer felt Nastase might have been too harshly treated.

'We were all acting on the assumption that all Ilie said when he walked off court was a sort of hot-tempered "I quit",' Kramer explained over lunch in Los Angeles. 'But sometime later the umpire, Boyd Morse, told me that what Ilie had really said was "I'll quit *if you don't remove that line judge.*" Now, to my mind, that puts a whole different complexion on the thing. I think every player has the right to ask for the removal of a line judge if he has lost confidence in that person's ability to call the line correctly. But in this instance Ilie's request seemed to get buried in the confusion created by his rather tempestuous behaviour. I always used quietly to ask that the linesman I thought was doing a bad job be removed at the next change-over. It always worked with the least amount of embarrassment. The problem lies in the way Ilie goes about things. When the pianist flunks a note, you don't stop the concert. But Ilie is always stopping the concert.'

Why this never came out at the time is not clear. Certainly the rage the players felt at Ilie's behaviour centred on what they considered to have been a categorical statement that he quit, meaning that Rosewall should have been handed the match then and there. As we heard it at the time, there were no 'ifs' or 'buts' about it.

'I honestly don't know why this wasn't made clear at the time,' Kramer continued. 'I know I had it in my mind that Ilie had done it deliberately to throw Rosewall off and that was why I felt he should be fined, although the $500 was nothing. Now I feel kind of badly about it considering all the abuse Ilie took.'

Although people who have had to face him across the net in his all-conquering championship years, and those who dealt with him when he was master-minding the future of professional tennis, may not have noticed this particular trait in his character, Jack Kramer has a soft heart. His biggest fault as executive director of the ATP was his almost total

117

reluctance to levy fines against those players who deserved it. But somehow this aspect of Kramer's nature never transmitted itself to Ilie. Probably the basic differences in their temperaments and upbringing made it impossible for them to speak the same language and, as we shall see, their relationship deteriorated rather than improved as Nastase's stormy year progressed.

Two months after Tucson, Nastase arrived in Bournemouth for the British Hardcourt Championships in a nervous frame of mind. Captain Mike Gibson, for many years the referee at Wimbledon, always made Ilie nervous. Gibson ran his tournaments like a military exercise. The players were his troops and troops are not expected to answer back or query an order. Many players found Gibson's autocratic manner hard to swallow so it goes without saying that Nastase suffered from a permanent state of indigestion whenever the good captain was in command. Like any experienced officer in the British Army, Captain Gibson knew how to banter with the men on the eve of battle and during the early part of the week he and Nastase were frequently involved in jocular arguments over scheduling of matches and practice courts—always in short supply during rain-drenched Bournemouth.

But the current of tension that ran between them became increasingly frayed as the days passed. Nastase had talked his way through an early round match against Hans Kary and driven the Austrian—normally a man who has a lot to say himself—to both distraction and defeat. Gibson had wagged a cautionary finger at him after that performance and Nastase smouldered.

I had to spend a lot of time on ATP business in the referee's office during that week and I remember watching, fascinated, as the two of them probed and parried, each nipping away at the other man's nerve ends.

Captain Gibson, a straight-backed man in his forties with wavy brown hair and a heavy moustache that covered a large upper lip, would be standing erect and still behind his desk as the Romanian burst in—the panther facing the sphinx.

'Why you put me first on court at 11 tomorrow when I have a late doubles tonight?' was the kind of question Nastase would throw out for openers.

There would be a barely perceptible twitch of the moustache and then the throaty upper-class accent, well-suited to lecturing in large halls at Sandhurst, would waft back across the desk.

'Ilie, you know you are a round behind in the doubles so you'll probably have to play two doubles tomorrow after the singles,' Gibson would reply. 'And anyway we need a good opening match for the Centre Court.'

'Why do you have to put me on the Centre Court? Put me on one of those shitty ones outside. Nobody will care, anyway.'

This is Nastase being deliberately provocative. He would be mortified

118

if he were not put on the Centre Court at this late stage of a tournament and he knows that more people care about him in England than anywhere else. But he is also damn sure Captain Gibson isn't one of them. (Which, probably, is also not quite true.)

'Now come on, Ilie. You know everybody loves you.' But Ilie does not fall that easily for condescending remarks. Staring balefully at the man whose British phlegm he would dearly like to pierce, he would shrug and flounce out with a parting threat.

'O.K., maybe I play, maybe I don't. We'll see.'

Nastase, of course, was there at the appointed hour just as he had always intended to be. But, nevertheless, the fuse was running short and when he played Patrick Proisy in the quarter-final, it blew.

Nastase was leading 5–4 when, not for the first time, a close line call went against him. Ilie argued. The linesman stared impassively, infuriatingly, into space. Umpire Eric Augur, a senior member of the autocratic British Umpires Association, told Nastase to play on. But all the pent-up tension of the week was pouring out of him now. He gesticulated, he pleaded, he cried out for justice. He even managed to remember not to swear.

'Please look at the mark. Just look at it. Look ... look.'

But umpire Augur was unmoved. 'Play on, Nastase,' he said, and then repeated the imperious order. But Nastase wouldn't listen. Finally Augur told him twice that he would be disqualified if he did not resume.

Ilie was standing in the middle of the court, manacled by a deep, burning conviction that justice was not being done, when Augur looked over to where Captain Gibson was standing like an expressionless executioner. With the faintest inclination of the head, Gibson nodded. Augur turned back in his seat and announced 'Nastase you are disqualified. Proisy wins.'

Although Gibson hotly denied that any prior decision had been taken to 'get' Nastase at the first legitimate opportunity, the referee's presence at court-side, which is not normal, coupled with the readily understood signals with which he and the umpire communicated, suggested that some premediated act had taken place.

Dominique heard the news on the car radio as she was driving down from London to join her husband for the weekend. She was furious. 'I could not believe this would happen to Ilie in England. In America, maybe, but not here.'

She was not the only one to feel that Ilie had been given a rough deal. Throughout the week the standard of line-calling had been atrocious and the situation had not been helped by the unbending attitude of the umpires. And before the day was out, Ilie received purely coincidental moral support from an unexpected source.

Without bothering to argue about it, Roger Taylor picked up his rackets and walked off court when Manolo Orantes led him by a set and 1–0. Again it was the line-calling that caused the problem. Taylor had simply reached the limit of his patience. For Nastase to complain and carry on was one thing but when the biggest name in British tennis went as far as defaulting a match in protest then it was time for everyone to sit up and take notice. Derek Hardwick, the canniest politician in the game who was president of the ILTF at the time, hurriedly issued a statement sympathizing with the players' viewpoint and just managing to stop short of censuring the umpires. The press flailed about, blaming everyone in sight, including the Bournemouth weather; and Robert Harland, publicity officer of Coca-Cola which was sponsoring the event for the first time, managed to hide his delight at the amount of front-page coverage the Championships were getting behind a suitably serious countenance.

So once again, quite by chance, Taylor found his name linked with Nastase's as another major row swept through British tennis. It was ironic in that, although the Yorkshireman is an admirer of Ilie's talent and finds him pretty amusing as long as he is not on the other side of the net—a sentiment shared by many players—he has never been close to the Romanian.

'How can you get close to a guy who only says "Sheffield Steel" every time he sees you?' asks Taylor. Not very easily, I suppose, but it is odd how often Nastase and Taylor seem to act in concert.

The standard of umpiring and line-calling remains the single biggest problem facing professional tennis. Bournemouth 1975 and various other unhappy incidents spawned a break-away umpires' association in Britain with a somewhat younger membership assembled by Roy Cope-Lewis, and numerous electronic devices are currently being tried in an attempt to overcome the problem of human frailty. But nothing will be solved until enough money is found to produce a world-wide group of professional officials, uniformly trained and uniformly respected by the players.

Obviously Nastase goes about the problem the wrong way. Taylor's simple but devastatingly effective act of saying 'Thank you, but I no longer wish to play' elicited far speedier action than a whole symphony of histrionics. But Ilie still had a complete repetoire to play that year and unfortunately the jam session wasn't over.

8

DR JEKYLL AND MR HYDE

'Where's Ramirez?'. It was mid-afternoon on the Saturday of the Italian Championships 1975 and suddenly the question was being asked all over the elegant restaurants, bars, administrative offices and locker-rooms of the Foro Italico.

'Anyone seen Raul?' No one had. The sense of acute urgency with which that question was being asked centred on the fact that the Mexican was due to play Ilic Nastase in the day's second semi-final like ... NOW. Ramirez wasn't there.

Someone in the referee's office put through a frantic phone call to the Holiday Inn, which has become the headquarters for most of the players in Rome. One of the desk clerks, a lovely Eritrean girl called Doris, who, like most of the staff knew the players personally, confirmed that Ramirez had rushed out just a couple of minutes before. Taking into account the unpredictable flow of Roman traffic that would mean he would be between twenty and thirty minutes late.

In the locker-room Nastase started to fume. Although Ilie has transgressed against most of the rules in tennis at one time or another, I cannot think of a single instance when I have known him to be late for a match. He had every right to be angry. Ramirez had absolutely no excuse. The day's schedule was posted every night in the lobby of the Holiday Inn and, although he had checked it, he had committed the naive and unacceptable error of *assuming* that the women's final and the first men's semi-final—which were scheduled before his match with Nastase—would take a 'normal' amount of time. But there is no such thing as 'normal' when predicting the length of a tennis-match. It can take three hours or a player can pull a muscle in the first game and default. There is only one thing to do. Play safe. Get there early.

Ramirez was unlucky in that both matches had taken an inordinately short length of time. Chris Evert had destroyed Martina Navratilova 6–1, 6–0 and Manolo Orantes, making the game look so easy, as he always does when in top form, had out-classed Guillermo Vilas 6–2, 6–2, 6–2. So by playing so well Chrissie and Manolo had caught Raul on the hop.

'So you give me walk-over? When do I get walk-over? Rule says fifteen minutes and he's scratched, right? So now it's twelve minutes. He has three to go.' By this time Nastase was pacing up and down the spacious locker-room like a caged lion. As usual he was exaggerating a bit. It was only about eight minutes since the match had been called but nonetheless, the time was fast approaching when a decision on whether or not to default Ramirez would have to be taken. Ostensibly that responsibility lay solely with the referee but, as European director of the ATP, I knew I would get dragged into the issue, at least in an advisory capacity. During the two years in which I ran the ATP's Paris office, I found myself frequently acting as a sort of joint tournament director-cum-referee at many tournaments I attended purely because harassed local officials felt that players were more likely to accept rulings and judgments made by one of their own directors.

Nastase had gone one further than that by assuming that I was going to make the decision as to when to default Ramirez on my own. In deference to the tournament committee that I could not do, but I was certainly prepared to weigh in with an opinion if the situation demanded it. Actually, the referee and I saw things in much the same light. As soon as it was verified that Ramirez was on his way, I agreed with him that the match should go on. I came to that conclusion with a clear understanding that in doing so I was allowing the ATP rules—as they stood at the time—to be broken and was therefore being unfair to Nastase. For the rules clearly stated that if a player was not ready to play fifteen minutes after the match had been called to court, he should be fined *and* defaulted.

As I explained to the ATP board of directors later, that looks a very fair and reasonable rule when it is written in the peace and quiet of a conference room in a hotel in London, Paris or Palm Springs. It is the sort of rule that would work perfectly in Palm Springs. One would just walk up to the microphone and announce that, on account of one player arriving sixteen and a half minutes late there would be no further tennis that day. Assuming that the match was not being nationally televised—in which case the ATP rule-book would be torn up and thrown in the referee's face—everyone would boo and hiss for a couple of minutes and then climb elegantly into their Cadillacs and Thunderbirds and drive away.

But try implementing it on a hot Saturday afternoon in Rome with 6,000 Italians already restless over the fact that their money has been spent on two matches that barely warrant the name. Instead of a rout, they are now wanting a contest—some value for their money. Try telling a crowd like that they have seen all the tennis they are going to see and it is quite possible you will have a riot on your hands. Not a very big riot by today's standards, perhaps—just big enough to get a child trampled to death by angry spectators as they jump down from the marbled terracing and charge across the court. Then what do you tell the child's mother? Do you hold up your little ATP rule-book and say, 'Well, I'm terribly sorry but you see it says here under Section Three, sub-clause 15 ...'

You give the crowd a tennis match, that's what you do. And if you want to call that mob rule, that's quite all right with me. At least it's peaceful. No matter how carefully we write the rules nor how much we want to see them implemented in a uniform and impartial manner, blindly to ignore special circumstances and situations is merely abdicating one's responsibility as a human being. Computers might do otherwise, but when it comes to the crunch I'd rather bend a rule than a limb. So Ilie got screwed. Sorry, Ilie. But, in similar circumstances, I would advise the referee to do exactly the same thing.

With due deference to Raul, who had simply made an honest mistake, it would have been more just if Nastase had managed to keep calm about the whole thing and gained his revenge on court. But that would be like expecting Muhammad Ali to become a trappist monk two weeks before a world title-fight. For the first twenty minutes that we waited for the errant Ramirez, Ilie was in a state of near hysteria. He shouted at me; he shouted at the referee; and he shouted at the Italian Federation general secretary, Gianfranco Cameli.

Then, as the fifteen-minute mark came and went and there was still no sign of Ramirez, he fell silent and seemed to become reconciled to the fact that he was going to have to play the match. I think Cameli might have had something to do with Ilie's sudden change in mood. Gianfranco had reminded Ilie that he was to receive a presentation on court before the match to mark his appearance in every Italian Championship since 1966, apart from the one year in 1971 when it had been primarily a WCT event. Either Ilie did not want to let Cameli down or he rather liked the idea of receiving a presentation. Probably it was both. At any rate when Ramirez finally swept in half an hour late, Nastase never said a word and calmly waited for the Mexican, who looked slightly embarassed but otherwise unruffled, to change.

Ilie duly received his presentation and then proceeded to go to pieces once the match got under way. He had no feel, no touch, and the harder he tried the less he seemed able to time the ball. Ramirez, playing cool, steady tennis, moved swiftly to 6–2, 5–2 and, at the change-over, Nastase picked up his rackets and stormed off court amidst a barrage of boos and high-pitched whistles.

'I'm too nervous, I can't play. I don't concentrate. Shit, I shouldn't be playing anyway. I should have had walk-over.' Ilie, shaking with a combination of nerves, anger and frustration, babbled away as he made the long walk down the tunnel to the locker-room. Barging his way through a rapidly growing bunch of reporters crowding the door-way, he eventually slumped down on the locker-room bench. He looked exhausted.

'It's your fault,' he suddenly screamed at me. 'You're the bloody ATP. You should have defaulted him. That's what you're here for. Why should I have to wait forty minutes to play my match?'

He needed a target and at that moment I was as good a one as any. There was no point in arguing about it. He wasn't rational and, in any case, looking at it strictly from his point of view, I wouldn't have had much ammunition with which to argue. The rules, as written, were in his favour and they hadn't been obeyed for reasons that I have tried to explain. It had been the referee's decision more than mine but there was no point in pretending I hadn't backed him up. If Nastase wanted to blame me, so be it. Frankly I felt sorry for him.

It had been a peculiarly peaceful Rome prior to that horrendous Saturday and I had almost ignored my instincts and returned to Paris. It was a good thing I didn't because, incredibly, Ramirez was not the only player who contrived to be late for his match that day.

Dick Crealy, one of the circuit's more colourful characters and by no means your average Aussie, stampeded into the locker-room frothing at the mouth over what he claimed was a scheduling bungle. The fact that Nikki Pilic, his partner that week, had been changed and ready to play for about half an hour—as had their opponents Manolo Orantes and Juan Gisbert—made little impression on Dick. And when, at Gisbert's insistence, the Spaniards were given a walk-over, Crealy did his ape-man trick and went bananas, which is quite a sight to behold. Loping around the Foro Italico like some wounded jungle beast, Dick managed to insult just about everyone he came across in the most wondrously incoherent language. Needless to say I got it in the neck again and when he eventually roared back into the locker-room, I thought someone ought to padlock the door and certify the place as a lunatic asylum.

There was a worried-looking doctor stuffing tranquillizers down a distraught Nastase's throat in one corner while Jimmy Connors, who had condescended to play doubles in Rome that year, danced around in attendance looking as if he was ready to hit the first Italian who criticized his pal Ilie. Across the room, Gisbert, whose greying temples gave him a distinguished look at the best of times, was playing the Spanish grandee to the hilt, standing erect and indignant in the face of Crealy's verbal barrage.

'It is correct that we demand a default, you understand,' said Gisbert. 'It is in the rules.' Then, turning to me with a pompous flush of disdain, he thrust a fistful of lire, peseta and dollar bills into my hand. 'Here, take this and give it to them or whoever you like,' he said proudly. 'You must understand it is not for the money that we do this but the principle.'

'Fuck the principle,' Crealy spluttered in basic Australian. 'You can take your bloody money and stuff it up your arse. The fact is I was told by that bloody referee that we were third on court ... whatever and then ...

and anyway, you bastard, listen ... Ramirez gets away with it so why shouldn't we?'

And there Crealy had a point. There was no real answer to it. Of course he was right when he said that there should not be one rule for himself and one for Ramirez. The fact that his doubles was scheduled for an outside court where the crowd problem did not become a factor was, quite reasonably, not going to alter his thinking on the matter. The real problem lay in the writing of the rules which did not take into account the rights, feelings or reaction of the paying public. But as it stood, one had to make the best of a bad job and I still maintain the referee was right in not risking trouble by allowing Ramirez to play, while following the letter of the law with Crealy because there was no outside threat involved. Of course it was unfair but badly thought-out rules do not beget fair play.

But they do help create ludicrous situations and the locker-room of the Foro Italico had turned into a theatre of the absurd as Nastase trembled, Connors glared, Crealy frothed and Gisbert and I stood there thrusting a bundle of money back and forth at each other like a couple of demented fools. Orantes, who basically has the temperament of a saint, sat in a corner looking concerned and slightly hurt that he, too, had been singled out for abuse. I made Crealy apologize to Manolo afterwards but the next day Orantes needed more than kind words of humility when Ramirez, riding his luck all the way down to the wire, played shrewd and sometimes brilliant tennis to beat him in three long sets.

When all was said and done even Crealy, who is really a very lovable guy, admitted that no player ever has a proper excuse for being late for a match and, as with many passing storms on the pro circuit, there was no aftermath of bitterness.

Ramirez was fined, although less than he should have been considering the $16,000 he picked up for winning the title. But his sharp Washington lawyer, Lee Fentress, argued a good case which was helped by the fact that Raul did not have a reputation as a bad boy in official circles.

But for Ilie, of course, the whole thing had been a disaster. He had ended up being in the wrong, too, by walking off court once he had agreed to play the match but not even his worst enemy could accuse him of having instigated the problem. Many players would have been able to cope with it, but this turned out to be a classic example of Nastase's nerves getting the better of him. He had worked himself up into such an emotional state that he really did need those tranquillisers before he and Connors could play doubles later in the day.

So by June 1975 Nastase had already been involved in three highly publicized furores and was already becoming guilty by association. No matter what the facts of any particular rumpus might be, if Nastase was in any way involved then, in the mind of the public, he tended to be considered the cause of it. That, of course, was not always fair but at the Canadian Open Championships in Toronto in August there were no excuses. Nastase was guilty.

He was playing Orantes in the final and an excellently fought first set had reached three points to one for Nastase in the tie-break when Ilie hit a first serve that seemed to clip the line. But it was called out. So Nastase went into his rant and rave routine which achieved nothing. The linesman refused to change his call. So, quite inexcusably, Nastase went into a major sulk. He didn't stop playing, he didn't even stop running. There were points when he actually looked as if he might be trying ... a little. He hadn't switched the engine off. But from overdrive he had simply changed down to let it idle. Not even when your name is Nastase do you win championship matches that way and Orantes, looking faintly embarrassed, walked off with the title 7–6, 6–0, 6–1.

It was not difficult to fathom what was going through Ilie's mind. 'So they screw me again,' he was thinking. 'So, OK, I screw them. I don't care any more. If they want Orantes to win, he can win.' It was the classic, petulant reaction of a sulky little boy. But Nastase was supposed to be a great tennis champion with a responsibility towards the crowd, the sponsors and the game. And he had let them all down. As Bud Collins wrote in the BP *World of Tennis Yearbook*, 'Ilie insulted his opponent, Orantes, as well as a sell-out crowd of 6,000 and nation-wide television audiences in Canada and the US ... even his staunchest admirers were saddened by the episode of August 17th at the Toronto Skating, Curling and Cricket Club.'

CBC sportscaster Don Chevrier voiced the opinion of many Canadian sports fans when he told me, 'That was the most disgraceful exhibition by a top athlete I have ever seen in any sport. If Nastase is not thrown out of the game for a long time as a result I shall lose all respect for pro tennis.'

During the match Ilie's language had also been a disgrace. I was sitting on the side of the court taking photos when something caught his eye in the crowd and he yelled over my head, 'Go fuck yourself!' Apart from being vulgar and embarrassing it was unnecessary. but such was his state of mind that he didn't care. Inside, he was threshing about with his own emotions, scared, angry, unhappy and, as a result, vindictive. He wanted to strike back at a world he was rapidly losing faith in. Pressures he often didn't understand and could rarely control were becoming too much for him to handle. The more he struggled, the tighter the web of disaster clung to him and although there were times when he was innocent, it was he who had spun that web. Ilie was his own spider.

When I interviewed him for John Chanin's 'World of Sports' radio programme on the ABC network that evening, Ilie denied having thrown the match, just as he continued to deny it to everyone else.

But there was something he had said to me the instant he walked off court that made it clear he had not tried. I will not attempt to quote his exact words here because I cannot remember them with any precision. But the impression they left was absolutely clear. In my mind, there was no doubt at all that he had not cared whether he won or lost. That makes the whole thing a charade and I firmly believe it is the worst sin a professional athlete can commit.

As Marty Riessen said in his book *Match Point*, 'As a paid performer, be it boxer, singer, juggler or tennis-player, there is no way you should be allowed to cheat the public and get away with it.'

Some people will feel that Nastase's foul-mouthed outbursts of anger are as bad. In an article written for *World Tennis*, the comedian, Bill Cosby, who is a good player himself, made the following valid point: 'There are millions like me who want to see the game executed as beautifully as Ilie Nastase can, but when he goes off into one of his tirades, our minds are clouded by his arguing; no longer is his chipped backhand down the line a thing of beauty ... He must stop because, in truth, he is wasting the time of the people who have paid to see a great tennis-player play great tennis.'

I take Cosby's point which, basically, I agree with. But in response I would just say this. When Nastase goes off into one of his tirades at least he is interested. At least he is trying. It is, in fact, *because* he cares so much that he is spitting fire. One should not condone it nor hold it up as an example of how a young player should behave. But a man who behaves like Nastase has to be competing with every fibre of his being and as long as he is doing that, professional sports retains its one magic ingredient—its unpredictability.

Of course people pay to see professional sport so that they may marvel at the precision of Ken Rosewall's backhand; or swoon over Denis Compton's late cut—I weep for those too young to have seen that man bat—or gasp at Richard Sharp's outside break. But it is the fact that you never know when or how those incredible moments are going to happen that gives sport its extra magic. As a form of entertainment, it is what separates sport from art. The thrill of watching Nureyev dance or listening to Olivier speak such lines as 'He which hath no stomach to this fight, /Let him depart, ...' is just as mesmerizing for the connoisseur of the classics. Yet the lover of Shakespeare has not gone to find out what happened to Henry V. The verse and the way it is spoken is reward enough.

But sport is unrehearsed. That might make it less perfect art but it gives it the edge in raw excitement. Yet as soon as one competitor ceases to compete, the whole enterprise becomes meaningless. The public are cheated as surely as they would be if, unannounced, Laurence Olivier was replaced by an incompetent understudy.

In tennis, no one in their right mind would stage an exhibition match between Nastase and Borg in London or Paris. Exhibition matches are only worthwhile in places where the local fans have never had a chance to see either man in the flesh. Then, and only then, will curiosity overcome the absence of the competitive ingredient from which all exhibitions suffer. The final of the Canadian Open was no exhibition and that is why Nastase's insult to his audience was so great. By having no stomach for the fight, he deprived them of what they had paid to see—namely a competitive match.

The scene in the referee's tent after the debacle against Orantes was chaotic. The sponsors, Rothmans, whose loyalty to tennis over the years is deserving of special thanks, wanted to prevent Nastase from playing in the doubles final.

At first Nastase himself seemed too distraught and belligerent to want to play. But Jan Kodes, his partner that week, talked him into it after a blazing row with the tournament director, Don Fontana.

'I blew my stack at him which wasn't too smart,' Fontana admitted when we talked about the unhappy episode some time later. 'But I couldn't agree to Rothmans' request to put on an exhibition doubles instead of the final. I felt that would have been cheating the public still further.'

Typically, Nastase's mood changed completely when he got back on court and large sections of the crowd were ready to forgive and forget by the time he and Kodes lost a thrilling match 7–6 in the third set to Cliff Drysdale and Ray Moore.

But quite rightly, that was not the end of it. Fontana filed a report on Nastase as well as on Bjorn Borg and Kodes, both of whom had been involved in other incidents during a trouble-strewn week. After a series of hearings held by the Pro Council during the US Open in New York a couple of weeks later, Nastase was fined $8,000—the equivalent of his runner-up money in the singles.

The Romanian authorities were beginning to be concerned over Nastase's problems and it was at about this time that Mitch Oprea was called in to act as trouble-shooter.

'The situation with McCormack at the hearings in New York was a little absurd,' said Oprea. 'They were not only Ilie's agents but they were also representing the Canadian Lawn Tennis Association. How could they plead in front of the Pro Council for parties on both sides of the arguments? They should have disqualified themselves.'

To amend this situation Oprea called in New York lawyer Fred Sherman who immediately appealed against the Council's decision, complaining of 'procedural defects' at the hearing. So a second hearing was set up in London later in the year, this time with a panel of independent arbitrators consisting of two former Wimbledon champions, Jaroslav Drobny and Lew Hoad, and an eminent British judge, Sir Carl Aarvold, who was also President of the British Lawn Tennis Association. After listening to Sherman and considering reams of written evidence, the

2 The start of a notorious partnership—Ilie and the almost hairless Tiriac.

In India Ilie learned how to play on grass—and how to complain. Asian Championships referee Mustafi and Romanian coach Gheorghe Cobzuc listen while Nastase disputes a line-call against Jaidip Mukerjea in Calcutta.

1 Skinny and short haired—Ilie in the beginning.

21 Ilie and his parents.

8 Laurie Pignon (London Daily Mail) and Bud Collins (Boston Globe) watch Ilie in action at the Foro Italico. Under the straw hat, Ion Tiriac's face adds its own comment on the state of play.

19 Constantin Nastase, Ilie's 44 year old brother, leaves the practice court at the Progresul Club.

28 The Romanian Davis Cup teams line up to meet the United States at the Progresul Club in Bucharest in 1972.

17 And if you have been really naughty, a gallant gesture will usually put matters right.

Ilie acclaims his own great shot to the amusement of the crowd during his victory over Jan Kodes in the 1977 French Open.

5 An engagement picture in the snow outside the Kunglihallen in Stockholm, November 1971.

9 Left-handed Dominique has become an accomplished tennis player thanks to some rather special coaching.

22 The first wedding ceremony in Brussels.

25 Nastase, the father, outside his house at La Basoche.

23 In action on Wimbledon's Centre Court.

24 Major Nastase of the Romanian Army.

31 Nastase in Autumn.

7 Stan Smith's victory leap at the end of one of Wimbledon's greatest finals in 1972.

14 Nastase captured at Wimbledon by the much-missed photographic skills of the late Ed. Lacey.

2 Ilie decides he can do without his shoe during the first Benson & Hedges Championship at Wembley. But he still couldn't beat Wojtek Fibak.

16 And if you miss, there is always the foot.

18 But sometimes only a confrontation will do.

11 Ilie surrounded by admirers at the Royal Albert Hall.

20 Ilie and his favourite car outside his house in Bucharest.

7 The Duchess of Kent and the late Herman David, the All England Club chairman who made Open tennis a reality, applaud while Ilie and Rosie Casals raise their mixed doubles trophy aloft in the Royal Box.

0 The scratch team of Lew Hoad and Frew McMillan take on the Romanians in the Italian Championships.

15 Nastase captured at Wimbledon by the much-missed photographic skills of the late Ed. Lacey.

26 Ilie and Jimmy Connors camp it up during the Dewar Cup at the Albert Hall.

'Please may I be excused?' Ilie asks referee Capt Mike Gibson (left) before a call of nature sent him trotting off to the clubhouse during the British Hardcourt Championships at Bournemouth in 1972.

LEADING MEN AT 8/5/72

POS	PLAYER	POINTS
1	I. NASTASE Rumania	203
2	M. ORANTES Spain	170
3	S. R. SMITH U.S.A.	152
4	A. GIMENO Spain	94
5	J. KODES Czechoslovakia	89
6	J. FILLOL Chile	55
7	J. CONNORS U.S.A.	52
8	F. PALA Czechoslovakia	48
9	P. BARTHES France	44
10	A. J. PATTISON Rhodésia	42
11	B. J. PHILLIPS-MOORE Australia	41
12	G. BATTRICK Great Britain	37
13	T. W. GORMAN U.S.A.	37
14	J. GISBERT Spain	34
15	P. PROISY France	34
16	V. ZEDNIK Czechoslovakia	29
17	H. RAHIM Pakistan	28
	BARANYI Hungary	23

Ilie racks up the points in the early years of the Grand Prix at the West Hants Tennis Club in Bournemouth.

29 The sweetness of success.

30 Consolation for Ilie from the World's No. 1—Wimbledon 1976.

arbitration panel decided to reduce the fine from $8,000 to $6,000, having found the allegation of swearing proven but dismissing the suggestion that Nastase had thrown the match. It was, I admit, a difficult charge to prove and apparently Sir Carl was loath to uphold it because of what he described as the inadequate and legally worthless constitution with which the Pro Council was trying to govern tennis at that time.

'A lot of people in the game wanted to see Nastase suspended,' Hoad told me. 'But Sir Carl said there was no way we could legally suspend the guy. Apparently there were just too many loopholes for Nastase's lawyer to wriggle through.'

So a cheque was sent to the Canadian LTA for $6,000—a contribution, according to Nastase's lawyers, to the development of Canadian junior tennis. In my opinion he got off lightly.

Despite a great deal of heavy criticism in the Canadian press, Ilie returned to Toronto the following February to play in a WCT event and went a long way to silencing his critics.

'There was no personal animosity on my part,' said Fontana, 'although Ilie was, quite understandably, a little wary of me to start with. But he accepted my invitation to attend the Ontario Sports Celebrities Dinner at the Royal York Hotel one night and helped us out on another occasion by agreeing to play an exhibition with Vitas Gerulaitis when we were short of a match. On the whole he couldn't have been more cooperative. He's really a pretty harmless guy and it's hard to dislike him.'

In other words, it was the same old story. Once Dr Jekyll re-emerges, one wonders how on earth Mr Hyde can exist in the same soul.

Arthur Ashe was left pondering the enigma that is Nastase after the Commercial Union Masters in Stockholm at the end of the year—a year that for Ilie had become a series of running battles with officialdom all over the world. The night before their memorable encounter at the Kunglihallen, Nastase had staged a little scene-setter for Ashe's benefit in the bar of the Grand Hotel. That the preview turned out to be a lot funnier than the main act was unintentional but perhaps predictable. Off court few people mind if Nastase gets a little outrageous. On court, especially against a man like Ashe, it is different. At any rate when Arthur strode into the bar for a nightcap, Ilie was already holding forth. Perched on a bar stool he was chattering away with a whole group of people from the tennis world including Spence Conley, then with Commercial Union's Boston office; Susie Trees from San Francisco and the *World Tennis* editor Ron Bookman.

'Ah, Negroni,' exclaimed Ilie, addressing Arthur in his customary manner. 'How you feeling? Good, I hope. Tomorrow night you will need to feel good.'

Ashe, who genuinely enjoys Nastase in this kind of mood, smiled and sat down next to the Romanian. Without saying much, but laughing heartily at times, Arthur sipped a drink and let Ilie rattle on.

'Such a good serve you have, Negroni. Such a pity for you they put Supreme Court over the tiles. The tiles they are so much better for your serve, no? But it does not matter because I beat you anyway. Tomorrow night I do things to you that will make you turn white. Then you will be a white Negroni.'

Although most of the people in the bar were falling about by this stage, it was nothing new for Ashe. He had heard it all before. He also knew how to handle it. Pushing his drink tab towards Nastase, he leaned across and with an air of quiet authority, said to the barman, 'That'll be on Mr Nastase's check.' With that he slipped gently off his stool; tapped Ilie on the shoulder by way of recognition and, with a satisfied grin on his face, walked out. It was the kind of exit only Arthur Ashe could have pulled off with quite so much dignity and timing.

Twenty-four hours later the contrast was total. From the serene, understated, imperturbable human being I had always known, Ashe had been reduced to a screaming, nerve-ruined wreck. I have never seen him like it before or since. And the cause of it was, of course, Nastase.

It had started in a drearily familiar way. Ashe was leading 1–6, 7–5, 4–1 and seemed set for victory. Then Ilie started arguing over a line call and a heckler in the crowd began baiting him. Almost invariably that triggers a response in Ilie which I do believe is instinctive and compulsive. He shouts back. A lifetime's training might have made him able to ignore the lone loud-mouth but it is too late for that now. He just has to answer back. And so it started. Every time Nastase would bounce the ball and begin his service action, the man would call out. Each time Ilie stopped, turned and shouted back. This happened four or five times. The umpire repeatedly warned Ilie that play must be continuous but Ashe suddenly decided there would be no play at all.

Striding up to the umpire's chair, simultaneously shaking his head and waving his arms in front of him to signal termination, Ashe's high-pitched voice cut through the sudden buzz of the crowd. 'That's it,' he said. 'I'm not putting up with it any longer. He's contravening the rules and I'm not taking it any more.'

With that Ashe picked up his rackets and was off the court before the West German referee, Horst Klosterkemper, could reach the court-side and activate the decision he had taken seconds before the American's dramatic exit—namely to disqualify Nastase.

When I got down to the locker-room a few minutes later, confusion reigned. Klosterkemper, the umpire, John Beddington of Commercial Union and Hans-Ake Sturen of the Stockholm Open were milling round trying to decide what should be done. All that would have been normal under the less than normal circumstances had it not been for the condition of Arthur Ashe. I have known Arthur a long time. I have seen him in dire situations on court and even tougher situations off it, as when he faced a militant group of black students in South Africa. I have seen him angry, sometimes very angry. But never before had I seen him lose control of himself.

'I'm not taking any more of that crap,' he screamed, his voice a whole octave higher than normal. 'There's no goddamn way you're getting me back on that court. He's broken the rules, goddamm it. I helped write them. I ought to know.'

Ripping off his damp shirt he flung it down on the bench, his whole lithe body trembling with emotion. 'That son of a bitch isn't going to get away with it any more. I'll damn well see him run out of the game before he tries that kind of stunt with me again.'

The subject of this tirade was sitting somewhat sheepishly behind a row of clothes and towels that almost completely hid him from Ashe's view. It was not difficult to see that he had been shocked by Ashe's sudden flare-up. 'What you go so crazy for?' he asked plaintively a couple of times in between long bouts of brooding silence. 'Shit, what you want me to do, say I'm sorry? I'm sorry. But that guy kept yelling at me, what could I do?'

But Ashe was not about to get drawn into a verbal slanging match with his antagonist. He knew his emotions were running wild in a manner that was quite foreign to him and he thought he had better try and channel his anger as best he could. So he ignored Nastase and confined his attention to the various officials who were trying desperately to come up with a solution. The problem was that Ashe, by walking off court, had committed an offence just as grave as Nastase's. The fact that Klosterkemper was on the point of defaulting Ilie when Ashe made his move was, technically, of no consequence. Instead of remaining on the court and demanding that the referee implement the rules, he had taken the law into his own hands and left the arena. And, even some fifteen minutes later, as the argument raged on, it was still Ashe, not Nastase, who was refusing to continue the match.

But no one wanted to default Ashe and give the match to the Romanian. The fact that Arthur had been provoked also had to be taken into consideration. It was also impossible to overlook the fact that he was not merely president of the ATP but one of the most orderly and respected players ever to grace a tennis-court. Orderly, however, did not quite describe him at this point. Half-naked, dripping with sweat and still taut with rage, he caught the gist of several half-whispered discussions between Klosterkemper, Beddington, Sturen, myself and others and quickly interjected, 'Don't think you're getting me back on that court—there's no way. I've quit and it's his fault. You guys work it out any way you like but I'll tell you this—if you penalize me I'm walking straight out of this tournament right this minute.'

147

We all stared at him like men hit with a sudden attack of migraine. He was not making it any easier. As the Masters is partially played under a round-robin format—two groups of four play round robin to produce two semi-finals that are then played off on a knock-out basis—any player walking out on the first day would leave a nasty hole in the scheduling. But the round-robin format also offered Klosterkemper the possibility of a compromise solution. I don't know whether I was the first to suggest it to him or whether he had already thought of it himself but I remember whispering the suggestion to him as he talked on the locker-room phone with the ILTF President, Derek Hardwick, who was back at the Grand Hotel, having left the Kunglihallen half an hour before the incident occurred.

The solution was to default them both. In a knock-out format this would, I agree, have been too hard on Ashe. But in round-robin play, it is quite possible for someone who loses his first match to go on and win the whole tournament. Nastase himself had done it in Boston two years before and, as it turned out, was destined to repeat the feat that week in Stockholm.

By simply depriving both men of the point one of them would normally have gained for a victory, they would be left joint bottom of the White group after the first round of matches—a handicap certainly but not an insurmountable one. Klosterkemper liked the idea and initially Hardwick agreed. 'It's your decision, Horst,' the ILTF president told him on the phone. And so indeed it was. One of the younger and more progressive members of the European tennis hierarchy, Klosterkemper had made his reputation in the game by organizing the Grand prix event in Düsseldorf each year—a tournament considered by most of the players to be one of the best-run in the world.

But nothing he had had to face in Düsseldorf had posed as many delicate problems as the situation facing him now. Emotionally he wanted to overlook Ashe's indiscretion because he knew how genuine Arthur was in wanting to make a stand against the kind of behaviour he felt was intolerable. But his teutonic respect for rules could not allow him totally to ignore the fact that Ashe had committed a serious offence by leaving the court. So Klosterklemper finally decided on the double default solution and, rather bravely, considering the American's frame of mind, walked over to Arthur to tell him.

'I'll appeal against that,' Ashe retorted. 'You won't get away with it.'

Incredibly, he was right. In one of the stranger decisions professional tennis has witnessed over the past decade, a tournament committee, consisting of Hardwick, Klosterkemper, Beddington and his Commercial Union boss, Geoff Mullis, voted to overturn Horst's original decision and award the match to Ashe.

It was an enormous compliment to Ashe's standing and reputation in the game that he was able to convince the committee that this was the correct course of action. I understand how important it was to him to be officially exonerated from blame. And to an extent I sympathize. But I cannot honestly say that I consider it to have been a good thing for the game. For an ATP president to use his position and his influence to have an official decision overturned on his own behalf throws up too many ethical question marks. But he got away with it and if one views it as a somewhat unorthodox bonus for all the esteem he has brought to his sport over the years, then one should not complain too loudly. During the particular match in question he had, if not technically, then in essence, been more sinned against than sinning and, to his credit, Nastase was the first to admit as much. Even now he looks back on the incident and says, 'That time I think I go too far. It was not intentional. Arthur had such a big lead I think he would have won the match anyway but this guy keeps talking to me as I try to serve and what could I do?' He still does not have the answer.

He did, however, find an immediate method of soothing the last remnants of Ashe's anger. Having practised after the committee meeting in the morning, Arthur was having a late lunch by himself in the Grand Hotel dining-room, gazing out at the panoramic view of the steamers and fishing-boats riding at anchor in front of the Royal Palace. There weren't many other people in the room but even those unconnected with tennis could not have missed the significance of the little scene that was about to be enacted. Appearing at the door-way half hidden by a huge bunch of flowers, Nastase almost tiptoed his way across the room and then, with the half-scared look of a child who is trying to make it up with his father, laid the flowers across Ashe's table.

'Please forgive me,' he said with a smile.

Of course everyone laughed but in many ways it was an action, as Oscar Wilde once said, 'so sweet and simple as to hush us to silence'. Certainly he knew how and in what spirit he should approach his rival and as he flitted away as silently as he had come, Arthur lifted his hands in a gesture of despair and smilingly shook his head. 'That was so typical of Nastase,' he said when we talked about it later. 'You can't be mad at the guy for long.' Ashe also maintained that he was angrier at the officials than he was at Ilie. 'Nastase was just being Nastase,' Arthur said. 'I was just furious that everyone was letting him get away with it.'

Yet, incongruous as it may seem, I think Arthur helped Ilie reclaim his Masters title. If he had lost that opening match in the normal way, he would have fiddled and footled his way through the rest of the week, bemoaning his luck, complaining about his lack of form and getting himself into more and more trouble. But the intensity of the row with Ashe both shocked him and knocked him into shape. Even he realized he had gone one step too far and he suddenly became desperately keen to make amends. And in doing so he played some of the most brilliant tennis in his career.

It is a sad but seemingly inescapable fact of life for Nastase that he needs one good blow-out before he can settle down to play serious tennis. In a normal tournament this means he needs to survive one gigantic row without disqualification or defeat—otherwise, of course, it is all over. But in the Masters, the round-robin format allows him that one early setback without putting him completely out of the tournament. As he proved both in Boston and Stockholm, he can overcome any penalty or handicap just so long as he is still allowed to play.

At the Kunglihallen, in front of the knowledgeable Swedish crowd who were already inclined to forgive him his trespasses because he was working diligently with their Davis Cup squad, Ilie battled his way back to form and favour. But he still required Ashe's assistance to reach the semi-finals. Ilie produced two workmanlike victories to beat Manolo Orantes and Adriano Panatta and then had to sit and wait while Ashe played Orantes in the last of the round robin maches. If Ashe had lost, the Spaniard would have advanced to the semi-finals in Ilie's place. But Arthur was in commanding form and won 6–4, 6–1.

From then on Nastase needed no further assistance. John Barrett, editor of the *World of Tennis Yearbook* and an important figure in the British tennis scene, described Ilie's semi-final like this: 'Nastase, wielding his racket like a wand, conjured pure magic from the ball in destroying Vilas 6–0, 6–3, 6–4. The young bull of the Pampas was reduced to impotence—every charge was parried; every attack blunted until the despairing Vilas was executed at last by the flashing Romanian rapier.'

Borg stopped Ashe in the other semi-final but then discovered that Nastase, on this form, was an altogether different proposition. Disappointingly for the crowd, the final only lasted sixty-five minutes. Shrugging with despair and obviously embarrassed by his inability to match magic with magic, Borg found himself served, volleyed and drop-shotted into a 6–2, 6–2, 6–1 defeat. Ilie was ecstatic. A fraught and worrying year had finally produced a ray of sunshine minutes before the Nordic night closed in on a chill November afternoon. But no matter how brilliant the finale, it could not obscure the sour memories of the past months. Fined in Tucson and Toronto, disqualified in Bournemouth, Washington DC and Stockholm—it was not a happy record.

I did not witness the incident at the Washington Star event but, in his customarily erudite style, Barry Lorge of the *Washington Post* described it thus:

'The disqualification episode was filled with low comedy. Down match point at 30–40 on his serve, Nastase was called for a foot-fault which some people thought he committed intentionally to start a furore. He argued at length and eventually took off his shoe and flipped it in the direction of the foot-fault judge.

'At the other end, Cliff Richey—who had said the day before that his long-running feud with Nastase was over—was steaming. Finally he walked off court, packed his gear, and departed. As the crowd howled and confusion reigned, an official sought out Richey and told him he would be defaulted if he didn't return to the court. Eyes bulging and his complexion the colour of a tomato, he stomped back like a man possessed. Nastase asked for two serves, and when the umpire ruled he should only have one, he began to argue again. Off went Richey a second time, shoving an official as he went. Once more he was coaxed back on court and the umpire told Nastase he had fifteen seconds to serve. The Romanian kept arguing as the crowd counted down, and at the stroke of fifteen he was defaulted.

' "Nastase has pulled that crap 49,000 times," Richey said afterwards. "It was time to stand up to him. He'll go on intimidating officials, ruining his opponent's rhythm and concentration until his bluff is called. Otherwise there's no telling how far he'll go. Maybe next time he'll pull off both his shoes and drop his pants." '

Although the hot-tempered Texan was not perhaps the ideal person to start lecturing Nastase on how to behave, he was voicing an opinion shared by many players, not to mention the public. Yet, in America especially, the difference between the public's attitude towards Nastase and those who knew him personally was considerable. The players understood that Ilie was a very different character off court from on and the majority of them were prepared to accept this, often liking and enjoying Jekyll while hating Hyde. But the average American tennis fan never got close enough to recognize the difference. And watching him at his worst moments on court many true-blue citizens from the great American middle class were mortally offended by what they saw. To a far greater extent than in Europe, a deep puritanical streak still runs through the core of the American psyche and often Nastase's behaviour simply blew its collective mind.

The cables that poured in after the match against Rosewall at the American Airlines Tennis Games showed how easily people could be roused to righteous indignation. It took Ilie some time to realize this but by the time he did I think he was past caring. He had, by then, been the victim of so many bad line-calls and been abused so frequently by spectators using language every bit as abusive as his own, that he saw no reason to spare anyone's feelings. The more vicious the criticism, the more outrageously he reacted and by the end of 1975 he was, on the sports scene at least, public enemy No 1.

He had his problems in Europe, too, but somehow they never reached the same intensity. Even when crowds in Rome or Madrid turned against him, he never felt as threatened or as alienated as he did in the States where the culture gap between the emotional Latin and Mr Middle America is wider than the Grand Canyon.

Even in Britain, where the stiff upper lip syndrome is supposed to abhor an excessive display of emotion, Nastase has always been much more warmly received than in the United States. In fact there is probably no country in the world that has taken Ilie to its heart as Britain has. This is not so strange as it may seem. As a nation, the British not merely tolerate but actively enjoy eccentrics. Acutely aware of the primness of their society, a sizeable minority of British people are forever seeking ways of expressing themselves in an extravagant manner, either by deed or dress. In tennis no one provides a better example of this than the inimitable designer, Teddy Tinling. And even little old ladies who have spent a life-time in twin sets and pearls seem to get a kick out of those who have trodden a more daring path. After watching Nastase behave in a manner that would induce heart failure if copied by their sons or family friends, I have heard them talk of Ilie being 'terribly naughty' but 'such a dear boy'. The American matron tends to take a less tolerant view.

Of course, Ilie does ask for it. There is no quicker way to stir up a hornet's nest in the States than by making racial remarks in public and before 1976 was halfway through, Nastase had done it twice.

The first incident occurred in January at the indoor event in Baltimore. Nastase was involved in a close match with that gritty little fighter Harold Solomon, whose home town of Silver Spring, Maryland, is a mere thirty miles away. Both players had received a few bad calls and when Nastase began reacting in his usual manner, some of Solly's numerous fans in the crowd started heckling him. So, true to form, Ilie decided to hit back. And, of course he went straight for the jugular. 'Not only do I have to play you here,' he said to Solomon across the net. 'But I have to play 2,000 Jews as well.'

Harold returned the compliment by calling him a Romanian Commie bastard and all hell broke loose. Solomon couldn't help smiling when he looked back on the incident some time later.

'Jewish people were going nuts all over the country,' Solly told me. 'They're very defensive about things like that. You should have seen some of the letters written about him in the papers. He knows what he's saying, of course, but I think he just wants to strike back. He's not really a racist. Actually I enjoy him a bit. Off court I don't mind him at all but on court he's an asshole.'

A few months after he had alienated the most influential ethnic minority in America, Ilie turned his attention to the most populous—the blacks. If ever a politician with a death-wish is looking for ways of how not to get elected, he should ask Nastase to write a pamphlet for him. He makes Spiro Agnew look like a beginner.

Dr Jekyll and Mr Hyde

This time it was in the final of the WCT Challenge Cup in Hawaii and once again Arthur Ashe was the player involved. Having won the first set, Ilie was trailing 1–5 in the second when he began muttering away to himself as he so often does when he loses his grip on a match. During the course of a long monologue, the sensitive NBC microphones at court-side picked up the inflammatory phrase 'bloody nigger'. Few spectators heard it—merely a few million television viewers across America. Again the complaints started flooding in. Ashe never heard the remark and even when he was told about it afterwards, he kept his cool. Nastase's stalling tactics in Stockholm might have roused his ire but Arthur was not going to get upset over the names Ilie calls him or anyone else. He had heard them too often. Echoing Solomon, Arthur commented, 'Whatever he said, I don't think he's a racist.'

Both players are right. Nastase's carefree way with racial nicknames derives largely from what he has picked up from the essentially healthy locker-room banter. In any other company the names that are flung around with the wet towels and smelly socks would be sufficient to start ground wars on five different fronts at once.

As a group, tennis-players are neither politically insensitive nor naive. By virtue of their constant travel itinerary which takes them to every corner of the globe, they are far more sophisticated than most athletes in matters of religion, race and political regimes. They are well aware of the absurd distinctions that mankind insists on magnifying to antagonize his fellow-man. But through a more natural desire to co-exist with one another, they choose to make light of their differences. Whenever delegates at the United Nations ('That concrete slab of hope and optimism,' as journalist James Cameron once described it) start hurling insults at each other, I often wish they could be replaced by members of the ATP who, short of Eskimos and pygmies, represent just about every religious and racial grouping known to mankind. They would quickly reduce the whole debate to a suitable level of genuine farce and the world would be better for it. It is said that familiarity breeds contempt. In my experience it is far more likely to breed tolerance and understanding. And if this expresses itself by way of lighthearted insults, that's a great deal better than the other kind.

For the past several pages, I have, perhaps, presented the reader with a distorted view of the atmosphere that exists in tennis locker-rooms around the world. The genuine rows that I have recorded here are the exception, not the rule. Even now, as the intensity of pressure and competition mounts, the vast majority of players co-exist in an ambiance of friendship and humour.

Taken out of context, the name-calling that goes on may not seem particularly amusing. But when Nikki Pilic and Cliff Drysdale were playing doubles together one year, it was always a source of much entertainment when the South African call Nikki a 'Commie bastard' and was, in turn, referred to by his partner as a 'racist pig'. At the height of the Arab–Israeli conflict another interesting doubles partnership was formed, on a few occasions by Tom Okker, a Jew, and Egypt's Ismail El Shafei.

Thinking mainly of his good buddy Gerald Battrick, whose politics lie somewhere to the right of Genghis Khan, the socialistically-inclined Ray Moore once announced gaily that 'some of my best friends are right-wingers'. Even when their countries were at war there was never any problem between Pakistan's Haroon Rahim and the Indian players and the suggestions of what the turbanned Sikh, Jaz Singh, could do with his uncut hair when he uncoiled it in the shower are as unmentionable as a certain caste in his country are untouchable.

Because of the brilliance of its timing, perhaps the most genuinely funny racial remark I have heard on the tennis circuit came during an ATP players' meeting at the Gloucester Hotel in London. Addressing the meeting in his capacity as a member of the ATP board, Arthur Ashe hesitated for a second while trying to explain some controversial rule that had been passed at the directors' meeting the night before. While he searched for the right words, a voice from the floor called out, 'Now come on, Arthur, don't be afraid to call a spade a spade.' Amidst the general hilarity, no one was laughing harder than Ashe.

Taking his cue from those around him when he first joined the circuit it was not surprising that Nastase, as we have seen, learned fast. Kodes was quickly dubbed 'Russian', Ashe became 'Negroni' and the inseparable pair, Solomon and Eddie Dibbs, were often referred to by Ilie as 'Jew-boys'. Naturally he didn't bother to make any adjustment when he discovered that Dibbs is, in fact, of Lebanese extraction.

Nastase himself has been referred to as a 'bloody Romanian gypsy' which has incensed him no end for about three and a half minutes and then it ceased to matter. Therein lies the beauty of it all. An insult repeated often enough soon dissolves into a rather unoriginal joke. Like Enoch Powell.

So, given this background, it should not be difficult to understand why the players, not least Solomon and Ashe themselves, shrugged off Nastase's so-called 'racial slurs'. The fact that so many people were offended by his remarks was more a condemnation of those political and religious leaders who play on people's intolerance and fear for their own devious ends than on Nastase. We only have ourselves to blame if a tennis-player can use words like 'Jew' and 'nigger' as a weapon and have them wound so deeply.

Amid all the uproar over Nastase's unfortunate aside in Hawaii, it had been conveniently forgotten that he had played doubles with Ashe less than a year before on the US summer circuit and on that occasion the two players' racial differences had been subject of much hilarity.

The funniest incident had occurred at Louisville where the popular Sam English runs one of the players' favourite American tournaments. Ilie could not resist exploiting to the utmost the fact that he was playing with 'Negroni'. So, finding a couple of willing accomplices in Ismail El Shafei and the voluble Austrian prankster, Hans Kary, Ilie sent them off in search of something with which he could blacken his face. Eventually they produced a weird mixture of charcoal and cream and did a thorough make-up job on the Romanian just before his doubles. When Nastase, looking like an athletic Al Jolson, ran out to join Ashe the crowd collapsed in hysterics and, as usual, no one was quicker to see the joke than Arthur. Even though Ilie's colour rubbed off, their harmony on court was more than skin-deep and they managed to beat an experienced pair—Jaime Fillol and Patricio Cornejo—on their way to the semi-finals.

But despite the controversy that swirled around his head during the early months of 1976, Nastase's tennis was showing signs of regaining the consistency it had lacked the year before. Winning the WCT Avis Challenge Cup over Ashe, which Ilie achieved by virtue of some brilliant stroke-play after the American had led by two sets to one, was a major achievement, and little more than a month later, he came within one match of fulfilling his life's ambition. But, for the second time in his career the final hurdle at Wimbledon proved too much.

Although seeded third behind Ashe and Connors, few experts had given Nastase much chance of winning one of the few major titles that had eluded him. But by the time Ashe, who never looked like retaining his crown, had gone down to Vitas Gerulaitis and Connors had been served into oblivion by Roscoe Tanner, only Borg had been able to match Ilie's majestic progress through the Championships. Apart from one lapse when he and Connors had created a few unholy scenes in a doubles match, Nastase had both played and behaved impeccably.

'Ilie is so calm just now,' said Dominique who was desperately trying to conceal her own nerves so that she should not transmit them to her husband. 'He is concentrating so well and nothing disturbs him. That is why I think it is good he does not go to press conferences. Some of those questions just make him nervous.'

Nastase did indeed refuse to attend the post-match press conferences that are held beneath the locker-rooms in the bowels of the All England Club. Although I feel it is something the ATP should be stricter about, there is no rule which says a player *must* attend press conferences and on this occasion Nastase was taking advantage of the fact for a calculated reason. He wanted to cut out every possible source of aggravation and annoyance that might conceivably destroy his concentration. Naturally the press criticized him for it, but, from a purely selfish point of view, it was a wise decision. It also revealed that, at the age of thirty, Nastase was beginning to undestand himself well enough to avoid some of the more obvious pitfalls.

In his relaxed state of mind and fine physical condition, Ilie breezed through the early rounds, providing one of the few cool and unruffled sights during that stifling fortnight. By the time he reached the final neither he nor Borg had dropped a set and in describing his quarter-final victory over Charlie Pasarell, Rex Bellamy of *The Times*, who consistently wins the ATP's Writer of the Year award, wrote, 'There was nothing Pasarell could do about a tennis genius who made the difficult look easy, the improbable likely and the impossible possible.'

That kind of performance, which had been repeated during his semi-final victory over Raul Ramirez, altered the critics' minds and, considering Borg's earlier lack of success on really fast surfaces, most of them made Ilie the favourite to win the final.

But in a decade that has produced an extraordinarily high proportion of memorable finals, this turned out to be the most disappointing the seventies has seen so far. Ilie raced away to a 3–0 lead in the first set, had three break-points for 4–0 and then, as Bellamy wrote in *World Tennis*: 'The Romanian became inhibited and indecisive. He could not take the initiative to let himself go and attack as a man must in order to win a big match on grass. He had trouble putting the ball away because he was not aggressive enough to thwart Borg's astonishingly fast footwork.

'Borg had taken cortizone injections and at every change-over he sprayed a worrying stomach muscle with a pain-killing aerosol. But he was a bundle of fidgety energy and attacked whenever discretion permitted. He hit harder and to a better length. He served very well. He made fewer errors.

'In mid-match Nastase was so subdued and cautious that at times it was embarrassing. But at the end, as at the beginning, he showed us what he could do. From 3–5 down in the third set, he counter-attacked, saving a match-point at 4–5 and breaking for 5–5. The crowd was roaring him on. But at 7–7 he lost his service, hitting a reasonably easy backhand volley into the net instead of into an open court. So Borg served for the match a second time and, on this occasion, clobbered everything that came his way. He won the game to love, flung his racket high and buried his face in his hands. Nastase, disguising his disappointment, jumped the net and put an arm around a youngster who was momentarily overwhelmed by the triumph all tennis-players dream about.'

And so what had happened this time? For almost two weeks Nastase had been a model of decorum in victory only to be suddenly transformed into a sad and generous figure in defeat. Why?

'For six matches I try so hard to be good and to concentrate all the time,' Ilie told me recently. 'Then, I don't know what happened. Suddenly I couldn't play. I feel as if I have no energy. I wasn't even nervous when I went out to play the final. Maybe that was the problem.'

Certainly it would have been a contributing factor. As any actor, performer or athlete will certify, a total lack of nervous tension before a big occasion is a very dangerous sign. Often the greater the apprehension, the greater the performance. In his fascinating biography of Laurence Olivier, John Cottrell reveals how Olivier was so distraught on the opening night of an Old Vic production of *Richard III*, that he called John Mills into his dressing-room to warn him that his performance was sure to be dreadful and that Mills should tell everybody out front not to expect too much. The result was a night of what Cottrell describes as 'sheer theatrical magic' in which Olivier gave a performance that many critics feel he has never surpassed.

Nastase is well-equipped with the kind of stomach-knotting desperation that gripped Laurence Olivier before the curtain went up that night. His only problem was that he did not experience it before he went out to face Borg. In the locker-room before the match he was relaxed and quietly confident. The critics thought he would win and so did he. For a player of Nastase's temperament that kind of mental preparation was all wrong.

He was not the first Wimbledon finalist to suffer from lack of nerves. In 1963, as an innocent little bundle of energy called Miss Moffitt, Billie-Jean King went out to face Margaret Smith in her first Wimbledon final. 'I was so happy to be playing the final, I wasn't nervous at all,' Billie-Jean told me. 'As a result I never got into the match and lost in straight sets.'

Like Nastase, Billie-Jean needs to be hyped up to play her best tennis. Against Borg, Ilie was so wound down one could scarcely believe this was really a Wimbledon final. It was equally difficult to believe one was watching Ilie Nastase. Rarely has he given a more untypical performance. There was no spark, no verve, no histrionics and only fleeting glimpses of the skill that had demolished opponents throughout the fortnight. At times it was pathetic to watch him slap his thigh in exasperation like a man turning the ignition key in a car with a flat battery. No matter how hard you pump the accelerator, all you get is that dreadful heaving whine of an engine being turned over by too little power.

In my view, Nastase had run out of power. Not the physical kind but what I believe is referred to in the trade as 'psychic energy'. Mentally he was drained as dry as the deadest battery. You couldn't have electrocuted a fly with the amount of energy he was giving off that day. The mental effort of containing his normal impulses; of concentrating totally through six matches in ten days; of never once allowing that fast-flowing temperament to burst its banks, had in the end proved too much. For Nastase the Wimbledon final of 1976 was, quite simply, one bridge too far.

Nastase

The eminent Los Angeles psychiatrist, Dr Mike Franzblau, basically agrees with me while having some reservations: 'I think one should make it quite clear he was not physically fatigued,' said Dr Franzblau. 'No one crept up in the middle of the night and drained him of a quart of blood. But that does not mean to say he could not have *felt* fatigued. I see people all the time who tell me that they slept well but are still tired. In reality they are mentally depressed and that manifests itself through a feeling of weariness. I believe Nastase felt drained out there for psychological reasons. Some form of anxiety; a state of fear at the thought of defeat, perhaps—all these could be subconscious factors. But without a deep personal analysis one can only guess at the real root of Nastase's problem that day.'

Within eight days, Nastase proved Dr Franzblau right as far as not being physically tired was concerned. Combining a spell of tennis and travel that would have turned most people into a zombie, Nastase flew straight back to Hawaii after Wimbledon to pick up his interrupted World Team Tennis career. He played three matches for them on the Monday, Tuesday and Thursday nights of that week following Wimbledon and then got on another plane and flew all the way back across America to Myrtle Beach, South Carolina. There he won the new Pepsi Grand Slam television spectacular with victories over Connors and Orantes on the Saturday and Sunday, and by the Monday night was back in Hawaii playing against the San Franciscan Gaters. And it was all achieved with the minimum fuss, few complaints and not even a hint of that bad old Nasty.

So the adrenalin was flowing again and Ilie had it under control—for a while. When age finally begins to mellow him and he gets away from the competitive arena, things may change but for the moment there is no way a temperament like Nastase's can be kept permanently bottled up. Like the thunder which follows hot tropical nights, Ilie's calm summer erupted in September.

For anyone heavily into horror shows, Nastase's second-round match with Hans-Jurgen Pohmann at the US Open was a classic. Vesuvius erupting would have been hard put to challenge the sheer ferocity that Nastase's temper spewed forth. The linesman who refused to go and check the mark after a call against Ilie was either incredibly brave or turned instantly to stone by the piercing glare of the Romanian's eyes. Along with Dominique and Mitch I was sitting in a little group of seats to one side of the base-line in the Stadium Court and was not more than eight feet away when Nastase's first temper tantrum rent the air. The veins pulsating in his forehead; his whole body jerking in rhythm to the epithets that were pouring out of his mouth, he swung round on the linesman and yelled at him like a man possessed. It was really quite a frightening sight. But that was only for openers. Pohmann, a little blond Berliner with an awkward but effective style, is also a showman at heart and, as the match headed for a dramatic third set tie-break finale, he was not beyond milking the situation to a point where Nastase was in danger of being upstaged.

Having reached match-point twice and twice been thwarted on the brink of victory, Pohmann eventually collapsed with cramp and after that it was cabaret time. There was no doubt at all that Hans did get hit with a bad attack of cramp in his thigh. But, equally, there was no doubt that he made the most of it. Writhing in agony at the net, Pohmann let out a half-stifled scream of pain as he clutched his leg. Quite contrary to the rules, the umpire allowed a doctor to attend to Pohmann on court and for a minute or two Nastase merely paced up and down on his side of the net. But soon he could stand it no longer.

'That's not allowed,' he yelled at the umpire. 'You should give me default.'

Nastase was right. But the doctor continued to treat Pohmann; the umpire continued to ignore Nastase whose language was becoming more obscene by the minute; and the crowd were as loud and as abusive as a New York crowd can be.

Finally Pohmann staggered to his feet, hobbled about in dramatic fashion and managed to wince his way through a few more points before collapsing once more. Nastase ranted; the crowd yelled; Pohmann writhed—the din was ear-spitting, the atmosphere electric. But the shrillest crescendo of noise was reserved for the end when Nastase, having squeaked through to a 7–6, 4–6, 7–6 victory, not only refused to shake Pohmann's hand but spat in the German's face. It was all very unpleasant.

As usual Nastase received 99 per cent of the blame—a bit more that he probably deserved. In the *World of Tennis Yearbook*, Bud Collins' summary put it in perspective:

'The Bucharest Buffoon appeared to set new standards of bad taste ... With victory came a $1,000 fine and, eventually, a twenty-one-day suspension because Nastase had exceeded $3,000 in penalties for the calendar year. Yet Ilie had been treated unfairly, too, in that Pohmann was permitted too much time to recover from cramp and was even examined on court by a physician, wrongly summoned by the umpire. More offensive even than Nastase was the audience of 12,553 who, like the worst of hockey or football nuts baited and taunted him viciously. He felt cornered.'

Collins was correct in his indictment of the crowd. That particular year they were as bad as any tennis crowd I have known. True to form, Nastase's behaviour did a 180 degree turn after he had drained it of all the vitriol against Pohmann, but the crowd, if anything, became worse.

Both Marty Riessen and Roscoe Tanner who lost to Nastase in subsequent rounds, expressed sympathy for Ilie after they heard some of the things spectators were yelling at him.

'They were on him before we had hit a ball,' Riessen said. 'I have never had any great problem with him personally and, just as I expected, we had a perfectly normal match. But it couldn't have been easy for him to ignore that crowd.'

After beating Dick Stockton in the quarter-finals, Nastase once again seemed to have exhaused his supply of nervous energy when he faced up to another meeting with Borg. Right from the start the Swede never let go of the firm grip he took on the match and won in straight sets. But two days later, Connors thwarted Bjorn's hopes of adding the US Open title to his Wimbledon crown.

The twenty-one-day suspension to which Collins referred did not begin immediately. It was not that simple. All sorts of legal ramifications were involved and for a while no one seemed able to decide precisely when the suspension should or could begin. Mitch Oprea, who had a few lucrative deals set up for Nastase in Venezuela and Norway, wanted it to start as soon as possible. However the Pro Council informed Oprea that the suspension could not begin until Nastase knowingly waived the right to appeal.

'So I quickly sent them a cable saying that Ilie "knowingly" waived that right,' said Oprea. 'I have a certain amount of sympathy with the Pro Council. It is necessary that there should be such a body but the current composition of the Council is entirely dishonest. It is supposed to be split into three groups ... three from the ITF, three from the ATP and three tournament directors. Yet at one stage no less than seven members of a nine-man council were responsible for running tournaments. Everybody seems to represent everything on that Council and they all appear to work in cahoots—or at least a majority do.' [1]

By chance more than design, the delay in starting Ilie's suspension did help one Council member, Jack Kramer, whose Pacific Southwest Championships in Los Angeles follow Forest Hills two weeks later. Kramer badly needed a big foreign name for the tournament and as they don't come any bigger than Nastase he was delighted to secure Ilie's services. It was a close thing. The final Council decision was that the suspension should start as soon as Ilie was beaten in the Pacific Southwest.

The real farce lay in the fact that there was no law to prevent Nastase from earning a fortune through exhibition matches during the period of his

1 The Pro Council at that stage consisted of Bob Briner, Pierre Darmon and Cliff Drysdale (ATP), Philippe Chatrier, Paolo Angeli and Stan Malless (ITF) and Jack Kramer, Owen Williams and Lars Myhrman (tournament directors). As president of the ITF, Derek Hardwick acted as Council chairman. Although it would be a little difficult to find six qualified people totally divorced from any involvement in tournaments, Oprea makes a valid point. Only Drysdale and Angeli were not involved with the organization of a tournament somewhere in the world.

suspension. Oprea reckons he picked up about $80,000 in the three weeks he was supposedly banned from the game. But as Fred Sherman was quick to point out, the pro Council only had the right to ban him from Grand Prix tournaments. They would have been leaving themselves open to a lawsuit under American law if they had tried to prevent Nastase from earning a living on a tennis-court. After all that happened it was ironic that Nastase should end up helping Kramer's tournament even though Jack had voted for his suspension, not merely in this most recent instance where the $3,000 limit on fines gave him little choice, but also a year earlier following the Toronto fracas.

'I had it in my mind that he tanked against Orantes,' Kramer told me. 'And as a member of the Pro Council I was prepared to be as difficult as possible, in an attempt to try and cut out that kind of crap which is so bad for the game,'

Evidently Kramer's attitude did not go unnoticed by Nastase. It resulted in an incident at the US Open in 1975 which Jack laughs about now but which could not have been too amusing at the time.

'It was just after he had lost in the quarter-finals at Forest Hills and Ilie was walking back to the club-house over the grass courts,' Kramer recalled. 'I happened to be walking parallel with him along the pathway. There was a small fence and about twenty-five yards separating us. Suddenly Ilie starts yelling at me. "You did it" he screams. "You went after me, you dirty son-of-a-bitch." He was swearing away at me in English and Romanian and soon a lot of people started yelling back in my defence. I remember thinking that if I was half a man I should climb the fence and go after him. But I suppose it would have been a bit undignified. Eventually he just goes in one side of the club-house and I go in the other and that's the end of it. Neither of us mentioned it again. Frankly I feel sorry for the guy. I've often had this great urge to try and help him sort out his problems because I have always felt that if he could learn to handle himself better and try to emulate some of the great champions like Don Budge or Fred Perry, he could amass the record of an outstanding player. With his super ability he hasn't won as much as he should have.'

The balance of the $3,000 fines had been accumulated at the American Airlines Tennis Games and, ironically considering his general deportment during the fortnight, at Wimbledon. Apparently Connors and Nastase had damaged the court during their rather over-boisterous doubles and for that Ilie was docked $500.

The American Airlines incident was more serious. Even though the tournament had been moved from Tucson to the Mission Hills Country Club at Palm Springs, it was all the same desert as far as Nastase's fortunes were concerned. It was obviously not an event at which he was destined to enhance his reputation.

161

After an ill-tempered match with Dick Stockton which ended with the American standing pointedly at the net with his arm outstretched while Ilie ignored the customary post-match handshake, Roscoe Tanner came on court to face Nastase in the next round with his ATP rule-book tucked under his arm. It had been the general opinion of the players that Ilie had got away with murder against Stockton and Tanner was determined not to let it happen to him.

In fact, he need not have bothered. Charlie Hare, the former British Davis Cup player who twice reached the Wimbledon doubles final, had decided to emulate Mike Gibson in his role as tournament referee and keep a close eye on the whole match. In view of Nastase's behaviour earlier in the week, it was a perfectly reasonable decision for Hare to make but, in fact, the sight of the referee sitting next to the umpire's chair probably ruined whatever chance there had been of Ilie playing through the match without incident. His reaction was typical and it is not difficult to interpret what went through his mind. So if you come expecting trouble, I'll give you trouble, was Ilie's belligerent response to the sight of encroaching officialdom. And, inevitably, there was trouble. The details become repetitious but I seem to remember that at one stage he responded to a provocative remark from a spectator by climbing into one of the court-side boxes and unzipping his shorts.

'Some woman made a remark about my underwear so I thought maybe she ought to have a look at it,' Ilie explained mischievously afterwards. Other ladies present, who kept their fantasies to themselves, were justifiably disgusted.

With Ilie in that kind of mood, the outcome was a foregone conclusion. Before Tanner had a chance to start waving his rule-book around, Hare disqualified the rebellious Romanian. After the various misdemeanours Nastase had committed throughout the week had been totted up—$250 for hitting a ball out of court, $500 for abusing an umpire, etc,—the grand total was judged to amount to $4,100.

'That would have meant immediate suspension and with the Davis Cup coming up it would have caused serious problems with the Romanian Federation,' Oprea explained. 'So after long negotiations with the ATP and the tournament officials we managed to get it reduced to $2,200.'

The $500 at Wimbledon increased it to $2,700 and the $1,000 levied at Forest Hills as a result of the Pohmann affair put Nastase over the top.

Even after the farcical—and highly profitable—suspension period was over, an unrepentant Nastase was not finished for the year. There was a bad scene at the end of his final against Ken Rosewall in Hong Kong and more disruptive incidents when he played Wojtek Fibak in the Benson & Hedges Championships at Wembley the following week.

But if 1976 showed no improvement in Nastase's record of behaviour

Davis Cup campaign. On the face of it, that was not too much to ask for what Nastase was getting in return, as he was allowed to keep all his world-wide earnings; travel as and where he pleased; and even obtain permission to take both his parents to France for extended holidays.

However, as the Davis Cup is now the last amateur cog in an increasingly well-coordinated professional wheel, the dates on which Nastase was required to appear for Romania frequently jarred against the natural flow of events on the international circuit.

The week of Romania's tie against Belgium clashed with the World Championship doubles finals in Kansas City for which Ilie had qualified with Adriano Panatta. They had in fact formed a highly attractive and effective partnership and would have been a good bet for the title had they played.

The following week when Czechoslavakia were due to visit Bucharest—providing of course that both nations won their opening round ties—Nastase would have been a most welcome addition to the Alan King Classic at Caesar's Palace.

Had he won both those events—a feat well within his capabilities—he would have been $75,000 richer, not an inconsiderable sum of money even by his standards. So when one says playing Davis Cup for free was a small price for Nastase to pay, it is true, but only in relative terms.

Ilie was disappointed at missing Kansas City. It is frustrating in the extreme to have worked towards a certain goal for three months and then to have to pass up the finale. But his complaints were muted and more a matter of genuine regret at not having the opportunity to win something big with Adriano than any resentment at losing out financially. And anyway the prospect of being at home in Bucharest for two weeks appealed to him. He had not seen his parents since his last visit in December and he was anxious to have a look at the state of his house after the earthquake.

He would have preferred Dominique to go with him and her refusal to do so revealed the more stubborn side of her nature. No matter how much Ilie pleaded with her, she was adamant. Her reasons seemed to be threefold. Seismologists were predicting another earthquake six weeks after the first disaster and the six weeks were up. So that ruled out any possibility of taking Nathalie. And quite apart from the earthquake, she was suffering from some quite illogical fear that the Romanian authorities might somehow try to keep the child in the country. The only logical answer to that was that governments can be stupid but not that stupid. The third reason was more personal. Nikki obviously dreaded the thought of having to withstand the family pressures and duties that inevitably befall her whenever she is with Ilie in Bucharest.

Initially she had made a great effort to learn Romanian so that she could converse with Ilie's parents. But Mr and Mrs Nastase were not really the problem: it was the hordes of relatives, well-wishers and hangers-on who inevitably surrounded Nastase as soon as he set foot inside the country that made her recoil. She knew that for Ilie's sake she should go. It was awkward for him to turn up without his wife when everyone knew she was merely sitting at home in France. But that was also part of the problem. La Basoche was a cosy family enclave that was not too easy to escape from. If Nikki had been entirely alone she would probably have gone. However there were too many of her own relatives saying 'Why go? It's not really necessary.' And that probably tipped the balance.

In the strictest sense I suppose it wasn't absolutely necessary. But there was no doubt that it did affect Ilie's frame of mind—a delicate mechanism that does not need too big an emotional nudge to send it spinning, God knows—and the fact that he brooded about it only contributed to the strain of the next few weeks which, even for a person who is used to the impossible travel and playing schedule of the present-day tennis pro, were fairly pressure-packed.

10

LIFE IN ROMANIA

On Wednesday, 27 April 1977, Ilie Nastase was due at Orly Airport to catch the 12.40 pm Air France flight to Bucharest. He had spent a couple of nights at La Basoche on his return from America and I had agreed to meet him at the departure gate so as to be sure we would not miss each other in the vast hall downstairs.

It was 12.37 pm when I eventually perceived the overloaded figure of one of the world's great athletes struggling off the moving walk-way, practically submerged in a mass of rackets, packages and plastic Felix Potin shopping-bags. 'It's OK, Richard boy,' he announced cheerily. 'Our flights's delayed.'

That much was true but Ilie seemed quite impervious to the slice of luck that had saved him from missing the plane.

'Shit, what can I do with all this stuff?,' he asked plaintively. 'Here, you look after it for a minute. I must get some wine. You sure I can buy some wine back there? OK, I be back in a minute.' With that he was off again, leaving me to examine the carry-on cargo we were going to have to haul on to the plane. There were eleven rackets—seven for Ilie himself; three huge Princes for his brother Constantin and my own Head Professional. There was a man's shirt he had obviously bought for a member of the family and stuffed into the plastic bags were boxes of cheese, shampoo, aspirin, Johnson's baby powder and several baguettes loaves of French bread. In addition there was a large cardboard box containing a coffee machine which his mother had asked for when she had phoned up that morning.

'The other one got smashed in the earthquake,' Ilie explained as he reappeared clutching a magnum of Bordeaux that carried a 75 franc price-tag. As it turned out, he didn't drink more than a glass of his wine—a fact about which he grumbled goodnaturedly when we left Bucharest. But, of course, he had bought neither the wine nor the rest of the stuff for himself. It was just Ilie, in his kindly, haphazard way, buying up anything he thought his family and friends might need or enjoy.

Having charmed the stewardess into allowing us to shove everything under empty seats and into every spare corner of the plane, we settled down

169

for the flight. Ilie, however, never settles for long. After lunch he was soon complaining restlessly.

'Four hours this flight takes just because we have to stop in Belgrade,' he said. 'With Tarom you go direct, Paris–Bucharest and it's just over two hours.'

'Yes, but at least this way we get there,' I muttered unkindly.

'Well, it's true Air France is a good airline,' he replied. 'You always get good food. Hey, and remember that time we flew from LA to Paris and they held the flight to Barcelona for us? There was just you and me and one other guy and they kept a full Caravelle waiting fifteen minutes for us. That was amazing.'

Ilie laughed heartily at the thought. 'And I won the tournament, you remember. Straight from the American Airlines Games in Tucson non-stop to Barcelona and, no problem, I win tournament easy.'

'You won Madrid the following week, too,' I reminded him.

'Yeah, that's right. I was playing so well then.' He turned and stared out of the window, gazing far over the snow-capped peaks of the Alps, reaching for those reassuring memories of tournaments won; of a game played with ease and mastery; of simply achieved success.

They were nice thoughts but like so many, they had become rose-tinted with time. To an extent it had been easy for Ilie but, apart from that glorious period in 1972–3, the success had never been sustained for more than a few weeks here or there. But in retrospect it all seemed a lot simpler than it did now. It was not just that the opposition was stronger: it was something within himself that had changed and he wasn't sure what. Maybe it was just some vital facet of his game that was missing. He was groping for it and it was worrying him. Throughout the following two months of missed opportunities, the nagging, desperate thought that he was not as good as he used to be haunted him continually.

But soon there was no time to brood. There was a welcome waiting at Bucharest Airport and Ilie was obviously looking forward to it. It is always reassuring when travelling in Eastern European countries to be closely associated with the passenger who gets a bear hug from the customs official. Such open expressions of warmth are usually followed by more practical assistance like being invited to by-pass the queues for baggage inspection and having one's visa stamped with few questions asked. Needless to say I hung on to Ilie's shirt-tails and encountered no problems.

Certainly I was spared the heart-stopping trap Ion Tiriac had laid for Tim Sturdza, when Switzerland played for the Davis Cup in Burcharest a few years before. To appreciate the story one must know that Sturdza, now a Swiss citizen, is a direct descendant of Ion Sturdza who was Prince of Moldavia before Romania became one nation in 1859 through the unification of Moldavia and Wallachia. As Tim is quite naturally fond of

170

pointing out, his family were a democratic bunch and the first Prince Sturdza incurred the wrath of several less open-minded people at the time by suggesting a new constitution based on elected assemblies. His son Michael, Tim's great-grandfather, put a lot of that thinking into practice when he became leader of the Romanian Liberal Party during the second half of the nineteenth century.

Along with King Michael and the ruling royal family of Romania, the Sturdzas found little in common with the new Communist regime that the Soviet Union installed after the Second World War and in 1947 they fled the country.

Although eligible to play for Switzerland in the Davis Cup—he has virtually been the backbone of the team for the past twelve years—Sturdza still felt too emotionally involved with the country of his birth to represent Switzerland against Romania. But, having elected not to play, he was still anxious to grab a rare opportunity of returning to Bucharest. Would it be possible? Or, more importantly, would it be safe?

'Don't worry,' said Tiriac, 'I arrange everything.' Indeed he did—Tiriac-style.

Despite these reassurances, Sturdza was still nervous as the Swissair flight landed at Bucharest Airport and he nearly panicked when he found an anxious-looking Tiriac standing at the foot of the gangway. 'Listen,' said Tiri in conspiratorial tones, 'the General in charge of the Secret Police happens to be at the airport just now so don't say too much and certainly say nothing in Romanian.'

Forgetting all his royal training, Sturdza freaked. Chased by Tiriac, he rushed back into the plane and strapped himself back into his seat.

'Come out,' roared Tiriac, 'What are you? A man or a mouse?'

'I'm a child—a dog if you want,' squealed Sturdza, 'but I'm not leaving this plane.'

By solemnly promising that if Sturdza was thrown in jail, he would go with him, Tiriac finally coaxed his reluctant guest out of the plane, through the customs and into the arrival hall. There, to Sturdza's horror, stood a Rumanian General, flanked by a posse of soldiers armed with machine-guns.

Marching straight up to this intimidating group, Tiriac said, 'Comrade General, I wish to introduce you to Comrade Prince Dmitri Sturdza who is here for the purpose of spying on the country of his birth.' With that the General drew his pistol; the bolts on six machine-guns snapped back in unison; and Sturdza dropped his rackets and stuck his hands in the air.

'I thought I was going to die with fright,' Sturdza told me. But before he had time to do that, Tiriac and the General collapsed on each other's shoulders in gales of laughter and Tim realized he was on the receiving end of a good Romanian joke.

Nastase

Happily, Ilie spared me the benefit of this local humour and we were soon surrounded by his mother, rather touchingly carrying a bouquet of flowers, and various relatives, including Constantin and Ilie's nephew, Vlad.

A little embarrassed by the fuss and impatient to get to the club before nightfall so that he could practice, Ilie embraced his mother quickly and, rattling away in Romanian to about four people at once, jumped into his Lancia Fulvia which was waiting for him outside. Vlad, a skinny, intense twenty-two-year-old whose spectacles always seem to be slipping down a flat nose, is entrusted with the care of the car while Ilie is away. Obviously he takes the job seriously. Gleaming in the afternoon sun, the yellow and black coupé with its owner's name painted down each side of the cowling, must have looked quite the spiffiest little sports car in Romania.

'I get it four years ago,' said Ilie as we roared out of the airport. 'They don't make them any more. Still goes well, eh? Great acceleration.'

It was a superfluous remark. Nastase had just jammed his foot down to produce a burst of power that carried us past six Romanian-built Dacias in one smooth overtake. Evidently driving with Ilie in Bucharest was going to be an experience.

We stopped at the house just long enough for Ilie to change and then we set off across town for the Progresul Club. As soon as we reached the downtown area the earthquake devastation became shockingly apparent. There were great gaping holes along almost every street where high-rise buildings had collapsed. A few, yet to come under the wrecker's hammer, were artificially supported, their innards grotesquely exposed. Ilie was horrified. 'I don't believe it,' he kept saying. 'Look, that was a big department store. Now nothing. It's just gone. And over there. Always I used to buy my petrol on the corner there.' He was pointing to an open space of levelled off brick and gravel.

To anyone who had known the city before it must have come as an emotional shock to see it in this state and Ilie, already excited and nervous at being home after a five-month absence, reacted emotionally. He reacted, in fact, just as he does on court when those taut nerves are strummed too hard with either pain, disappointment or apparent injustice. He reacted by seizing on some insignificant incident and engulfing it with his anger. As the world knows, it happens all the time with Ilie on a tennis-court but never before had I seen him release his emotions like that away from the competitive arena.

It happened when we were still in the downtown area. A car in front slowed down suddenly, forcing Ilie to brake, and then the driver seemed to go through a series of stop-start manoeuvres. Most people would simply have classified it as aggravating but somewhere inside Ilie it triggered an explosion. Blasting his horn, he yanked the wheel hard to the left and overtook, leaving precious little space between the Lancia and the dithering

172

driver. As soon as we reached the next traffic lights a few yards further on, Ilie leapt out of the car and ran back to berate the surprised driver in a screaming monologue of expletives that must have contained most of the swear words known to the Romanian language.

'Fucking son of a bitch,' he said as he climbed back into the car, switching profanities with his multilingual facility. Inevitably people had stopped to stare at this little scene for, quite apart from his behaviour, the yellow sports car and flame red Adidas track-suit were hardly items that passed unnoticed on the streets of Bucharest. Word that Ilie Nastase was home was spreading fast. But like a tropical storm the anger quickly passed and by the time we reached the club he was thinking about his tennis again.

'I've got to get a hit tonight to try and get used to these conditions again,' he said anxiously. 'I've only got one day and this court is so slow.'

Apart from scores of club members who leaped happily out of the way as Ilie swerved into his parking place and then clustered round to shake his hand, the ever-fathful Constantin and two members of the Romanian team, Dumitru Haradau and Gavril Marcu, were on hand to give him an hour-long work-out.

At Ilie's suggestion, that evening we went round to Ion Tiriac's house for drinks. Their relationship is stabilized again now with Nastase making most of the moves to bring them into each other's company. Tiriac, a prouder man, obviously enjoys Ilie as most people do but he will not be seen to be courting the superstar who was once his protégé. He has never yet, for instance, been inside Nastase's house. I discovered this when Tiriac dropped me home a few days later. Ironically Ion had been thinking of buying the house himself when Nastase snapped it up five years before. They were not speaking at the time and Ilie's fast purchase could not have improved the chances of their doing so.

'Ilie just walked straight in, in his usual lucky way,' Tiriac said with a tinge of resentment as he pulled up outside the Nastase villa. 'I had to spend almost double what I paid for mine on interior decoration. Ilie's was in perfect condition.'

After the earthquake neither house was any longer in exactly perfect condition. A couple of large cracks were visible on the outside wall of the top storey of Ilie's house and when Tiriac took us up into his attic one could see daylight between the top of the wall and the roof. The wall moved visibly when Ion pushed it but then one has the feeling a lot of walls would if pushed by the great bear-hunter from Brasov.

But Tiriac just shrugs. 'Listen, we were lucky,' he said. 'I have a friend living in my basement now whose whole apartment disintegrated.'

One strange idiosyncrasy of the 'quake was that it damaged furniture in some rooms but not others. In Tiriac's panelled study, decorated with large coloured photos of Panatta and Vilas and a couple of excellent

173

sketches of Ion himself, besides numerous photos of the lovely Mikette, a whole sideboard laden with cups and trophies came crashing down, just as it had at Ilie's place. But in the dining-room next door the only thing that was damaged was an eighteenth-century clock.

'That was a shame,' said Tiriac. 'Apart from it being a very beautiful clock it wasn't really mine.'

Evidently it had been bought by Heinz Grimm, the Swiss secretary of the European Tennis Association when he had been in Bucharest for that same Davis Cup tie that Sturdza had attended. However when Grimm tried to take it out of the country, the customs officer at the airport told him it was an antique and therefore could not leave Romania. Tiriac had offered to buy it from Grimm then and there but Heinz refused any money, telling Ion simply to keep it for him. In trying to preserve something precious from Romania's past, the authorities had unknowingly ensured its destruction. In Basle it would have been safe. Now it had been smashed to smithereens.

That Ilie's Lancia Fulvia has not been smashed, or even dented, is a tribute to the skills and reflexes of its owner. If there are speed limits in Bucharest, Ilie is blissfully unaware of them. With his favourite tape of his favourite singer, Elvis Presley, blaring full blast he is not beyond driving the car in time to the music ('Oh, What a night it was, it really was … such a night'—after a few days driving with him the words become embedded in the brain). Yet for all that one could not classify him as a thoughtless or dangerous driver. If he takes risks now and again, they are calculated ones based on the capabilities of the car and the driver and, like any top-class athlete, he is a good judge of speed and distance.

There is a woman in Bucharest whose name we shall never know who can be thankful for that. On the way home from Tiriac's house, Ilie moved into the outside lane of a three-laned avenue and put his foot down. The little car leapt forward like some eager colt let out of the paddock and was soon touching 90 mph. It was that bad time of the evening when dusk is just turning into night and the eye struggles to tell shadow from substance. A fraction of a second after I felt Ilie's foot come off the accelerator, I saw a bulky figure appear in the middle of the road about a hundred yards ahead. The woman had been intending to make a dash for it, which was a perilous thing to do in any case on an unlit road at that hour, but had been put off when she saw the speed of Ilie's on-rushing headlights. So, compounding her mistake, she stopped.

I shall not easily forget the sight of her silhouette arched in a pose of desperate indecision as Ilie's foot hit the brake. In fact, she was in danger not so much from the Lancia as from the car in the centre lane right alongside us. Although travelling more slowly than Ilie, the driver's reactions had been slower still and, as it was the centre lane in which the woman was now poised, it was he who would have to cope with whatever move she finally made. If she stayed where she was, he would have to brake to a halt—and he did not seem to be reacting fast enough to do that—or swerve out of her way. Which way would he swerve? Would he panic and yank the wheel left into our lane?

It is at such moments that the anatomy of an accident flashes through the mind—two cars, side by side, braking down from speeds of ninety and sixty miles an hour, a confused pedestrian rooted in fear to the middle of the road. Our only antidote to disaster was time. Those precious two or three seconds that so often mean the difference between life and death. In this case there was time. Making up her mind at last, the woman turned and scuttled back to where she had come from. Mercifully the inside lane was empty so she was safe. Nastase swore, hit the accelerator and moved the car swiftly back through its gears to top. We were almost late for dinner.

For as long as Ilie's mother is in charge of the kitchen no one is ever going to starve in the Nastase household. Several may die of flatulence, obesity or a diseased liver but starvation, no. One is given the distinct impression that nothing a guest could do in that house would be viewed with quite such dismay and even resentment as failing to eat enough. The problem, of course, lies in the definition of 'enough'. To Elena Nastase enough means a solid snack as soon as you walk through the front door and a huge four-course meal with plenty of second helpings not long after. Speaking only Romanian, she does not allow the fact that she cannot converse with many of her son's friends to stand in the way of the basics. Pointing, with as much delicacy as possible, to her mouth she nods her head hopefully to indicate the expected answer and promptly bundles off to the kitchen.

Dinner that night consisted of *mititei*, a kind of sausage baked in cheese, and Ilie's favourite dish, *sarmale*, which is stuffed cabbage. 'My mother makes the best *sarmale* in the world,' said Ilie, downing another mouthful. 'Just the way I like it. Have some more.' Mrs Nastase smiled and nodded encouragement. It was actually too tasty to refuse.

When Ilie is home one is never quite sure who is in the house. Odd relatives keep emerging from his parents' quarters in the basement and a whole stream of friends drop in by the front door. During this first visit Anna, Ilie's forty-six-year-old sister and the mother of Vlad, seemed to be in permanent residence which obviously suited her son just fine. It gave him even more of an excuse to be around the house and therefore closer to Ilie whom he obviously adores.

A sensitive person, Vlad is in the tantalizing position of glimpsing the good life through the fleeting visits of his rich uncle. He spoke of getting a job teaching tennis to children when he got out of the army later in the summer. But if the family connection helped him to find a job like that, the close association with one of the world's great players probably inhibited him, too. 'I just teach the kids, you understand,' he kept telling me earnestly. 'I work well with children.' When he was not rushing off on errands for Ilie, Vlad spent much of the time in the house mooning over his favourite song, 'Sylvia's mother says ...'—a hit of a few years back which obviously struck chords in his romantic heart. I just hope his ideas of love and life in the West do not include any romantic visions of Galveston, Texas.

After dinner a whole gang of people, including Anna, Vlad and Nastase's old coach Colonel Constantin Chivaru sat round drinking beer or scotch while Ilie took innumerable phone calls and generally looked harassed. He enjoys being at home with all the fuss and adulation it entails, but basically a shy person, even Nastase occasionally craves peace and there were moments when he obviously wanted to run out of the house and find a couple of friends for a quiet game of backgammon.

Frequently when we were out in Bucharest, he would avoid crowded places for fear of having to stand and talk to vague acquaintances from his past. Yet there were moments, too, when he visibly relished being the centre of attention. Certainly the spotlight was difficult for him to avoid. Celebrities are not exactly thick on the ground in Bucharest and when a home-grown superstar of Nastase's stature hits town virtually everyone stops to stare. To give them their due, people are mostly content to look and very few bother him for more than an autograph. There is none of the over-familiarity and unsolicited chit-chat that celebrities are subjected to in the West, especially of course in America.

A strict social etiquette, with personal privacy high on the list of priorities, still exists in Romania. It is, in fact, interwoven into the patterns of everyday speech. For instance, when one stops to ask a stranger the way, the correct form of address begins, 'Please don't be angry at my asking but ...' Contrast that with the 'Hey, got the time, buddy?' with which one is assailed in the States and there emerges a good example of the basic differences in the two cultures.

In retaliation, Americans could well point to Nastase's behaviour on court which is frequently obscene and the screaming, abusive partisanship of Romanian tennis crowds. Although I felt segments of the crowd at the 1976 US Open rivalled anything I had seen anywhere for cheap, abusive behaviour, the point is well made.

Then why this sharp contrast that exists not just in Romania but also in other Latin countries between the extreme personal civility that one encounters in everyday life and the animalistic screams of the mob at sporting events? The answer, I think, lies simply in the degree of contrast. Collectively Mr. Baseball Fan and his friends may not make quite such a shrill noise as a Romanian crowd but let us not forget that the American loud-mouth with his six-pack is at the game primarily to find a vocal outlet for his frustrations and prejudices. And yet when he leaves the stadium he can still behave with a freedom of speech and manner that would be socially, let alone politically, intolerable in Romania.

In adition, depending on his ethnic background, Mr Baseball Fan may or may not be saddled with the problems of a Latin temperament. Like compressed steam, the sheer volatility of the Latin character requires an outlet. Sporting occasions provide that outlet and, compared with America, the rigidity of their social structure makes the hissing sound seem all the louder.

With Nastase himself the explosion comes as a result of nerve ends that can no longer withstand constant irritation. Like worn electrical wires they sizzle and then the sparks fly. At that point Nastase is capable of anything. But that intensity of feeling is almost never reached off court. In the company of family or close friends he merely gets angry on occasion like any normal, highly-strung person. The driving incident referred to earlier was very much the exception to the rule.

Normally the inherent shyness in his nature becomes the predominant feature of his personality when he is away from the familiar surroundings of a tennis-court. Having every move you make watched by a room full of people can be disconcerting to the most self-assured person. For a shy one it can be acutely embarrassing. Another great tennis champion, Rod Laver, was equally shy and it took him many years before he could handle the daily needs of the public personality as opposed to those of the professional tennis-player.

When Ilie is embarrassed his natural reaction is to turn very stern, solemn and quiet. He certainly turned that way when a whole party of us walked into the Pescárusul Restaurant on our second night in Bucharest. The Pescárusul, which means seagull in Romanian, is set on the lake in Baneasa Park on the outskirts of the city. At lunch-time one can eat out on the large terrace and watch the rowing-boats drift by. In the evening the main building is crammed full on two levels, the upper level being in effect a four-sided balcony looking down on to the dance floor below. There was no music playing when we arrived but as soon as the diners caught sight of Ilie, the noisy chatter suddenly subsided. Virtually everyone stopped eating. Ilie, his head down, walked quickly to the table that had been prepared for us and behind him Tiriac strode in, his head rolling slightly on those massive shoulders, his face, as usual, a mask. Later, when the band worked up to a tempo that was almost as deafening as the Presley cassette in Ilie's car, they broke off from the rock and roll to play a couple of Romanian songs for the two tennis stars. Both Ilie and Ion rose, looking rather serious, to acknowledge the applause.

But Nastase's moods are nothing if not changeable and the following night, after he and Dumitru Haradau had despatched the two young and very inexperienced Belgian singles players in straight sets to give Romania a 2–0 lead in the Davis Cup, he was in a more expansive frame of mind. After a relaxed dinner with Mitch and his actor friend, Silviu Stanculescu, he was ready for a little night club action so we repaired to the Club Bucharesti, a sizeable establishment at the bottom of a large winding staircase. Having become inured to the sub-standard offerings served up under the all-embracing title of 'International Cabaret' at various dives around the world, I was expecting the worst. But in fact the floor show was rather prettily choreographed and even the mandatory acrobat was worth watching if only for the suppleness of her truly enormous thighs.

Ilie and Mitch were suitably impressed by the contortions of all that female flesh but it was the dainty little singer who received the benefit of Nastase's generosity. Although he had known the girl since childhood, he had not seen her for some time and was obviously in the mood to make an impression. So when the flower girl came round to our table, Ilie bought the whole basket. After her next song, the surprised singer found herself being presented with about £20 worth of red roses.

'When she saw me before the show she said she wanted a flower so now she has every flower in the place,' laughed Ilie. 'What the hell, I have all this Romanian money in my pocket and maybe the flowers make her happy.'

We left soon afterwards because Ilie had an early morning appointment at the Ministry of Defence. He was to become a major. Major Nastase? Well, Ilie was the first to see the funny side of it but not unnaturally, he was quite proud of the new red epaulette on his uniform when he brought it home. Ever since his national service, he had been kept on in the Romanian Army reserve and having received a commission, had steadily progressed up through the officers' ranks by virtue of age rather than any military prowess. Now at the age of thirty, it was time for him to become a major.

Back in more familiar surroundings that afternoon, Nastase and Tiriac won a routine doubles victory against the Belgians to give Romania a winning 3–0 lead. With the tie in the bag, Major Nastase led his troops into the celebration campaign with a little more gusto that night.

First there was a dinner in a private dining area of the Two Cocks Restaurant which is about half an hour's drive from the city. It was a typically boisterous Romanian feast with the jokes flowing as freely as the wine. Ilie, of course, was getting looser by the minute and when we eventually got back to the house around midnight, he decided to go in search of a wedding-party to which he had been invited. He also decided that the occasion warranted dressing up so on went the major's uniform and off went Ilie and Mitch into the night.

Life in Romania

I had elected to stay at home in the vain hope of getting some sleep. It was a fatuous idea on account of the cockerel. The bird lived in a cage in the courtyard just below my bedroom window. Now despite my city upbringing I know about cockerels. They crow. Ever since St Peter got caught out, they have been crowing at inconvenient moments. Nevertheless, however inconvenient dawn might be if you do not wish to get up that early, most cockerels I have ever heard of manage to stick to a fairly regular routine so at least you know where you are. But not the Nastase cockerel. Would you believe that the Nastase cockerel had a temperament that was totally incompatible with any civilized living pattern? This raucous bird would let rip with an ear-splitting cry at any old hour. 1.58 am; 3.15 am; 4.26 am and even, more by luck than good judgment, at dawn if it felt it had something to say at that particular hour. Its basic problem seemed to centre on the need to converse regularly with a friend which was no doubt locked in some equally restrictive cage somewhere across town. A few seconds after the Nastase bird cleared its lungs out, one could hear a plaintive reply echoing in the far distance. Sleep became something one grabbed desperately in between the damn creature's compulsive desire to converse with its pal and I never understood how the neighbours put up with it. The Congolese Embassy backs right onto Ilie's yard and every night I fully expected a raiding party to come over the wall and spear the bird to death. Unfortunately among their Embassy staff the Congolese seemed to lack daring warriors and I had to resort to empty threats in the hope that Ilie would take the hint.

'I'm going to wring that bloody bird's neck tonight,' I told him vehemently.

'Be my guest,' he shrugged. It was all right for him, his bedroom was on the other side of the house. Actually I had no intention of laying a hand on the cockerel. Ever since I saw a Haitian voodoo dancer bite a chicken's head off I have been a bit squeamish about those things. But although no relief was forthcoming on that trip, the first thing I noticed on my return a few weeks later was the blissful silence. Apparently Ilie's father had done the dirty deed.

Ilie and Mitch were in no better shape than I was the following morning when Mrs Nastase fed us lavishly on sausage, cheese, eggs, tomatoes and anything else she could lay her hands on. The wedding-party had gone on until four in the morning and the two late-night revellers looked as if they had already eaten and drunk enough to last them a week. Mitch's state of health was not improved by the fact that he had acquired a black eye. As he is built like a miniature Arnold Schwarzenegger, one of his favourite party tricks is to put one arm around Ilie's waist and lift him upside down.

179

'Normally it's no problem,' Mitch explained. 'But when you're a bit pissed you get careless and last night Ilie's heel caught me in the eye.'

Apparently Major Nastase had gone down a treat in his uniform but all that was last night. It was now approaching twelve noon and Ilie had a hangover and a match to play.

'Boy, I really don't feel like to play today,' he mumbled into his coffee. 'Maybe I don't play. No need, you know. We win the bloody match already.'

There are times when Ilie threatens not to do something and really means it. There are other times when a little bit of mumble and grumble help to shoo away the clouds that frequently darken his horizon. This was just a grumble. He had come to Bucharest to play for the Davis Cup and that was what he was going to do.

'The people like me to play,' he said later as we watched Bucharest Dynamo play another First Division side on TV at the club restaurant. 'I would have to practise today anyway so why not play a match? I need all the practice I can get before Kodes arrives.'

The Belgian tie had, in fact, been little more than practice. At the bidding of their two veteran players, Bernard Mignot and Patrice Holmbergen, both of whom had served Belgium valiantly over the previous decade, the selectors had decided to blood some of their younger players in order to lay the foundation of a team for the future.

Even in a dead Davis Cup rubber, playing against Nastase is always an experience and no doubt Jean-Pierre Richer was grateful that Ilie decided to turn out. It would not have mattered to the young Belgian that Nastase had not played a more meaningless match since he became a world-class player. The tie was won before he walked on court; he had nothing to prove against that standard of opposition and he was not being a paid a dime for his services. Contrast that with his Sunday exercise a couple of weeks earlier when there was $100,000 on the line for beating Jimmy Connors amid the media-mad hoopla of Caesar's Palace Hotel in Las Vegas. Some players would have found that contrast too deflating for their egos but not Ilie. Give him a stage, any stage, and whatever the circumstances or the financial return, he will contrive to enjoy himself.

Even before he played, he had caught the holiday spirit of the crowd. It was May Day in Bucharest and the weather could not have been more perfect. The city was draped in red bunting, with huge pictures of President Ceausescu hanging from government buildings. But there was no May Day Parade this particular year and no one seemed to be complaining about its absence. Away from the devastated downtown area, Bucharest didn't need any artificial decoration. The gentle breeze rustling the shell-like blossom from the tei trees and the vast areas of green beside the wide boulevards made the seventy-degree weather seem refreshing. Strolling by the lakes or sipping a beer at an open air café on a day like that, it was easy to understand why Bucharest was called the Paris of Eastern Europe before the Nazi jackboot and the Soviet sickle left their indelible mark.

Confident that Ilie would not let them down, some 4,000 people turned out to watch the final two matches against the Belgians. He was due to play the second singles but the crowd did not have to wait that long to get a glimpse of him. During a change-over in the first match, Ilie suddenly appeared with the contraption that whitens the lines and started to do the groundsman's job for him. Everyone cheered and clapped and Ilie was laughing like a child with a new toy. 'I did it because the guy wasn't there. Honest. I don't know where he got to but someone had to do it,' he told me afterwards. 'Anyway, I do it well, no? Very straight line.'

He hit some pretty straight lines against young Richer, too, winning 6–2, 6–2, 6–2 in a match that enabled him to give a lovely relaxed exhibition of his mastery with a racket.

There were sounds of much hilarity when I edged my way into the small Romanian dressing-room after the match. Apart from the players, the Romanian team doctor and the masseur, Virgil, there were two other short, stocky men I did not know. They were introduced as Prime Minister Verdet and General Stan who, in addition to being President of the Romanian Lawn Tennis Association is Chief of the Secret Police. One way and another there was a lot of fame, power and influence packed into a small space. The Prime Minister enjoys a game of tennis and, according to Nastase, plays quite well. He takes it seriously, apparently, but is not beyond cracking jokes about his efforts while hitting with Ilie. Although most of it was in Romanian, the mood of non-stop banter was infectious whether one understood it or not and once again one was reminded of the Romanians' extrovert humour.

Ever since our arrival we had been regaled with jokes about the earthquake. As with so many real tragedies, humour is often the only way of easing the pain. Certainly the Romanians did it in style.

One example which I heard—although not from the Prime Minister I should add—told of Brezhnev calling up the Lord to complain about the disobedient Romanians who were becoming much too independent. 'Can't you shake them up a bit with a big earthquake or something?' Brezhnev asked. A little reluctantly the Lord agreed to do the Soviet boss a favour. But when the earthquake struck it was so large that it caused a lot of damage on the other side of the Soviet-Romanian border, in a province that had been annexed from Romania by the Kremlin after the war.

Brezhnev was a bit peeved at this and couldn't help mentioning it when he phoned up the Lord to thank him for the effort. 'It was good of you,' said Brezhnev trying to hide his irritation, 'but I didn't ask you to make it so strong that it caused damage to property belonging to the Soviet Socialist Republic.'

There was a silence on the line for a few seconds and the sound of papers being shuffled. 'Oh, I'm sorry,' said the Lord eventually. 'I was looking at an old map.'

Ilie turned up late at the official dinner given at the Marul de Aur or Golden Apple Restaurant that night. But he had a good excuse. The Prime Minister had kept him talking over a beer.

General Stan, a fascinating character with a high, intelligent forehead and a ready smile that never quite reached all the way into his small, darting eyes, sat flanked by the vice-president of the Belgian LTA and the non-playing captain. If they had been chosen to reflect the ethnic division that exists between French and Flemish races in Belgium it would have been difficult to select two more typical types.

The Flemish vice-president was a ruddy-faced, grey-haired man with a rollicking, back-slapping personality—the type who absolutely insists that everyone has a terrific time. Daniela Moga, the pretty Romanian interpreter, was hauled on to the dance floor and, as he swirled her past our table beaming happily at everyone, I caught the look of prim disdain that crossed the face of the Franco–Belgian captain sitting opposite me. An altogether more introvert, fastidious character, it was hard to imagine him co-existing terribly well with his vice-president. However it must be said that when the captain himself was coaxed on to the dance floor he underwent a rapid change of attitude and suddenly did not look at all unhappy at being in close proximity to the enchanting Daniela.

General Stan, meanwhile, had been called away by his bleeper. 'There is nothing that goes on in this city that he does not know about,' whispered Ilie as the General and an aide swept out of the restaurant. One could well believe it. When he returned a few minutes later, even the state of Ilie's steak caught his eagle eye. Ilie had only muttered something about it not being cooked enough but that was sufficient for General Stan. The *maître d'hotel* was summoned and lectured on the need to produce a steak to the maestro's liking. The poor man looked mortified. Messing up Ilie Nastase's steak was bad enough but having General Stan complain about it was obviously having an adverse effect on his nervous system.

Possibly the need to get Ilie's steak right threw the kitchen into confusion because both the General and the Belgian team had excused themselves by the time the *tuica*, a very pleasant plum brandy, and the *crêpes*, a Romanian speciality, were finally served. 'There's typical Romanian organization,' said Mitch. 'They serve up the best part of the meal when everybody's left.'

Tiriac, who had obviously been under no pressure to attend the official dinner, was still serving lamb off the spit on his back porch by the time we got round there and the party continued into the early hours.

The next morning Ilie was given little chance for a lie-in. An 8 am phone call summoned him for a breakfast-time game of tennis with the Prime Minister and General Stan.

'Shit, I'm tired,' he announced when he returned to the house around 10.30, just as Mitch and I were finishing breakfast. 'I think I take a rest.'

When he re-emerged I made him put on his army uniform for a photo session before he drove me to the airport to catch the Air France flight to Paris.

Apart from the fact that it was getting late; that the car didn't have much petrol in it; and that Ilie was having difficulty standing still long enough to have his picture taken, everything was under control; the normal sort of chaos before leaving for an airport. As it turned out, there really wasn't time for Ilie to change out of his uniform and that gave him an idea.

'Kodes is arriving on a flight from Vienna at just about the time you leave,' he said as we raced for the airport. 'Maybe I play a trick on him. The Customs guys there, they are all friends of mine. They let me do what I want. So maybe I have big surprise for the Russian.' Ilie slapped the steering-wheel and laughed heartily at his idea. Finding little ways to play jokes on Jan Kodes, a rival since childhood, was always a pastime that amused Ilie. He called him 'Russian' precisely because he knew nothing could annoy a Czech more and Kodes had long since ceased to react to it. But Ilie never gave up and with the Davis Cup tie against the Czechs coming up at the end of the week, it was a good time for a little extravagant humour. To a foreigner, the uniforms worn by the Customs officials and Romanian army officers are virtually indistinguishable. Ilie knew this and intended to exploit it. Having arranged everything with his friends in passport control, he took his place in one of the booths where passports and visas are checked and, standing well back so that his face was in shadow, he waited.

Kodes eventually strode through and was guided to Nastase's booth by a willing accomplice. Like anyone who has been through the procedure too many times before, the Czech was not paying much attention as he handed his passport through the glass partition. He was, in fact, already peering through into the arrivals area to see if the Czech consulate had sent anyone to meet him. It was only when a voice in the booth said, 'This visa is not valid,' that Kodes swung around and took an interest.

'Why not?' he bristled.

'Because you're the biggest son-of-a-bitch in the whole world,' said Ilie, collapsing into gales of laughter. Recognizing his would-be inquisitor, Kodes stuck an arm through the glass partition and knocked Ilie's cap off and all the real Customs officials fell about. Unless you happen to be trying to get *out* of the country when the government does not want you to, Bucharest Airport can be a barrel of laughs. Dan Rowan ought to camp out there for a time and he'd soon have enough material for a Laugh-In, Romanian-style.

Actually Kodes got the last laugh that day because Nastase ran out of petrol on the way home and had to hitch a ride in the Czech's car to the nearest garage.

But that was about the last point Kodes and the Czech team scored in Bucharest. When the Davis Cup got under way a few days later, Jiri Hrebec who has a temperament almost as volatile as Ilie's, gave away one rubber by walking off court in protest against what he claimed were persistently bad line-calls. As the British were to discover a few weeks later that kind of attitude does nothing except play into the hands of the opposition. Having gratefully accepted the match, Romania clinched the tie when Nastase played dream-like tennis against Kodes, looking every inch the consummate artist running circles round the industrious but hopelessly outclassed artisan.

If he had been allowed to stay on that surface and in that relaxed frame of mind, there is no knowing how long the gold dust might have clung to his racket. But his schedule allowed no such luxuries. Another mad dash to the airport on the Sunday afternoon, where the plane for Paris had orders to wait for him in case he might be late; one night at home at La Basoche to change his suitcase and pick up Nikki and then off across the Atlantic again for the WCT finals in Dallas. An eight-hour time change; a different ball; Supreme Court indoors instead of clay outdoors—all those adjustments had to be made in three days. It is the sort of workload an artisan can survive, but not an artist.

11

THE CIRCUIT

For Ilie the 1977 World Championship of Tennis finals in Dallas were a disaster. It was not simply that he lost his first match against Eddie Dibbs. That was disappointing enough. But worse than that the long trans-Atlantic flight and the sudden brief switch of surface broke his rhythm and shattered his confidence.

There are moments when a great natural athlete can handle disruptive changes like that and shrug them off. Nastase had done it often in the past. But on this occasion he couldn't handle it. His mind was on too many things. Had he left his parents enough money in Bucharest? Where were the family going to stay in Los Angeles in the summer while he played Team Tennis? Would Nikki go back to Bucharest with him for the Davis Cup tie against Britain? All relatively minor personal problems, yet they piled up at a time when Ilie was uneasy about his game and a little confused about how he should cope with an expanding career. In both body and spirit he was scattered and that four-day trip to Texas right before the start of the European clay-court season did not help. Without the Davis Cup it might have been possible but Bucharest–Dallas–Rome within a week was asking too much.

Nevertheless Ilie did not pass unnoticed in the Big D. He and Nikki had arrived on the Monday night after a harrowing journey that had left them 'stacked' over New York in a snow storm. Surprisingly for a nervous flyer, Ilie seemed to recover from the experience quite quickly and was in good spirits when Nikki dropped him off to practise at the Moody Coliseum the next morning.

All eight finalists in Dallas are lent Cadillacs for the week but Nikki didn't want to drive Ilie's round a strange town, especially with her husband's name plastered on either side. So she accepted a ride with San Francisco's tennis writer Susie Trees to go on a shopping expedition to Neiman Marcus. Although she won't hesitate to buy anything she really likes, Dominique is not a frivolous shopper and on this occasion she resisted all temptation. Even when Susie pointed out a particularly pretty dress with a waistcoat top, Dominique rejected it and, in doing so, revealed more about her husband's mores than her own taste in clothes.

'You have to wear that with nothing underneath?' she asked Susie. 'It's nice, eh? But Ilie would never let me wear it. He doesn't like me showing too much skin.'

People who watched Nastase unzip his shorts in a court-side box in Palm Springs might have difficulty visualizing the puritanical side of Ilie. But it exists.

On the way back to the car Doiminique bought a copy of *Playboy*, which included an article on Ilie by Mike Lupica. Before letting Susie drive off, she sat in the parking lot, reading it intently.

'That's wrong what he says about the linesman looking at the mark,' she said when she came to Lupica's description of one of Nastase's many on-court arguments. 'That bloody man refused to get up off his chair.' But there was nothing else that her critical mind could fault. 'That's a good article,' she said finally. 'Mike writes well.'

Two nights later Nastase gave everyone more to write about but unfortunately some reporters were not quite as accurate in their analysis of Ilie as Lupica. Possibly the fact that WCT officials were obviously nervous about the prospect of Nastase throwing a spanner into the middle of their brilliantly oiled machinery only heightened the sense of drama, which, in turn, gave the press more of an excuse to exaggerate. But largely, of course, it was Ilie's reputation. Instead of being discreetly ignored, his hiccups now became headlines.

He did a bit more than hiccup against Dibbs but not nearly as much as the tennis public were led to believe when they read their papers next day. Had he indeed thrown a major tantrum, one would have expected him to be led away in handcuffs—summarily arrested by one of the red-blazered WCT officials who either sat next to him on court during the change-overs or lurked in the nearest box behind his chair. At one stage or another European director John McDonald, Bill Holmes, Larry Pease and the executive director himself, Mike Davies, were all in attendance on Ilie. It was an extraordinary sight and the significance of it was not lost on the sophisticated and knowledgeable Dallas crowd which now packs Moody Coliseum to its 9,300 capacity every night of the WCT Finals. Mike Davies' intention was to have enough people whom Ilie knew and could talk to nearby in case any problem arose and with luck to nip it in the bud. It was a risky exercise that looked dangerously like overkill and, as we have seen, Nastase can react adversely to the sight of officialdom encircling him in expectation of trouble.

But McDonald, Holmes (an experienced tennis official who had a spell with the ATP in Los Angeles) and Pease, the popular young road manager, are all sweet talkers in their varying styles and were probably as well equipped for the job as anyone. Certainly as a former New Zealand Davis Cup player and the only man Rod Laver relaxed with during his assault on the Grand Slam at the US Open in 1969, John McDonald understood the pressures a top player undergoes in a big match better than most. And so along with Davies, a firebrand himself in the days when he was British No 1 but now a mellowed Welshman, the quartet hung about in attendance while Ilie regarded them all suspiciously, not knowing whether to look upon them as instant psychoanalysts, pulse-takers or police.

A bit of each, perhaps, and although no arrests were made, the pulse-rate of the match was far from steady. That was probably inevitable with as volatile a character as Eddie Dibbs on the other side of the net. A loud, vastly humorous, well-liked little hustler from Miami, Dibbs gets as hyped up as anyone on the circuit before an important match and it was obvious that Ilie would need to do little more than twitch to get a rise out of Eddie. And so it proved. Dibbs reacted, sometimes humorously, sometimes impatiently, sometimes angrily, to every gesture Nastase made but only once—when hot words were exchanged during a change-over—did it get dangerously unpleasant.

On another occasion—one that the press totally misinterpreted—Dibbs chased a wide ball all round the court and ended up on Ilie's side of the net. Playfully Nastase pushed him back and Eddie went through a little belligerent 'don't shove me around' routine that was all in jest. The next morning the headlines were screaming about an angry Nastase being involved in a brawl. It wasn't much of a brawl but it was a fine tennis-match and Dibbs simply played too well. Nastase got back into it by winning the second set but generally the gutsy little American pounded his volleys with too much depth and made too few errors off the ground for a disorientated Nastase to make the score look any better than 6–1, 4–6, 6–2, 6–3 to Dibbs.

At the press conference afterwards, Mitch Oprea announced that he would act as interpreter as Nastase was too tired to talk in English. But it was merely a half-hearted attempt to camouflage the disappointment Ilie felt at having come so far for so little and within a couple of minutes he was answering questions sombrely in English, his haggard face wearing the mask of a sad clown.

Eddie Dibbs was more forthright. 'Sure, we said some tough things to each other out there,' he admitted. 'I get pretty nervous, too, you know, and I ain't about to take any bullshit from Nastase. But it's OK now. He just gets a little crazy, that's all.'

Most people seemed to have enjoyed the match and I heard very little criticism of Nastase from spectators afterwards. As gracious and diplomatic as ever, Lamar Hunt's lovely wife Norma played the understanding Texas hostess to the hilt by saying, 'I was just so sorry for the people of Dallas that they didn't have the opportunity to see Ilie at his best.

187

But what could you expect with him having to fly all that way and everything.'

However not everyone saw it that way. By the time the newspapers hit the streets Nastase was once again in disgrace with the sports fans of America. The extent to which the incidents in the match had been played up became evident to me when Dick Auerbach of NBC Television arrived from New York a couple of nights later in time for a cocktail party in the hospitality lounge of the Ramada Inn. Along with Slim Wilkinson of the BBC and Greg Harney of the public broadcasting station WGBH in Boston, there is no producer in the world with as much experience of televising tennis as Auerbach. Normally Dick's sardonic wit allows him to skate happily through the myriad pitfalls that bedevil a producer of live sports shows, but this time he looked worried.

'I just had a hell of a time with my network bosses over this Nastase business,' he told me. 'The agency reports played up the shoving and swearing real big and now people at NBC are asking how long we can go on televising these X-rated shows. It's getting to be a real problem.'

I sympathized with Auerbach and to a certain extent understood the concern of the NBC hierarchy who were obviously worried about public opinion and its effect on their precious ratings. But with the American sporting public at large I could not muster as much tolerance for this prudish reaction to Nastase's behaviour.

Of course if any individual—and there are obviously many—is sincerely offended by all forms of physical violence, verbal obscenity and lewd behaviour then one must respect their opinion and even applaud it. They would be absolutely correct in maintaining that much of Nastase's behaviour sets a thoroughly bad example for younger players and should never be condoned. But even if that kind of person makes up the majority of Nastase's critics in America, I am absolutely certain a very large minority fall into two rather different categories. Either they are the kind who are quite content to pay their way into tennis events expressly for the privilege of hurling abuse at the very man they so readily accuse of profanity, or they are the type who turn a blind eye to the blood-curdling fouls that take place in ice hockey or American football games every Saturday afternoon while still maintaining that tennis is a lily-white sport that should only be played by gentlemen. In my view both are enormous hypocrites. It is not good enough to point out that ice hockey and grid-iron football are physical-contact sports that, of necessity, contain a certain amount of violence. That much is true but there are also rules for both sports and I must assume that the rules of ice hockey do not embrace the freedom for players to flail about at one another like drunken boxers for minutes at a time. 'Ah, but you see,' my hockey friends tell me, 'that's what the public come to see, a good old punch up.'

Similarly I have known people who will in one breath tell me that Nastase should be thrown out of tennis for saying 'fuck' and giving the finger to the crowd while two minutes later, they laugh gleefully at an article in *Sports Illustrated* on Conrad Dobler of the St Louis Cardinals which quotes him as saying, 'I'll do anything I can get away with—eye-gouging, biting, face-mask twisting ...'

It reminds me of the woman I met at a party in Los Angeles some years ago who remained disdainfully calm and collected while I was describing the number of Vietnamese women and children who were being turned into charcoal by napalm but suddenly got terribly hot and bothered when I said 'shit'. It all has to do with one's sense of values, I suppose.

Nastase's values can most certainly be faulted but not, I would suggest, by the kind of person who finds Conrad Dobler funny. As for television, I would say only this. When the networks reduce the level of prime time violence to Nastase's level of obscenity, then perhaps they will have a case for taking both off the air.

Long before Jimmy Connors beat Dick Stockton in the final to win the WCT title for the first time, Nastase had flown away to Rome. There the atmosphere would be different but the problems would remain. He would be at odds with his temper and his talent and the crowd would yell abuse—but not for long. Italians never remain cross for long.

Although Ilie, Nikki and his brother Constantin decided to stay at the Cavilieri Hilton in an attempt to keep out of the tennis limelight, Nasty was still a topic of conversation down at the Holiday Inn. 'Nastase is very popular here,' the tennis-crazy barman Massimiliano told me one night. 'We like very much the showmen like Muhammad Ali and Nastase. Sometimes Ilie can do a little too much and then everybody is down on him. But really we like him.' That seemed to be a reasonably accurate assessment of Ilie's standing in Italy but on this occasion it wasn't the crowd that was down on him; he was down on himself.

The first problem was the weather. Badly in need of practice to readjust his timing to clay, he found it virtually impossible to secure any court-time for practice at the Foro Italico because of the rain which affected the first few days of the Championships. Then after struggling past Spain's Jose Higueras and Bob Hewitt of South Africa, Nastase was to throw all that excellent match practice down the drain by working himself into a needless frenzy when he played Phil Dent in the quarter-finals. The problem had nothing to do with Dent whom he had beaten easily enough on the same Centre Court two years before. It did seem to have something to do with the late arrival of Mitch Oprea although nothing made very much sense in the aftermath of disappointment and recrimination.

Oprea was delayed flying in from the States and only arrived a few hours before Ilie was due to play Dent. There was a problem about rackets which Mitch probably tends to be a little too insensitive about because he feels, with some justification, that Ilie could pick up any racket he found lying around the locker-room and win with it. Deep down Ilie shares that opinion but when his nerve ends are exposed the slightest variation in the grip, tension or weight of his racket will be sufficient to make him feel insecure.

At the start of the match Mitch sat in the front row of the marble-tiered players' enclosure with Constantin. Dominique, not wishing to be in the front of the firing line, sat a few rows back. From the moment Nastase lost the early service break he had gained in the first set, he began berating Mitch and his brother in between points. Screaming at them in Romanian, he let his mind wander completely from the task in hand and soon it had become an embarrassing ritual. After every single point he lost, whether as a result of his own mistakes or Dent's good play, he would turn and yell at Mitch—Constantin having quickly retreated after the first few salvoes.

The crowd didn't have any idea what was going on and after a few spirited attempts to cheer Ilie on lapsed into a sort of confused murmur. At Dominique's bidding Mitch finally withdrew, but it was too late. All the nervous energy and concentration he should have been using to defeat Dent had been expended by the end of the first set. In the second, which the Australian won easily, I did not see Nastase make a single aggressive shot. Blocked service returns; pitter-pat volleys—Phil fed off that fare like a man suddenly presented with a free banquet. 'I just hit the shit out of the ball: it's the only way I have a chance of beating the guy,' Dent said afterwards. 'If he's not thinking too well he'll always go cross-court off his forehand so I just sat on the net waiting for it, giving him anything he hit down the line, which wasn't much. I don't think he was concentrating out there today because we usually have really close matches. But seldom any problems. I told him a long time ago "Listen, mate, don't come complaining to me about line-calls. Complain to the linesman or the umpire but don't bother me because I'm not going to give you anything." So I just ignore him and it's worked out pretty good.'

Ironically, in view of the fact that they had agreed to play doubles together the following week in Paris, Hewitt had had plenty of problems with Ilie in the previous round. The big, balding expatriate Aussie had, of course, been involved before in on-court flare-ups. But, as is so often the case, it was less Ilie than the erratic officiating which caused the problem and it was quickly exacerbated by the fact that Nastase could speak fluent Italian while Hewitt barely understood a word.

So when the bad line-calls started becoming a subject for discussion Ilie inevitably had the upper hand, especially as neither the umpire nor the assistant referee who was called to the court spoke English. Since English is generally accepted as the official language of the pro circuit, this was an inexcusable lapse on the part of a tournament as important as the Italian Championships, and when, as a result of slamming a ball into the corner of the court and generally complaining about his lot, Hewitt was fined $200 he rather naturally felt victimized.

And when Ilie started laughing about it in the locker-room after the match, Bob didn't find it amusing. 'You just stay over on your side of the room or I'll break your bloody neck,' said Hewitt, looking as if he meant it. Ilie retreated and soon that large room which is situated directly under the Foro Italico snack bar, was invisibly partitioned into little sections, each player who had either just finished a match or was about to start one staking his claim to a patch of territory between the two long rows of wooden benches.

It is an ever-changing scene, of course, but just at that moment Hewitt's outburst—rare even by his standards these days—had made everyone self-consciously aware of each other's territory. Soon everything settled down and there was Hewitt still complaining bitterly to a couple of friends in his corner near the door; Nastase in his section by the showers was joking with the Italian trainer, Mario Belardinelli, and a small knot of Romans; and, further down that same bench, a world away in thought but only a few feet in distance, sat the man who was destined to win it all just a fews days later, Vitas Gerulaitis. Although a close friend of Ilie's, the ebullient New Yorker was too professional to allow himself to be dragged into someone else's argument just before he had to go on court. So he sat, his curly, blond head between his hands, staring at the floor. In another corner a body, its face draped with a towel, lay on the massage table, either asleep or feigning sleep in the hope of relaxing the muscles that would soon be called upon to last him through as much as three hours work on slow European clay. Each man was an island and, although it is not always so, at that particular moment everyone was especially careful to stick to territorial waters.

Nastase and Hewitt have too much respect for each other's talents and too much understanding of the problems a volatile temperament can cause to let their row in Rome spoil their plans for Paris and by the time the French Championships started at Stade Roland Garros they were acting like lifelong buddies. Hewitt felt sure he could help Nastase as far as talking tactics with him before matches and generally boosting his confidence was concerned and, even though Paris turned out to be as frustrating as Rome for Ilie, I think Bob was of some positive assistance.

I first found him in Ilie's corner, figuratively and literally, for Nastase had found another niche for himself in the comfortably modernized Roland Garros locker-room, when the Romanian trudged off the centre court two sets to one down against Tim Gullikson in the first round. The break in a

191

five-set match which brings both men off court in a state of acute anxiety creates a very special tension in a tennis locker-room. The normal free-wheeling banter tends to simmer down at the sight of two tense, sweat-streaked figures marching in.

The state of a match involving a top seed would be known to almost all the other players as many would have been watching the action on the close-circuit TV in the lounge area, and for those not in the know the news that Nastase was in trouble would soon be passed on to them in hushed tones.

Nastase yelled for a clean shirt; listened to some words of wisdom from Hewitt and disappeared into the massage room for a quick rub.

'Go and tell him he'll never win the match unless he stops talking all the time,' a friend told Adriano Panatta who, being closer to Ilie than most players, willingly went in and relayed the advice. Basically it had been the same problem as in Rome. Every error was followed by a plaintive sentence or two of complaint to Constantin or Dominique. Each outburst tore at his threadbare concentration and gave the inexperienced but talented American opportunities to build on his lead.

But after the interval all that changed, and not simply because Panatta had told him to concentrate. Dominique had taken more drastic action than that. She had removed the troops. When Ilie and Tim walked back onto the centre court there was not a single member of the Nastase entourage in sight. Constantin, his wife and their son Mihnea had been despatched to have tea and Nikki herself was sitting in the little ante-room that forms the entrance to the men's and women's locker-rooms flanked by France Dominguez, wife of Patrice, and Rosaria Panatta. It was quite a trio. Three raven-haired beauties, each exuding her own highly individual attraction, all looking as tense as relatives in a hospital.

'I'm not going back out there,' Dominique said. 'There's no way. It's better if he can't see any of us and then perhaps he'll concentrate.'

She was absolutely right, of course. During the first game of the fourth set, Ilie looked up as if to speak or gesticulate but finding no one there turned away, muttering quietly to himself. Eventually the muttering stopped and, as Gullikson made things easier by rushing his strokes in an effort to close the match too fast, Nastase levelled at two sets all and went on to complete a relatively straightforward victory.

'It was that bloody trip to Dallas that ruined my game,' Ilie complained as he showered after the match. 'Shit, and all for nothing too. I was playing so well against the Czechs in Bucharest. Now I have forgotten what to do. Sounds silly, eh? But it's true. I don't know whether to come in or stay back. I've lost the feel for it. I need time. I practised for one hour this morning and even then I played badly.'

Earlier Paolo Bertolucci, who had been Nastase's practice partner, had over the previous year, at least the tantrums had been punctuated with some worthy title-winning achievements. Apart from triumphs in the Avis Challenge Cup and the Pepsi Grand Slam, he had won singles titles at Atlanta, Salisbury and La Costa while reserving some of his best tennis for two of the most important events of the year, Wimbledon and Forest Hills. By December he had moved back up to No 3 on the ATP computer, behind Connors and Borg.

But at no time was Nastase—or Jimmy Connors for that matter—seen in better light than during the rain-afflicted John Player Tournament at Nottingham the week before Wimbledon. There is no more treacherous surface to play on than wet grass and the footing on a tennis-court has seldom been worse than it was when Ilie and Jimmy elected to play their singles final after a long delay because of the rain. They were both taking a considerable risk which would have been bad enough at any time of year, let alone on the eve of Wimbledon. Yet not only did they play, they played with such zest and flair that one would have marvelled at many of their strokes had they been playing in the most perfect conditions. Eventually after Connors won the first set and Nastase the second, the grass had become so slippery that the odds against injury were no longer reasonable. So they asked the umpire to abandon the match. Deservedly, the crowd gave them a rousing ovation.

'We had to do something for the people,' said Ilie afterwards. 'The place was full; 3,000 people getting wet and cold hoping to see some tennis. So we have to try.'

That was a side of Ilie Nastase that the Nottingham tournament director, Tony Pickard, had seldom seen before. In 1975 Nastase had refused to play the John Player event because of some injudicious remarks Pickard had made about what Nastase might or might not do, and until he proved himself a real trouper in the 1976 final, their relationship had been a little strained. Now Pickard, who had worked hard to bring top-class tennis to the Midlands, had discovered an unlikely ally in his bid to make professionalism a respectable word amongst the somewhat old-fashioned local tennis hierarchy. Not for the first time, Ilie had turned an enemy into a friend.

For that alone he could look back on the year with a modicum of satisfaction.

9

RETURN TO BUCHAREST

The opening months of 1977 were relatively uneventful by Nastase's standards. He played well intermittently on the WCT circuit, winning the title in Mexico City and generally playing consistently enough to make sure of a place in the eight-man Dallas Finals at the beginning of May.

He had managed to entertain without overstepping that ill-defined line which divides the comedian from the boor and apart from winning a considerable amount of money on court, had given himself the satisfaction of not merely retaining the WCT Challenge Cup but beating Jimmy Connors in that Caesar's Palace final.

In the minds of the tennis public, and indeed the majority of the tennis press, the Challenge Cup had not exactly taken its place alongside Wimbledon and the US Open as one of the world's great prestigious events. That was hardly surprising. The proliferation of big-money bonanzas in the pro game over the previous few years had left most people bewildered and to some extent bored by the meaningless array of new titles.

But the Challenge Cup, another brain-child of WCT executive director Mike Davies, was actually a far better test of a player's true worth than most. A selection of eight players from the world's top twenty were divided into two groups of four to be played off on a round-robin basis. The top two finishers in each section would then play a group final and the winners of those two matches would contest the final which alone would be worth $100,000 to the winner. All this was to be played over a period of several weeks.

Ilie had begun the defence of his title—he had won it in Hawaii the previous year when the eight-man contest had been played under Avis sponsorship—with a disconcerting loss to Manolo Orantes. But after beating Rod Laver and Harold Solomon, he had his revenge over Manolo 6–2, 2–6, 6–2, 6–1, in the group final and set the stage for the bitter showdown with Jimmy Connors which, as we have seen in Chapter 1, he won with lashing tongue and whirling racket 3–6, 7–6, 6–4, 7–5.

As usual there was little time to savour the euphoria of triumph. The week following Caesar's Palace, Ilie was due to rejoin the regular WCT tour at the River Oaks Country Club in Houston. It offered not merely a change to clay but a drastically different ambiance as well. From the gaudy Everyman's playground of Las Vegas where the amount of attention or adulation one receives is measured solely by the size of one's credit balance in the casino—or, for the selected few, by their superstar status—the rarefied atmosphere of River Oaks provides a quick insight into the varied worlds of the American rich.

In a land that strives hard to attain the utopia of social equality, River Oaks Country Club stands as a bastion of American snobbery. One might also say bigotry but that would be unfair to the majority of its membership who do not really deserve such an indictment. Here it is not enough merely to be rich. One has to be white, prefereably WASP and of good family pedigree. Those requirements are not simply laid down for membership but virtually for the most fleeting of visits to the club grounds in order to exercise one's democratic right to attend public events.

Five years before when Arthur Ashe was a member of the WCT group that played there, players were confined to the tennis-court and locker-room area and required special passes before they were allowed to eat in the club-house coffee shop. Worse still, the public were denied the right to buy tickets for the only major professional tennis event played in the Houston area that year.

The reason given by the tournament committee was that the demand for tickets for the 3,000-seat Centre Court was so great among members and their friends that there were no tickets left over. They did not mention—and would have denied it if asked—that the thought of Ashe's numerous black supporters tramping through their grounds was more than the redneck element in the club would tolerate. I remember writing a rather biting leader for *World Tennis*—at that time owned by Gladys Heldman and Houston-based—in which I suggested that if River Oaks had such scant concern for the needs of the tennis public they should terminate their tournament and go play with themselves.

As River Oaks members have never felt themselves unduly pressured by anything as sordid as public opinion, change came slowly. But at least a token offering of seats was put on sale for the general public in subsequent years and this was apparently sufficient for Lamar Hunt, who is usually more sensitive to the requirements of democracy, to continue WCT's association with the club.

Apparently the influx of a few non-members has done little to alter the overall atmosphere. Quite unsolicited by me, Ilie launched into a tirade against the River Oaks tournament on his return to Europe. 'Bloody stuck-up crowd,' he said vehemently. 'Such snobs. I wear jeans and old shoes all week just to annoy them. Apart from a few of the girls who work at the tournament and are always very nice I think everyone hates me in that club. It's OK. I hate the crowd. I hurt my ankle when I trod on a ball practising with Vitas during the week and had to default in the semis. Maybe at another place I try to play on a bit just because the spectators pay to see a match. But in front of that crowd I am happy to default. Screw them.'

It is amusing and also indicative of the importance he attaches to appearance that he should deliberately try to annoy River Oaks members and their studied Neiman Marcus elegance by playing a role that, in Texan eyes, could so easily be interpreted as that of the sloppy Commie. I am sure Ilie played the uncouth youth to the hilt, secretly delighting in the fact that his own wardrobe at home makes him a leading candidate for the title of best-dressed athlete.

In fact, by any standards, Nastase dresses with great elegance and taste. His suits and jackets and coordinating waist-coats from Guy Laroche and Saint Laurent in Paris and Battistoni in Rome, amongst other leading houses, are chosen with an instinctive flair for fashionable chic.

'I like to dress well although when you are travelling it is easier to dress casually,' Ilie says. 'But always I like a little style. The Americans dress better now but before they were terrible. They used to dress like rich Russians.'

On his way home to Europe, Nastase stopped at West Virginia Beach to pick up a cool $37,000 for losing to Guillermo Vilas in the final. 'The money is getting ridiculous,' Ilie admitted when he stopped to think about it a few days later. 'I play a couple of not-so-good players and get $37,000 just to get to the final. With the Challenge match and Houston that makes almost $150,000 I have won in three weeks. And I only play six matches. Unbelievable.'

Considering $100,000 was a top player's on-court earning target for a whole year in 1973 and 1974, the prize-money explosion in pro tennis has indeed bordered on the fantastic. Boosted by that one big win at Caesar's Palace which netted him a total of $170,000 for the whole competition, Nastase had collected in prize money something in excess of $400,000 by the beginning of May.

Contracts with the American television networks were often the source from which the prize-money flood gathered momentum and certainly the Tiriac-inspired promotion at West Virginia Beach—a non-Grand Prix, non-ATP approved event that was set up on an invitation basis purely for its monetary value—existed solely because of a good deal with local television. At any rate, it capped a profitable three weeks in the States for Nastase which adequately cushioned any deprivation he might have felt at having to play tennis for nothing for the following fortnight.

Two consecutive weeks of Davis Cup play in Bucharest were next on Ilie's agenda and it was part of the deal which gave him his passport to freedom that he should make himself available gratis for Romania's annual said much the same thing. 'Ilie's not playing well,' said Paolo. 'He has no confidence.'

On the first Saturday of the Championships, a cool breeze was rustling the chestnut-trees around the old renovated Stadium as the sun, making its first effective appearance of a hitherto wet summer, continued to shine out of clear skies. Nastase was due to play the West German No 1, Karl Meiler, and he was attending to the tiny details that loom so large for the professional athlete, such as examining the soles of his new Adidas shoes.

'They're good,' he said approvingly. 'I didn't slip so much when I practised today. The court's fast compared to Rome and I must get proper footing.'

Good footing was not what he lacked against Meiler. It was this increasingly strange refusal to hit his shots as if he meant to hit them. He was like a cat on hot bricks, running round in a lot of needless circles, not knowing half the time whether he was Tom or Jerry. Instead of killing the volley, he would pat it back into court so that even Meiler, who is not the fastest man on the circuit, could reach it.

This time Ilie led by two sets to one but after a match-point in the fourth set tie-break, he proceeded to lose it by eight points to six.

'*Je suis malade*,' said Dominique weakly and went into her disappearing act once again. Flopping down into one of the chair's outside the locker-rooms, she clasped her hands together in a temporarily effective attempt to stop her nail-chewing habit and shook her head. 'I tell you, sometimes I think it is worse for the wife,' she said. 'At least he is out there doing something. All I can do is sit and watch or sit and not watch. Trying to do anything else is impossible when I am at a tournament. Even if I could find a court to play tennis myself I wouldn't be able to concentrate on a ball. Not with Ilie in there losing matches he should win.'

But, quite quickly as it turned out, Ilie did win, running through the fifth set 6–1.

The post mortem was becoming familiar. 'Richard, I swear I don't understand myself,' he said with an expression of genuine bewilderment. 'I just don't understand. How could I lose that fourth set?'

'You're not putting away your volleys,' I replied.

'You're right but I just ... I don't know.' He shook his head and then brightened. 'But at least I'm getting some practice here. I need five hours a day.'

Sunday was a day of practice for Nastase, and his mood was altogether more relaxed as he prepared for his match against Jan Kodes in the round of sixteen on the Monday afternoon. Kodes was combing his hair when Ilie came bouncing into the wash-room. 'This bastard beat me in the 1971 final here,' Ilie reminded us. 'I had 5–3 in the first set and they changed the line-call.'

Both players laughed. 'You'd better watch out. I may do the same thing today,' Kodes replied. But it was only Czech pride that made him say it. After the way Ilie had beaten him in Bucharest he knew full well that he would not be in the match if Nastase played like that again. They had been rivals too long and knew each other's warfare now before their matches. All the banter was very lighthearted.

It was good that Kodes did not expect too much because Ilie did indeed produce almost as classic a performance of controlled artistry as he had done in the Davis Cup. His timing had returned; he was more decisive at the net; he concentrated well. And Kodes was beaten in straight sets. Suddenly it was all so easy again and Ilie, as much as those watching him, wondered how on earth it could have been so difficult just two days before.

After a win like that, Ilie's spirits rose and his irrepressible humour soon dominated the locker-room. It had been rumoured that Harold Solomon had been kept off the circuit earlier in the year by a rather painful complaint. When Ilie saw Solly later that day, he couldn't resist the obvious question.

'Hey, Solly, is it right you couldn't play Davis Cup because your balls hurt?' he asked innocently.

Solomon grinned. 'Yea, that's right, Ilie,' he replied. In a corner Eddie Dibbs yelled out something obscene in defence of his friend and everyone laughed.

On the surface this relaxed mood was still in evidence on Wednesday, 1 June when Ilie prepared for his quarter-final against Brian Gottfried. While the American sat on one of the locker-room benches engrossed in *Newsweek*, Nastase chatted amiably in the lounge area with Adriano Panatta, Stan Smith and Paul Kronk and then started to change into his yellow Adidas strip.

But as match-time approached, tension started to mount below the surface. Nastase knew he could win this match but equally he knew it was not going to be easy. Gottfried, one of the most decent and best respected men in tennis, was at that time the leader in the Colgate Grand Prix and he would play the only way he knew—straight and hard. He would not be intimidated or distracted by anything Nastase did on court and that in itself would put pressure on Ilie.

The preceding match on Centre Court was taking a long time and, as Ilie began pacing the locker-room, he began to look round for an outlet for his nerves. Just as happens on court when he can no longer control them, he picked on someone. Not particularly viciously but rather as a kind of absent-minded exercise to release tension. Eyeing Bud Collins changing nearby, he suddenly swung round and demanded, 'What you doing in here? This is the players' locker-room.'

'I just saw you and I'm going,' said Bud in mock seriousness, quickly recognizing the symptoms of a pent-up athlete.

An hour earlier it would not have entered Nastase's mind to challenge Collins' presence. As a player of sufficient stature to have played in the French Veterans Championships, Collins would have easily been able to defend his right to be there. But to argue that is to miss the point. Ilie might just as well have demanded to know why Stan Smith had blond hair. Logic had nothing to do with it.

Possibly it had the desired effect for when Nastase and Gottfried finally got on court at 6.25 pm, Ilie seemed totally at ease. And for two sets he played like a man in complete control of his talent. He was also in complete control of Gottfried. After he had put behind him some early problems with his service, he started sprinkling the court with magic. In the sixth game of the match, in which he broke the American's serve for the second time, he foxed Gottfried completely with a brilliantly disguised backhand down the line and then, when Brian tried a drop shot, Ilie loped on to it, lifted a lob over his opponent's head and sunk the desperate return into the red clay with a feather-touched drop shot of his own.

When Nastase secured a two set to love lead it seemed inconceivable that he could lose. But Gottfried came back strongly in the third, pounding his volleys with greater depth and precision and finally stinging the Romanian with a great forehand pass in the tenth game which took him to within two points of the set. Nastase, who had shown no sign of concern at the turning tide, acknowledged the shot and quickly lost the set.

Fourteen thousand people and a stadium cast in shadow greeted Nastase and Gottfried when they returned to the court. Ilie broke serve almost immediately and then, at 15–40 on his own serve in the fourth game, saw a lob which apparently landed on the base-line, called 'out'.

For the first time in the match Nastase lost his cool. He yelled at the linesman and then appealed frantically to Jacques Dorfmann who, along with the highly popular Bertie Bowron, must be one of the most experienced umpires in Europe. Expressionless as always when he is in the chair, Dorfmann glanced at the linesman to see if there was any hint of indecision, found none, and announced, '*Jeu Gottfried. Deux jeux partout, quatrième manche.*'

Twice Gottfried went up to the net to tell Ilie that he could not help him because he had not seen the ball land but Ilie was still gesticulating at the linesman and when someone in the crowd yelled at him to play tennis, he received Nastase's finger by way of reply. But the 'cinema', as the French might say, did not, by Nasty's standards, last very long. Quite quickly he lapsed into a sort of sudden despair as if he knew the match was slipping away from him and had forgotten what to do about it. The fourth set went to Gottfried 6–2 and by now the crowd were revelling in the drama, emotionally behind Nastase but almost equally appreciative of this solemn young American who kept on coming, seemingly stronger by the minute—a figure of total resolution and unwavering confidence. Apparently inexhaustible, Gottfried was chasing deep balls and wide balls and drop shots as Nastase desperately tried to probe for a chink in Gottfried's armour. But that was his problem. Once again he was only probing and pushing, apparently content just to get the ball back over the net rather than punch through his strokes as a champion must.

There was a flicker of a revival when Nastase checked Gottfried as the American served for the match at 5–2 but two games later it was all over. Brian thoroughly deserved his famous victory but Ilie, bitterly disappointed, could rightly ask himself how he could possibly have let slip a match that he had dominated with such masterful ease for two sets.

Screaming at reporters to get out of his way, Nastase stormed back into the locker-room and slumped on to the bench. 'If I play like that I should stop,' he said more to himself than to anyone in particular. Then Corneliu Manescu, the newly-appointed Romanian Ambassador in Paris who had known Ilie since childhood and is now one of his closest friends, came in to console him.

As they walked towards the shower together, two French reporters appeared and when Ilie saw them he turned at the doorway and, in a tone of controlled venom, said to one of them, '*Je peux dire, tu est vraiment con.*' In the harshest language, he was telling him that they were stupid to bother him before he had a chance to shower and calm down. But before anyone had a chance to argue the point, Ambassador Manescu, sensing a bad scene, grabbed Ilie by the shoulder and hustled him into the shower-room.

Later that night Ilie, Nikki, the Ambassador and a few friends gathered amidst the upper-crust elegance of the Brasserie Lipp on the Boulevard St Germain. But the plush surroundings were not enough to soften Ilie.

A few days at La Basoche were of greater benefit to Ilie's state of mind and by the time we boarded the Air France Caravelle 'Angoumois' bound for Bucharest and more Davis Cup action, this time against Britain, he was in fine fettle. By virtue of the Nastase name and my Air France 'Service Plus' card we had managed to get Ilie, Mitch and myself upgraded to first class but as two enormous suitcases stuffed with a lot of Dominique's old clothes for the earthquake refugees were included amongst our luggage, Ilie still found himself paying out 385 francs (£42) in overweight charges. But the hospitality on board soon made up for it. The crew turned out to be tennis enthusiasts and soon after take-off stewardess Michelle Jousseaume came back with an invitation from Capitaine Guillotel for Ilie to sit in the cockpit.

'For God's sake don't let him fly the bloody plane,' I told Michelle as she led Ilie away.

Capitaine Guillotel obviously enjoyed his guest. 'Such a nice fellow,' he told me as I wedged myself into the tiny Caravelle cockpit later on. 'Ilie's a great champion. I don't know how he manages to play so well with all the travelling he does. I told him he must always drink a lot on long flights because you know we have only 5 per cent humidity in a pressurized cabin.'

As the wine was flowing freely back in first class, Ilie and Mitch were doing all right and after he had presented Michelle with a signed Adidas racket, Ilie settled back to talk. By the time we stopped at Belgrade, the conversation had ranged over what political spokesmen like to call 'a broad range of topics'. After Ilie had reminisced about his first meeting with Jan Kodes and Alex Metreveli in Estonia, I mentioned the tragic case of Tomas Lejus, an Estonian by birth who had been the No 1 player in the Soviet Union a decade before. One had heard on the grapevine that Lejus had died in jail after being imprisoned for killing his wife. Ilie had not heard that Lejus was reputed to be dead and was shocked. 'That's incredible,' he said. 'Tomas was such a quiet guy. You know I can never understand getting to the point of really wanting to kill someone. We all get mad but to the point of killing ... no, I can't understand that. It's ridiculous. I don't think I could kill somebody. Hell, I've never even hit anybody, although sometimes when people start insulting me in the street I feel like it. But I always remember who I am just in time and control myself.'

It was interesting that a man who is renowned for his temper and who has participated in, if not always created, some of the biggest rows in sport should be talking this way. But it did not surprise me. The violent streak in Ilie's character is more a subconscious instinct than anything he readily perceives as part of his make-up. He also maintained that he never lost control of himself. With one or two exceptions I think that, also, is probably true.

'Even when I get really angry I always feel I have some control,' he went on. 'It's the same when I am drunk. It doesn't happen too often but even when I really have a lot I never get to the point when I am not in control of myself. I wouldn't like to feel I have no control at all.'

Obviously Nastase is often amazed at the way people react to his behaviour. To him and indeed anyone born with a volatile temperament a little flare-up, a passing flash of anger or emotion is the fire of life. Without it they would consider themselves dead. Ilie brought up the incident with Eddie Dibbs in Dallas as an example.

'We both talk a lot when we play and sometimes we call each other names,' he said. 'Once I pushed him in fun during that match and the next day all the papers say we fight. Everyone is suddenly asking me what is the matter between me and Dibbs and I say "What are you talking about?" '

The next player Ilie chose to talk to on a tennis-court reacted rather differently from Dibbs and the result spelt more trouble for the voluble Romanian.

12

DAVIS CUP—WIMBLEDON

One dark Romanian night I went driving with Ilie Nastase to a monastery by a lake where Count Dracula is supposed to be buried. It was, I admit, a little eerie but I only got really scared when I read an article by the brilliant *Los Angeles Times* columnist Jim Murray a couple of months later. It is one of Murray's more imaginative pieces and well-worth requoting at length:

'The first look you get at Ilie Natase ... you close your eyes and picture a lightning storm playing around this lonely castle and your car mysteriously breaks down and you knock to get in out of the rain and this big door opens and there he stands grinning in his evening cape and top hat and his eyes glow in the dark and he has this ghoulish pallor, and he says, "Goot evenink, von't you come in?" and he keeps staring at your wife's neck and his teeth start to drip. Off in the distance you hear a wolf howling and the pillow in the coffin in the corner looks slept on.

'You resist the temptation to ask him what time he turns into a bat or how his pet lycanthrope is doing.

'I mean, it's a great part for Bela Lugosi. Bram Stoker should cover his matches. "Count Dracula goes to Wimbledon." ... Crowds shout, "Hey, Ilie, your casket is ready!" Or, "Hey, Ilie how do you want your blood—straight up or over the rocks?"

'You're sure he lives in a place where the eyes in the portraits move and everyone is afraid to go down to the cellar. And the shutters bang all night and you don't want to know what it is that's howling in the basement or moaning under your window. You try not to look at the tombstones in the backyard.

'This is the image Ilie Nastase projects on a tennis-court. Linesmen are afraid to look into his eyes for fear they'll find themselves roaming across the countryside on moonless nights wearing a shroud and blank eyes.

'It is an image which is worth, perhaps, half a million a year to him and half a game a set. People love to come and shudder when he approaches the baseline, brandishes a racket at an umpire or goes after a heckler.

'His opponents buy the psyche and, nine chances out of ten, they come

199

on court tight-lipped, tense, jumpy and angry and ready to take desperate chances to teach this terrible Transylvanian a lesson. In other words, just the way Ilie wants them.

'Now, will the real Ilie Nastase please stand up?'

On closer acquaintance Murray, like everyone else, found Ilie a little different.

'The real Ilie Nastase would make as lousy a Dracula as Jimmy Stewart. Vincent Price would turn the part down cold. If he lived in a castle, the only howling would come from Elvis Presley records. He drinks 7-Up not Type O ... Take the racket away from Ilie Nastase and you go from Count Dracula to the Count of Monte Cristo, a suave, hand-kissing type, a lover not a lug.'

Perhaps it was a good thing I knew all that when on our first night back in Bucharest Ilie and I set off to find a dinner-party which was being held for Horst Dassler, the youthful boss of the vast Adidas organization. Dassler had landed at Bucharest Airport just a few minutes after us to begin a three-day business trip to Romania. For both professional and personal reasons he also wanted to spend as much time as possible with one of the biggest names his star-studded company has under contract. So when a dinner was arranged for Horst at a country lodge about thirty kms from the city, Ilie was asked to join the party as soon as he had finished practising at the Progresul.

'They say it's just ten kilometres past the airport,' said Ilie optimistically as we set out. 'I've never been there but we should find it OK.'

It soon became quite evident that we were not going to find it very quickly. Ilie may drive around the wide boulevards of Bucharest like James Hunt in pursuit of Nikki Lauda but as soon as we hit the smaller roads on the other side of the airport, he dropped his speed to little more than 25–35 mph. It was easy to understand why. The road had become a paved but narrow strip running between rows of self-built cottages. Apart from slits of dim light peeping from behind half-drawn curtains, the only other illumination came from the head lamps of the Lancia. It was a good thing they were powerful because practically none of the bicycles we encountered had rear lights and every few hundred yards an enormous black mass on the side of the road would finally materialize into a parked lorry. If we came upon one of these at the same moment as Ilie had to dip his headlights for on-coming traffic, some rapid braking was required, even at 25 mph.

'If a foreigner drives out here for the first time at night, he will kill many people,' said Ilie. 'It happens sometimes.'

It was easy to believe. After a while we stopped to ask for directions and Ilie was distressed to be told that the place was still twenty kms away. 'Shit, we're going to be late,' said Ilie, pushing the little car forward in

200

short burst of high-powered acceleration whenever he was absolutely sure there was a clear stretch of road in front of him. But that did not happen often and it was tiring work.

'Silly sons-of-bitches,' Ilie would exclaim as cyclists wobbled along the middle of the road. Eventually he fell silent—or at least verbally silent. For soon his strong, finely-drawn right hand, resting on his knee when he was not changing gear, became his voice. One quickly got to understand the language. When we circumvented a truck or cyclist without too much trouble, the hand would flutter briefly like the wings of a bird, denoting mild annoyance. But if danger loomed too close, it would take off in a full sweep of anger and then settle, twitching, as we continued to dodge the shadowy figures thrown up by the dark Romanian night.

Finally we reached a junction with a sign for a place called Snagdov. 'We're supposed to turn here and then turn left after the monastery,' said Ilie. 'You know the Wallachian prince they based the legend of Count Dracula on? Vlad the Impaler they called him. He's buried near that monastery. Down by the lake somewhere.'

Terrific. I thought that was probably all we needed: Dracula's ghost leering through the car window offering directions. In fact when we did make another stop to ask the way, the two characters who helped us were more likely to have been invented by Peter Cook and Dudley Moore than Bram Stoker, author of the nineteenth-century novel *The Passion of Dracula*. They were a couple of peasants meandering their way home, their wide-brimmed hats pulled down low on the forehead, baskets over their shoulders; too drunk to risk riding the bicycles they were wheeling beside them.

'We're looking for the lodge where the big party is,' said Ilie.

The tall one, 'Pete', stuck his head through the window, mixing the clear country air with the light alcoholic breath of wine and vodka. Grubby fingers stroked a long, stubbly chin and then the eyes flickered with comprehension as Ilie's question sunk in. Withdrawing himself from the car, he announced, 'Yes, sure I know where the party is. You must turn around.' He swayed convincingly to demonstrate the required movement.

'You sure you know the party I mean,' asked Ilie suspiciously. It was obvious that 'Dud' and 'Pete' had found a very good party of their own. In the background I caught sight of the little one, 'Dud', making faces and grinning inanely.

'Sure, sure I know,' replied 'Pete' with as much conviction as he could muster. 'Big party, lots of cars. You go back down this road and take the first left after the monastery when you have passed two signs.'

We left them standing in the middle of the road, going through sweeping movements with their arms like a couple of inebriated traffic wardens, chuckling happily.

201

They had given us tremendous directions. There weren't any signs and there was no first left after the monastery. After making another about turn just to make sure we hadn't missed it, Ilie pulled up in front of the huge wooden archway leading to the monastery. We both gazed up at it for a minute, a dark silhouette against the night sky. I knew what Ilie was thinking before he said it.

'You think we ought to take a look up there?' he asked. At that point Jim Murray might have run off screaming down the road but as Ilie looked just about as scared as I felt, I thought we might as well venture on together.

It really was a bit eerie. The long, winding pathway up to the monastery was overgrown and hemmed in by trees and shrubbery and when the Lancia's headlights finally hit the outer wall the whole area was suddenly flooded by a ghostly glow. Nothing stirred. It was about 9.30 pm by this time and the monks were either asleep or praying silently for Count Dracula's soul. 'Somehow I don't think there's a party round here,' said Ilie and our laughter broke the tension.

We made it back to the main road before anything fanged and frightening sprung from the bushes, and reverted to our original course, this time ignoring the turn off for Snagdov. 'Bloody people gave me the wrong directions,' said Ilie banging the steering-wheel in exasperation. 'Turn left the guy told me and so did those couple of idiots back there. Somewhere there's got to be a road to the left.'

But there didn't seem to be. We drove on for about a mile until a car a few hundred yards in front suddenly pulled off the road—to the left! When we reached the spot where the car had disappeared, there was no signpost, not even a road. All we could see was a barely discernible track leading across an unkempt field.

'We might as well try it,' I suggested. 'There don't seem to be too many alternatives.'

After a few hundred yards the rear lights of the car in front disappeared around a bend and when we made the turn, we found that the driver had pulled over to the side under the cover of some trees. Leaning across me, Ilie rolled down the window and called out. 'It there a lodge further on? We're trying to find a dinner-party.' The young man in the driver's seat stared at us blankly for a couple of seconds and then his face took on an expression of suspicion and disbelief. Ilie Nastase, possibly the most famous Romanian alive, was obviously not the person he had most expected to find in the middle of a field in the dead of night. 'Yea, I think so,' he replied cautiously. 'There's a house or something a few metres further on just by the lake.'

Just as we drove off I caught sight of a pretty blonde in the passenger seat. She had been leaning back to avoid what little light was filtering into the car.

'It's a good thing those two were looking for a place to make love otherwise we would never have found the place,' I said.

'You mean there was a girl in the car?' Ilie asked. 'I never saw her. Jesus, that's great. I hope they have a good time!'

The young man had been more than just a determined lover. He also knew what he was talking about, which made a refreshing change. The lodge was there all right and we were led straight through it out into an untidy garden at the back where some twenty people were seated at a long table. The grass was ankle-high and the cluster of trees stretched down to the lakeside where the throaty chortling of frogs could be heard competing with the babble of human conversation. And directly across the lake, huge, dark and forbidding in the moonless night, stood the monastery. Before anyone noticed his arrival, Ilie bounced up to the top of the table and greeted the guest of honour. 'Horst! So sorry we are late but we would never have found it at all if we hadn't followed a couple looking for a place to screw!'

From then one, it became a pretty good party.

This was more than could be said of the Davis Cup against Britain. The odds on a Davis Cup tie passing without incident in Bucharest are never very good. But they verge on the ridiculous if you have two personalities like Ilie Nastase and David Lloyd in opposite teams. They simply become lightning-rods for disaster.

With three brothers, David, John and Tony, all playing at international level the Lloyds have become the first family of British tennis, rivalled on the world scene only by the Amritrajs from India who also have three brothers on the pro circuit. The Lloyds have been great for the game in Britain, giving our national teams a competitive backbone they have often lacked in the past. As that is such a vital ingredient of any successful campaign at international level, it might seem counter-productive to complain that, on occasions, the Lloyds as a family and David in particular suffer from a surfeit of nationalistic feeling. Their laudable competitive spirit is too often fired by an innate and somewhat old-fashioned belief that anything foreign is suspicious, probably devious and possibly not to be trusted at all. As David fights like a bulldog as soon as the action starts this can often lead him into situations of unnecessary ill-feeling. And so it was in Bucharest.

But there was, as usual, a calm before the storm. On Friday, 10 June, Britain battled through a hot and humid afternoon at the Progresul Club and ended up two rubbers down. That came as a disappointment to the young British captain, Paul Hutchins, who had expected that his No 1 singles player, John Lloyd, would defeat the inexperienced Romanian No 2, Dmitru Haradau. When Lloyd won the first set 6–2, there seemed every chance that he would. But Haradau proved himself a powerful and determined competitor and when Lloyd started to get cramp in his racket hand the match slid away from him.

In the opening singles John Feaver had performed creditably against Nastase in his first ever Davis Cup rubber. Like all players who suffer from periodic neurosis about various aspects of their game—which is 98 per cent of pros on the tour—Feaver had, at that time, lost confidence in his serve. As the big West Countryman has one of the deadliest first serves in tennis, it was a considerable handicap to go into a match against Nastase in Bucharest with one's best shot on crutches. But when John started slicing his first serve instead of hitting it hard and flat, there was no doubt that it was in need of mental, if not physical, repair. Yet even without that potent weapon, Feaver showed a surprising aptitude for sticking to it on slow clay and, after winning the third set, he led 4–2 in the fourth before Ilie capitalized on a few English errors and ran it out 6–4.

The day's play had presented few problems for the experienced Spanish referee, Jaime Bartroli. The line-calling had been above average and, to the occasional surprise of the large crowd, what few dubious calls there were tended to be called in favour of Britain. And from the point of view of clashing personalities, there was no problem between Nastase and Feaver. They had played doubles together once on the US Indoor Circuit and had always got on.

But the next day the players on court produced very different vibes. Ilie Nastase and David Lloyd should never be separated by anything as frail and inadequate as a tennis-net. A concrete wall, perhaps, or, if they insisted on being able to see each other, bullet-proof glass might suffice. But nothing which allows their high-voltage nerve ends to rub themselves raw. With two people who basically find each other irritating, it is only a question of time before the sparks create an almighty explosion.

On this occasion it took a little over an hour. Nastase and Tiriac had won the first set 9–7 and the Lloyds were leading 2–0 in the second when, in play reminiscent of Dibbs in Dallas, David Lloyd chased a wide ball at such speed that he ended up on the Romanians' side of the net. As fate would have it, David and Ilie were in the net positions as John Lloyd prepared to serve the next point and so verbal contact became all too easy.

Nastase began making some funny and relatively harmless remark about David trespassing on Romanian territory. Whether David heard what Nastase said correctly or not is a moot point. What is clear is that he had been waiting for Nastase to make a wrong move. And at the first suggestion of it, Lloyd, bristling visibly, pounced.

'What was that you said?' David snapped back, cocking his head in

Nastase's direction. Even from the stands, his whole stance, expression and attitude seemed provocative and from a distance of five feet across the net there was no way that Ilie was going to have enough self-control or sense to resist what seemed to him to be a challenge.

So he replied with a phrase that threatened to give oral sex a bad name. David heard that clearly enough and still not satisfied that he had hooked his fish, said, 'What was that? I didn't hear.'

Nastase was probably quite well aware of what he was letting himself in for but there is something in his character which will not allow him to back away even if the bait is clearly marked 'DANGER—DON'T TOUCH.' So once again he repeated the insult and Lloyd had got him.

'That's it, that's it,' David shouted in a fit of moral indignation. 'I'm not taking any more of that.' And he strode off court. The crowd, who had heard nothing of the conversation at the net, were momentarily stunned but quickly added their own cacophony of boos and whistles to a state of total confusion which had erupted on court.

At first David said he was going to quit in protest. Then in quick succession, David and Ilie started to walk towards each other gesticulating; Tiriac and Bartroli got between them; Nastase tried to tap Lloyd over the head (David later maintained that Ilie hit him with his racket); Paul Hutchins tried to talk to Bartroli; the British coach, Roger Becker, raced down out of the players' enclosure to have a soothing word with David who had been frog-marched backwards off court by Bartroli and Constantin Nastase, the Romanian captain; and up in his chair the umpire made vain attempts to attract somebody's attention. Only John Lloyd stayed on his side of the net, aloof from the chaos.

After a full ten-minute hiatus, Bartroli got everyone back on court and publicly warned Nastase for insulting behaviour. The line-calling continued to be generally good and even the British players acknowledged later that Tiriac had been excellent throughout, never disputing a call and once even signalling a dubious decision in Britain's favour. Tiriac seemed to be enjoying his role as the elder statesman in this tie. With much shaking of his curly head and shrugging of the shoulders, he adopted a gently superior air to any dispute that arose, as if admonishing little kiddies for getting up to such childish games. The American Davis Cup team that had battled with Tiriac on the same court five years before would not have recognized him.

But even Tiriac in this benign mood could not prevent further arguments from flaring up as the match progressed. The score had reached 8–7 to Romania in the fourth set when Bartroli changed a call in Britain's favour, thus making John Lloyd 15–30 down on his serve instead of facing three match-points. Then it started to rain in earnest. Obviously the Romanians wanted to continue and just as obviously Hutchins wanted to get his team off court. Anything to break a spell when it is going against you. Once again David Lloyd was the most visible advocate for stopping and when Bartroli finally decided to call the players off, David, swathed in a huge towel that made him look like a senator in Ancient Rome, gave the hissing crowd a deep, facetious bow and marched out of the arena.

In the corridor leading to the locker-room, Nastase confronted Hutchins. 'You running this match, Mr Hutchins?' Ilie asked coldly. 'Or perhaps David Lloyd is?'

'It's the referee's decision,' Hutchins replied.

When the match resumed, David netted a forehand volley; John hit a smash out of court; and Romania had gained an unassailable 3–0 lead in the tie. But the drama was not over.

That evening an extraordinary dinner took place in the large restaurant of the Inter-Continental Hotel. The hotel is evidently not very busy at a weekend for the British team virtually had the place to themselves. A group of Africans occupied one nearby table and over in a far corner, John Parsons of the *Daily Mail*—the only British tennis-writer farsighted enough to have made the trip—entertained Christopher Bullock, the chairman of the LTA to dinner.

Hutchins' team were seated at a large circular table in the middle of the room. Apart from the Lloyds and John Feaver, the party included Roger Becker, a Davis Cup player himself back in the early sixties, and Richard Lewis, a big, blond left-hander who was the fourth man on the squad.

Evidently Hutchins had been at a series of meetings since the end of the match, both with members of his team and with Jaime Bartroli; but none seemed to have helped to alleviate the feeling of acute disappointment and nervous tension that still pervaded the group. And one major and quite startling suggestion remained unresolved: a move was afoot for the British team to pack their bags and leave without completing the remaining two rubbers, as both Davis Cup rules and sporting etiquette demanded. Needless to say, it was David Lloyd who was advocating this drastic action and he was supported by Roger Becker.

'Even if there's a small chance of it doing some good it would be worth it,' said David. 'Sometime, somewhere, someone's just got to take a stand against Nastase's type of behaviour and we have a golden opportunity to do it right now. How is anyone ever going to be able to persuade kids that Nastase's antics are not the proper way to behave on a tennis-court if we go on condoning it?'

'But we've lost,' Feaver interjected. 'It would look like sour grapes.'

'Quite apart from that, we've got a problem with Bartroli,' Hutchins added. 'He says he never heard Ilie make those remarks to David and never saw David being hit over the head with a racket. He feels that in the circumstances he cannot put those incidents in his report to the ITF. So without evidence from the referee to back our action, I think we'd just risk having ourselves banned from the Davis Cup next year.'

'Then it's not worth it,' said John Lloyd. 'British tennis would lose and the Romanians would get off free. What would be the point in that?'

Becker shook his head. 'I tend to agree with David. No matter what the consequences, I just think it is time someone took a stand.'

'That's right,' said David vehemently. 'You guys can do what you want but I'm on that early flight in the morning no matter what.'

'How can you leave the team now?' Lewis shot back heatedly. 'We've worked as a team, trained as a team, played as a team and we should stick it out as a team. How can you bugger off now just because you're upset?'

'Well, I'm sorry but I'm going and that's that,' David replied. 'If you're gutless enough not to come to a decision either way, I can't help it.'

'Well, I wish you'd fuck off right now,' Lewis retorted, his blond features suddenly turning crimson with rage. 'And if you're going to call me gutless, you can step outside and we'll discover who's gutless. No one's ever called me that before.'

If honour and moral behaviour are close relations then one could argue, somewhat ironically, that it was David's complaint about the lowering of the standard of behaviour which had created the row in the first place.

Even so the elder Lloyd had to keep a very firm grip on himself to avoid getting dragged into a brawl. For Lewis suddenly slammed down his soup spoon, jumped up and grabbed David by the collar, twisting it in a large fist and in an effort to yank him to his feet. Refusing to react, David stared down at his plate and said nothing. Everyone round the table froze in a mixture of shock and embarrassment. The French-speaking Africans at the next table were the first to react.

'*Eh, doucement, mon ami,*' one of them said.

'Oh, shut up,' snarled Lewis who eventually responded to the more recognizable tones of his captain and his coach by resuming his seat.

'Bloody idiots,' someone muttered as the Africans cracked jokes about what to them must have seemed an amusing scene.

'I think,' said Feaver, 'they would have more right to call us idiots.'

'Look, try and calm down,' Hutchins interjected. 'We're all up-tight and it's getting to us.'

'You mean, *he's* got to us,' replied Lewis who was slowly returning to his normal colour. 'Bloody Nastase's the one who got through us.'

And of course Richard Lewis was right. With one obscene and insulting phrase repeated twice across a net, Nastase had set friend against friend and temporarily disrupted the excellent team spirit—so eloquently voiced by Lewis in his moment of anger—that Hutchins had carefully nurtured. That was much more than Ilie had intended, if, indeed, he had intended anything. Having had the red rag waved in his face, he had simply unsheathed his horns and gored. The wounds, as usual, had run deep.

If any player but David Lloyd had been on the other side of that net it would probably never have happened. (But Kipling did not write 'If' with Nastase in mind. 'If you can keep your head when all about you/Are losing theirs and blaming it on you ...' No, no—Ilie can never be counted on to handle stuff like that.) Occasionally, Ilie can surprise everyone with his reaction to adverse circumstances, as he was to demonstrate at Wimbledon just a few days later, but generally it is no use lingering over 'ifs' with Nastase. (A lot of things could have turned out differently for him if ...)

But there weren't many question marks left when this particular situation had run its course. After a long, heart-searching talk with Hutchins after dinner, David Lloyd reluctantly agreed to stay with the team. But when the ITF pronounced judgment several months later after reading Bartroli's report, David was partially vindicated even though he did not escape mild censure himself. For the International Federation decided to get tough with Ilie and banned him from all Davis Cup play in 1978—Bartroli having finally decided to back up Hutchins' sweeping condemnation of Nastase's behaviour in his own report. The Spanish referee did, however, point out that Lloyd himself had acted in a provocative manner. It was a fair judgment.

With the need to change surface again—this time to grass in preparation for Wimbledon—Ilie got himself excused from playing the dead singles rubber on the Sunday so that he could catch the afternoon plane for Paris, change suitcases, and be in London in time to practise on Monday. Before leaving for the airport, he dropped in at the Progresul and spent some time with two people close to him who should not be ignored if this story is to be complete, for both are remarkable in their vastly differing ways. In age, they also happen to be virtually a life-time apart.

The first, whom Ilie took obvious pride in introducing me to, was Father Pietreanu, the seventy-nine-year-old priest who baptized him. With his flowing white beard and sparkling eyes, Father Pietreanu has one of those faces that once seen can never be forgotten. Too often one sees sadness in old age. In this holy man's face there is nothing but joy, serenity and life. He told me he has never had a day's illness and has never experienced physical pain. One suspects the secret lies somewhere in his soul but it may be assisted by the fact that he is a vegetarian who neither smokes nor drinks.

He told me proudly that Ilie had been the five-thousandth baby he had baptized and that, predictably, he had screamed a lot. Ironically Father Pietreanu and Nastase share the same birthday, 19 July, but, presumably, rather different astrolological charts. By all accounts, however, the priest is a shy, emotional man who had stayed out of the limelight to such an extent that he had not got to know Nastase properly until he was twenty-seven, which one feels was Ilie's loss.

The other person was a child of ten, Mihnea Nastase, who is Constantin's son. I had met him during my first visit to Bucharest and again in Paris when he was with his parents at the French Championships. At first glance, it would be easy to dismiss him as a precocious little brat. At times his expression takes on the look of a mean, over-spoilt seventeen-year-old. But there is a sweetness and sensitivity about him as well which already suggests a character every bit as complicated as his uncle's. And that is not all. He spends five hours a day on a tennis-court and plays better than Ilie did at his age. Eight or nine years from now when the sports page headlines have the name Nastase plastered across them, it is a good bet they will be referring to Mihnea, not Ilie. It is not just his total dedication to the game he plays so well that makes one believe this but also his inbred attitude of singular determination. He was just four years old when he first poked his uncle on the chest as Ilie bounced him on his knee and said gravely, 'One day I am going to beat you.' Ilie has long since ceased to doubt it.

Revealing still more of his highly developed personality, Mihnea recently told Ilie, 'I know I have low marks in school for behaviour and deportment but I am only ten and have time to improve. What are you going to do about it at thirty?' And just so that the tennis world has fair warning of what lies in store, it should be added that Mihnea has already walked off the court because of a bad line-call.

'He has exceptional ability,' says Ilie's old coach, Colonel Chivaru. 'But he needs more discipline.' For everyone's sake, I hope he gets it.

Nastase arrived in London to find huge cartoon posters of himself and Jimmy Connors plastered all over the town—a piece of imaginative advertising by Rawlings, the soft-drink company, whose sponsorship had revived the pre-Wimbledon London Grasscourt Championships. Unfortunately Ilie reserved his best performance at Queen's for the following Sunday, the day after the tournament was over. A big-serving American called Hank Pfister had removed him from the Rawlings event one dark and drizzly evening early in the week and it was something of a coincidence that so many people were on hand to watch him practise with Connors on the Sunday. But, as it happened, Crockford's, the gambling club, were running a pro-celebrity tennis-cum-backgammon tournament during Wimbledon and much of the tennis action was taking place at Queen's that day. Everyone had a lot of fun watching former Australian Open champion Mark Edmondson team up with Aussie cricketer Doug Walters to win one flight while Bob Hewitt and racing driver Jody Scheckter cleaned up the other. But it was impossible to ignore the additional bonus that was being offered on a nearby court as Nastase and Connors put on a virtuoso performance of free-hitting stroke-play. It was mesmerizing stuff and one could also not help marvelling at the fact that the pair of them were getting on so well together again. After the ugly scenes in St Louis and Las Vegas, their relationship was unlikely to be as close again but Ilie, who knew how deeply the death of Connors' father the previous January had affected Jimmy, was prepared to forgive if not entirely forget.

Ilie was relaxed and confident that day at Queen's but as soon as he walked on to court 2 for his second-round match against the Texan-domiciled Rhodesian, Andrew Pattison, the little gremlins were busy snipping away at his nerve ends again. He had every reason to feel a little apprehensive for Pattison is not merely a classy performer who can beat the best on his day, but he had actually upset Ilie at Forest Hills back in 1973 when he, Ilie, was the reigning champion. So it was not particularly surprising when Nastase found himself in the kind of special jam a player faces when he is two sets to love down against top-class opposition. For Ilie, it was becoming an all-too-familiar situation. And the general anxiety that growing acquaintanceship with disaster was creating began to have a deeply detrimental effect on his style of play.

One remembered the surprised reaction of Patrice Hagelauer, the French coach and tournament player, after watching Ilie at Stade Roland Garros a few weeks before when he said, 'Ilie has completely changed his style of play. He doesn't hit his volleys any more. He seems only to go for placements and, apart from his first serve, he has no attacking shots at all.'

There was truth in that assessment at the best of times but on the bad days it was especially true. And, of course, on grass aggression is the name of the game; against even the most rudimentary serve and volley player on a fast surface, defence is death.

As Pattison is several notches above the rudimentary, it was no wonder that Ilie was in trouble. After a few complaints about the crowd packing the small arena and a few disruptions over line-calls (one of which was severe enough to lead to a call for the referee, Fred Hoyles) Ilie battled his way out of the third set 7–5 but was soon in danger again in the fourth when he dropped serve for 3–4 after being foot-faulted.

That began a fifteen-minute interruption of the match, the blame for which was placed squarely on Nastase's shoulders in the press next day. For the record this was the sequence of events. As Pattison walked back to his chair to towel off, Ilie started complaining to the foot-fault judge. Pattison was on the other side of the umpire's chair and should not have been unduly distracted by it. Ilie went through his usual gesticulating act but not for longer than the legal change-over period. However, when he walked out on court to receive, he held up his hand and called out to the policeman stationed at the far end of the court—the end from which Pattison was about to serve—and asked him to remove the long row of faces that were peering up from under the canvas back-drop. Not having seen all of the previous three sets, I do not know if the kids had been peeking through there before. But there is absolutely no doubt that they were causing a distraction directly in the player's line of vision and Ilie was well within his rights to ask for them to be removed. That, however, was easier said than done. No sooner had the bobby battened down one end than the kids popped up again while he was attending to the other. It was a pantomime that could have been written specifically for Nastase. And, of course, the temptation to exploit the situation was irresistible. So he started joking with spectators at his end of the court and eventually disappeared from view altogether by hiding behind the tarpaulin.

Obviously all this was to Nastase's considerable advantage as Pattison was waiting to serve for a 5–3 lead and not being temperamentally equipped to handle fanciful flights of comedy at important moments of his career, he was anxious to get on with it. But no matter how much one sympathized with Pattison, it was not Ilie who was causing the delay. He had made a legitimate request, albeit at a highly propitious moment, and now it was its implementation that was creating the hiatus.

It was nearly ten minutes before the poor policeman got things relatively under control and Ilie had reappeared to take his place on the base-line to receive serve. Then by some weird piece of timing, Fred Hoyles, who had been called for at least half an hour earlier, appeared at the umpire's chair. So before a ball had been hit the delay was prolonged while Hoyles conversed with the umpire, both about the previous incident and the one he had happened to stumble upon.

By this time a distressed Pattison had wrapped a towel round himself and gone back to his chair. Quite understandably he protested against the delay and that in itself took up a few more seconds. So by the time everything had been sorted out, it was very nearly fifteen minutes since Ilie had lost his serve in the previous game. And that, of course, was the news that flashed back to the pressroom. A fifteen-minute delay on court 2? Nastase's court? And then on checking with the tiny handful of reporters who had witnessed the whole incident to verify that Nastase had indeed been acting up, the obvious conclusion was reached: Nastase had caused a fifteen-minute delay. Some reports conscientiously carried some of the details I have described here, but that did not alter the headlines or the general impression relayed to the public at large that Ilie had been directly and solely responsible for holding up a tennis-match for fifteen minutes for the purpose of upsetting his opponent. I am in no way attempting to defend Nastase when I say that in my view that conclusion represents a distortion of the facts.

Of course, Ilie was being found guilty by virtue of his reputation as well as by the fact that at certain moments during his match he did not behave well. Nor did the fact that the whole delay so obviously helped him to relax assist those who maintained he had been unfairly accused. For when Pattison did serve, Ilie hit two majestic cross-court backhands off the service return and broke back for four-all.

Standing next to me on the players' balcony which directly overlooks court 2, Jeanie Drysdale, the lovely lady Cliff had the good sense to marry, was suffering during every second with Andy Pattison, who is her neighbour at the Lakeway World of Tennis at Austin, Texas. A fine player herself, Jeanie knew exactly what Pattison was going through and was highly critical of Nastase as a result. And when he eventually lost the match in the fifth set, Pattison, normally a mild-mannered man, was livid.

Later a group of us, including Erik Van Dillen, Tommy Tucker, the bearded tennis *aficionado* from San Francisco, and Colin Dibley, were sitting in the players' tea-room discussing the problem of what to do with Nastase in those situations.

'You have to do one of two things,' said Dibley firmly. 'Either you ignore him completely and make absolutely certain that nothing he does gets through you, or you threaten him. You can't mess about somewhere in between. That's disastrous.'

Given that the special circumstances of the one major hold-up in the match made it difficult for Pattison to do anything except wait, he should probably have made a greater resolve before going on court not to let *anything* bother him. No one is suggesting that is easy. In fact, it may be the most difficult thing some players have to face on the circuit today; this very special problem of how to deal with Nastase. Some have resolved it better than others but many still react just as the audience does when a door bangs in a Dracula movie—they take fright before anything really sinister has happened. Just because they expect it.

No one quite expected the scenes which erupted when Nastase played his second-round match at Wimbledon against Eliot Teltscher, the promising American teenager. This time it was impossible to point the finger at Ilie because he turned out to be the hero rather than the villian. His only crime was his popularity. In his customary succinct and vivid style, Rex Bellamy described the match for *The Times* like this:

'The tennis, though, took second place to the ugly and frightening crowd scenes. It was noted here yesterday that far too many people were admitted to Wimbledon and that the area around court 14 presented particular hazards. Yesterday the sparks flew a little too close to the powder keg. Ilie Nastase was assigned to play on court 14. That was a mistake because he draws spectators the way lights draw moths.

'The crush was appalling. The weight of people behind them pushed teenage girls over the canvas and on to the court. There were screams, tears, incipient hysteria. One six-foot stretch of canvas was ripped down. The police were reinforced. Play was repeatedly interrupted. The bedlam was awful. It contained the seeds of panic, the threat of widespread injury. Luckily all those in the firing-line kept their heads—none more so than Nastase himself. He was concerned for the girls and concerned for his opponent, Eliot Teltscher, a qualifier from California. ... His response to yesterday's scenes was exemplary. Nastase scores a lot of minus marks during his tumultous progress round the international circuit. Yesterday he scored a big plus.'

He also scored a straight-set victory and so advanced in a pattern remarkably similar to his progress in the French Championships. For in the round of sixteen he faced not Kodes but another old rival in the Dutchman, Tom Okker, a player of exceptional ability whose talents have never flowered to their full potential at Wimbledon. Just as did Kodes in Paris, Okker found Nastase relaxed, serious and unbeatable. Playing one of his finest matches on Wimbledon's Centre Court, he recovered after losing a long first set to win the last three 6–4, 6–4, 6–4. Each set was keenly contested with skill and guile between two men who are still as fast as anyone in the game. They provided a feast fit for Centenary Wimbledon.

And so, for the third major championship in a row, Ilie reached the quarter-finals ... and there he fell. This time it was Bjorn Borg, the reigning champion who had been looking increasingly sharp as the fortnight progressed, who brought him down. And if it was Borg's brilliance that lost him the match, it was his own nerves that made his exit from this very special Wimbledon such an unhappy one.

To the casual observer, Ilie might have looked calm enough, munching some boiled potatoes and nasty-looking veal in the players' tea-room a couple of hours before the match. But in reality he was already taut with tension. It it always a question of degree with Nastase and his nerves. A year before when he faced Borg in the final he was not sufficiently nervous. This year, in the match against Okker he was probably tuned to exactly the right pitch—keen, confident and just a little nervous. Now, facing Borg again, he was strung so tight he felt he might snap.

Until he got into the match, it was obvious that the slightest incident would cause his temper to flare. And from that point of view Nastase had no luck. The match was just one *point* old when Ilie got a late and dubious call on his base-line. He swung round and glared at the official and the crowd groaned. 'Oh, not already,' someone said in the press box and it just about summed up the general feeling. On the next point Ilie complained to the net-cord judge about the lack of a call and eventually became directly involved with umpire Jeremy Shales, a thirty-four-year-old Bank of England official, who tried hard to bring Ilie to heel and got it all wrong.

That is not meant as a criticism of Shales. He did what he thought best and acted in the only way he knew how. But to Nastase that merely came across as a vaguely familiar face of authority booming down at him in an autocratic British accent, and nothing makes the Romanian's hackles rise faster than that. Had it been Bertie Bowron in the chair, Ilie might have been allowed to let off steam with a couple of arm-waving complaints and then settle down to handling his real problem which was Bjorn Borg.

But, as he admitted afterwards, Shales had decided beforehand to 'stamp on him hard' if Ilie started fooling around. Everyone agrees that umpires should be stricter with Ilie—even Nasty himself does not dispute that—but there are ways and ways to do it. Calling out on the microphone on the Centre Court at Wimbledon, 'Come here, Nastase!' is not the way to do it. Few people in England realize that the players become accustomed to being called 'Mr' whenever they play in America and it suddenly sounds very rude to be ordered around by one's unadorned surname in front of 15,000 people. If, at the time, you happen to be in a state of hyper-nervous tension, it simply heightens your anger until you start behaving very stroppily indeed. Especially if your name is Ilie Nastase.

Ilie's most shocking act was to flick a ball between Shales' legs as he walked past the umpire's chair. That was a new one. The swearing, both at the umpire and at the court-side photographers; the finger-signs; and the stalling and arguing, all that was a re-run of an old and very bad movie. Much more stimulating was the awesome power of Borg's hitting. Lashing each stroke with top-spin he hit some of the hardest shots ever seen on the Centre Court. Like a batsman who is good enough to get a touch and pays for his superior skill by getting caught, Ilie was made to look stupid because he was good enough to get his racket to some of Borg's drives when he advanced to the net. But, of course, he couldn't control them. No one could have. They came too fast and carried too much spin. Most players would have missed them altogether ... But Ilie actually managed to parry a few in the process of losing the first set 6–0.

It was to Nastase's considerable credit that he managed to gather himself together sufficiently to work his way into a 4–2 lead in the second set. But Borg regrouped quickly and came on again like a Nordic storm, cold and steely-eyed, his shots piercing Ilie's defences from back-court or fore-court. Off the ground or off the volley, Borg's racket, strung tight as a board, powered shots of breathtaking accuracy to every corner of Nastase's court and when the Swede won the second set 8–6, the match became a formality.

'What a Nasty way to go' was the front-page headline in next morning's *Daily Mail*. Reporter William Langley wrote: 'His cursing, raging, ill-tempered retaliation led match umpire Jeremy Shales to label his behaviour "atrocious". Nastase quickly lobbed one back—accusing Mr Shales of "acting like a schoolmaster".'

Langley quoted Nastase as saying, 'I did not have any argument with the umpire, he picked one with me. He was giving Bjorn balls he hadn't won. That's why I threw a ball at him. He seemed totally biased. He knew of my reputation and deliberately tried to start something.'

If one detects a streak of paranoia in Ilie's remarks, it is not entirely misplaced. While one could never suggest that Shales 'tried to start something' he did react to Nastase's reputation as much as to anything that happened initially on court. And there have been other instances where the question of whether or not linesmen have deliberately made calls against him is open to considerable speculation. But if it can be argued that Nastase made his own reputation and now has to live with it, that still does not solve the problem.

On the *Mail's* sports page, veteran tennis-writer Laurie Pignon said that Shales treated Nastase like a 'rebellious fourth-former' and in the *Evening Standard* columnist Neil Allen called for Ilie's expulsion from the game. Although he took pains to present both sides of the picture, Allen remained firm in his conviction that Nastase was bad for tennis. 'The chief reason why I think he should have been expelled from this game for a long time is that his gross bad manners, his neurotic petulance and his sometimes vile tongue are a bad example to the young who may think it trendy to ape his "fingers-up" attitude when things go wrong.'

The example he sets is really the greatest case against Nastase and Allen was not the first to have demanded his expulsion from tennis. Neil Amdur of the *New York Times*, writing in *Tennis Magazine* a few years ago, also called for his banishment.

I tend to think everyone gets a little hysterical about it. As a journalist, I am only too well aware of what marvellous copy Illie makes. He is a godsend to headline writers: a terrific villain to have around on a slow news day. Of course he can be bad and of course he sets a bad example but I cannot accept the hypocrisy that banishment entails. Every one of us who has interviewed him, written about or even simply paid money to see him perform is responsible in some small degree for having made him what he is. And that, in terminology the modern commercial world can readily understand, amounts to the biggest draw the game of tennis has ever known and one of the biggest draws any sport has ever known. Like it or not it is a fact that tournaments and sponsors get more publicity when Nastase plays; more people pay at the gate when Nastase plays; more people who never go near a tennis tournament talk about the event when Nastase plays and in the long run, his fellow pros earn more because more prize-money becomes available when Nastase plays.

Of course the game can survive without him.

13

SHOWMANSHIP

Even for those familiar with its concrete and perspex world of tilted walk-ways and space-age tunnels in the sky, Charles de Gaulle Airport at Roissy is not the place to be with a hangover. And after a night at Castel's and Le Privé, Ilie was hungover. Fifteen minutes before the scheduled departure time of TWA's flight to Los Angeles, he and Mitch struggled into view, shovelling rackets through the X-ray machine and fumbling for boarding cards.

Once again Ilie need not have worried about being late. A computer breakdown was causing a one-hour delay, thus ensuring that a long journey was going to be even longer. We were already on board when Roger, the chief purser, gave us this information so Ilie spent the time surrounded by more than half the complement of stewardesses on the 747. At least it took his mind off the Davis Cup tie against France.

Immediately after Wimbledon, Nastase had flown to California to begin his new World Team Tennis career with the Los Angeles Strings, and then after two weeks had flown back to join the Romanian team in Paris.

It was a tie Romania could have won. But it all rested on Ilie winning two singles and that he failed to do. In a match so similar to the one he had played against Brian Gottfried on the same Centre Court at Stade Roland Garros, Ilie toyed with the veteran Davis Cup campaigner, François Jauffret, for two sets, dropping only three games in the process. He then reached 40–15 at 4–3 on his serve in the third and promptly let his concentration snap. Someone was talking too loudly in the court-side boxes. Ilie yelled at them and started to fret. Suddenly his serve was gone and two games later Jauffret had the set. After that the Frenchman battled his way dourly and effectively back into the match and won in five sets.

After a long dispute with his Federation, Patrick Proisy had been restored to the French team by the non-playing captain, Pierre Darmon, after winning the Hilversum title a week before, and with Patrice Dominguez still not fully recovered from a football injury, it was a wise piece of diplomacy. Proisy's experience was needed to make sure that Dmitru Haradau did not pull any surprises and when Patrick duly secured a 2–0 lead for France, Romania had little chance of recovery. Jauffret, whose comeback against Nastase was as dramatic as anything he had achieved in a long and distinguished Davis Cup career for France, put the issue beyond doubt by defeating Haradau on the Sunday and then Nastase fought for nothing other than his pride to beat back Proisy's stubborn resistance in the otherwise meaningless fifth rubber.

The French victory was a shot in the arm for the nation's tennis which had been starved of success for too long. By a happy coincidence Philippe Chatrier, the driving force behind the game in France for many years, had been elected to succeed Derek Hardwick as President of the International Federation just one week before. For Philippe, it was an auspicious beginning.

Ever since Nastase's defeat on the opening day, the mood in the Romanian locker-room—they had taken over the ladies' changing accommodation for the tie—had been subdued. Virgil, the team's masseur, still worked away feverishly at everyone's limbs and Alexandru Lazarescu, the Romanian Secretary-General, tried to put a bold face on things. But he was deeply disappointed, feeling, with some justification, that this had been the last year his country had a real chance of winning the Cup. Tiriac, obviously, could not go on forever and Nastase was over-extending himself with his various commitments around the world.

But no one felt the pain more deeply than Ilie. 'I don't know how I could lose that match,' he muttered on the Sunday afternoon. Nobody attempted to offer any explanation. Haradau stared morosely at the strings of his racket like a man hoping to conjure up some latent magic before he faced Jauffret, and away in a corner Tiriac beat out a tom-tom rhythm on his thighs with plastic *Eau de Badoit* bottles.

'My mistake was to come in the first place,' Ilie went on. 'Having got myself into trouble I didn't have enough strength to get out of it in the fifth set when he started playing well. But that was the jet lag. Two days just isn't enough time to prepare.'

Then, with a sudden flash of mild anger, his mood changed. 'They're blaming me for the whole thing, you know,' he said. 'Shit, I can lose like anyone else. I'm not a machine. They rely on me too much. Like Tiriac says, what happens if I'm injured? What do they do then?'

A night on the town with Mitch had done much to wash away the anger and the regret and by the time we finally got off the ground after a stop-over in London, Ilie was ready for the big sleep.

The 747 was practically full but an understanding stewardess managed to move someone into another row, thereby creating a row of three empty seats in the centre section. And there the great body lay, prone for most of the ten-and-a-half-hour flight, the dark head resting no more than six inches from the lap of a rather prim woman in her thirties whose eyes never seemed to stray from a book on Eastern mysticism. I would love to have seen her reaction if Ilie had groped at her in his sleep. But exhaustion had set in with a vengeance and he barely moved.

With rather more interest than his mystic neighbour, one of the TWA stewardesses gazed down at him somewhere over the Atlantic and asked me when he next had to play.

'Tonight,' I replied. 'In Fresno.'

She looked suitably shocked. 'You're joking,' she said incredulously. 'But he told me he only finished playing in the Davis Cup in Paris last night. My goodness, that's really rough.'

Perhaps it required a fellow professional traveller to really appreciate just what kind of a body-bending, mind-blowing itinerary Nastase had embarked upon when he had left Los Angeles the previous week. Normally it takes about five days to recover completely from the nine-hour time change involved in the LA-Paris trip which, like any journey going against the sun, is always more difficult to handle than east-west travel. But he had only spent a total of six nights in Paris before heading straight back again and Fresno, an hour's flight north of LA, was by no means going to be the end of it.

On the Tuesday night, the Los Angeles Strings were scheduled in Salt Lake City and then it was all the way back east to Boston for a Thursday-night match, St. Louis on Friday and New York on Saturday. Of course by the time he got back to Dominique and their rented house in Beverley Hills, Ilie didn't know where he was.

When we touched down on the Monday afternoon at Los Angeles International Airport one hour late, TWA ground personnel had been informed of the tight connection Nastase needed to make if he was to have any hope of getting to Fresno in time for a 7.30 pm start. An efficient ground hostess took us to the top of the immigration queue where one of the officers, a middle-aged lady called Mrs. Manzanares, peered at Ilie from behind her spectacles and said, 'I'll take him right away or maybe he'll get mad at me.'

'No, he never gets mad off court,' someone told her.

'Yes, I've heard that,' Mrs Manzanares replied and having made sure Ilie wasn't wanted for crimes against the Federal Government by checking in that ominously bulky folder all US immigration officials keep on their desks, she waved him through. A car was waiting to whisk Ilie and Mitch across the tarmac to where the PSA 727 already had its engines running and less than half an hour after landing, they were airborne again.

As a child I used to have a record by Danny Kaye in which he sang about Fresno and pronounced the name with a funny warble. For a long time I had tended to think of Fresno as a funny town. In fact it is not. I discovered that when I first stopped there as a member of the Nixon press entourage during the 1968 presidential campaign. Nixon and Fresno—the combination does not make for a lot of laughs.

In reality, Fresno is a flat, farming town whose originality runs as far as naming its streets after presidents and states of the Union. Huge hoardings advertising termite killers and secondhand tractors line the highway into town and on this Monday afternoon, like most other afternoons, the whole place shimmered in 90-degree heat. But what Fresno does have, in common with so many other American cities, is a convention centre/sports hall that makes Stade Coubertin look like an annexe. With 5,177 people waiting to see the great Romanian perform, the place was about half full. But it was, by WTT standards, a good crowd.

Whether the great Romanian was in a fit state to perform was, however, another question. He was changed and ready to go on court against Tom Okker, leading light of the San Francisco Gaters, when I arrived and checked my watch. It was thirty-three hours since he had hit the last ball against Patrick Proisy on clay in Paris and twenty of those hours had been spent travelling. If he was going to play anything remotely resembling tennis, it would be done purely by instinct.

There are those who maintain that World Team Tennis does not remotely resemble tennis in any case and the traditionalists would certainly have been scratching their heads when Dennis Ralston, the Strings coach, calmly trotted on court to substitute for Nastase after three games of the one-set match against Okker. Substitution being allowed at any time under WTT rules, Ralston was quite right to try something different in a losing situation, for Okker had whipped the first three games off Ilie and there seemed little likelihood of things getting any better. Nastase, to put it mildly, was having difficulty timing the ball.

'Quitter!' screamed someone in the crowd who had paid his $4.50 and didn't give a damn if Nastase had just flown in from the moon. Quite right, too. This was show business.

Back in the bare, concrete locker-room, Nastase slumped on a bench. 'I think they've had enough of Nastase tonight,' he said in a toneless voice. 'Three games, that's enough. Shit, I can't even see the ball.' Then he sniffed the shirt he had used in Paris the day before. 'Anyway I smell,' he added disgustedly. 'Then stay away from your partner,' said Charlie Pasarell who was due to play doubles with Ilie later in the evening.

Dennis and Mitch had to gently coax Ilie into the idea that it would be nice for the team and the crowd if he did play doubles, as his natural inclination was to roll over in a ball and collapse. Eventually Ilie agreed to make a second gallant attempt to get his act together when his equilibrium was still trying to sort out the eastern hemisphere from the west and 35,000 feet from ground level—not to mention a Sportface carpet from Parisian clay.

In fact the second attempt turned out to be a lot better. The Strings were trailing by 13 games to 22 when the fifth and final one-set match began. Although they had no mathematical chance of catching up, the flexible rules of WTT say that the team winning the last match cannot lose then and there, no matter how far behind they might be. So the action continues until the team that is leading in total games wins one more game or the other team catches up. In the event of the latter happening a super tie-breaker is played.

When Ilie connected with a superb forehand cross-court, it was obvious that he and Pasarell were going to give Okker and John Holladay a tough fight.

In fact they won it in the tie-break and so the match continued until the Gaters duly won one more game and so ended up the overall victors by 29 games to 21. The crowd seemed to have enjoyed it, which offered some consolation for having just flown halfway round the world to spend the night in Fresno.

In the dark, red dining-room of the Fresno Hilton, the female members of the Strings, Rosie Casals, Julie Anthony and Valerie Ziegenfuss, were playing their usual word game—making up as many words as possible from a limited number of letters—when Ilie joined the table for a late supper. Mitch and Charlie arrived a little later and soon everyone was discussing the merits and drawbacks of World Team Tennis.

'I think some rules should be changed,' said Ilie, tucking into a huge salad. 'First of all the balls; they're too fast. And then the court, certainly you should have lines on the court. It's impossible to tell whether the ball is in or not as it is now.'

One of the most inventive quirks of WTT was to produce a multi-coloured court in which the only demarcation lines were the different colours of the strips of the court itself.

'Yes, I definitely think there should be lines,' agreed Pasarell. 'I lose orientation on a coloured court.'

'And another thing,' said Ilie. 'Why they introduce me as Temperamental Nastase? That only makes me worse. If they want a real circus then I can give them a real circus, but in that case, not so many rules, please.'

'Yeah, I agree,' laughed Charlie. 'I wouldn't like to be introduced as a bow-legged Puerto Rican bum.'

'But you *are* temperamental, Nastase,' interjected Mitch. 'It's not just a rumour.'

'That's why you draw the crowds,' said Valerie Ziegenfuss, a pretty, well-liked girl, who had been a regular member of the Virginia Slims circuit ever since its inception in the early seventies. 'That's why your pay packet's bigger. It's because you're a personality.'

'No, that's not right,' said Rosie Casals, long regarded by most other girls as the most influential woman player after Billie-Jean King. 'Introducing someone should be positive. You can call someone brilliant, or artistic or something, but not temperamental. That's negative.' Valerie eventually accepted Rosie's point and at about that time, Ilie announced he'd had it. No one was surprised.

Needing something other than smelly shirts for the long road trip ahead, Ilie and Mitch had arranged to fly back to Los Angeles in the morning, swop suitcases, kiss Dominique and little Nathalie hello and goodbye and rejoin the team in Salt Lake City in time for the evening match against the Soviets.

By spending no more than ninety minutes at the house, they made it to the Mormon City in good time and Ilie even hit balls for a few minutes before the match got under way. However, it was hardly what one could call practice.

The Soviet team, who were supposed to have set up temporary headquarters in Philadelphia but who had in fact become the nomadic members of the League, were all decked out in bright red Adidas track-suits that matched the red seating of the huge Sports Dome that sits on top of a hill on the University of Utah campus. Alex Metreveli couldn't play that night because of injury but even so Vadim Borisov, the young substitute, proved too wide-awake for Ilie, closing a closely fought set 6–4.

Nastase's game was basically in tatters by this stage. Occasionally the odd streak of innate talent would gleam through the confusion but in reality his whole game was splintered by fatigue and disorientation. At times he was angry; at times just gently hysterical; and on occasions very entertaining. There was a moment when a lob drifted long and Nastase blew on an imaginary ball with an act of delicate mime that would not have disgraced Marcel Marceau. In that mood, no matter how fleetingly it lasts, he is not using his art as a tool of intentional distraction, and the Salt Lake City audience were quick to realize it as they laughed and applauded this clever clown.

It was amazing that Ilie still found the energy to be funny, but the fact that he did only confirmed just how much a part of his natural character is this talent to amuse. Nor could he stop kidding his friends.

'Hey, Olga, they permit you to smile yet?' he called out to Olga Morozova during the interval.

'Yes, Ilie,' Olga replied, recognizing an old joke. 'I told you, we have a new constitution now. It permits us to smile. You must read it. You still understand Russian?'

'Sure I do,' replied Ilie and meandered off to find some other distraction.

The Strings, who were bottom of their division and destined to remain there, couldn't handle the Soviets that night, going down 33–29. Ilie, of course, could have turned the match for his team had he beaten young Borisov, but once again he and Pasarell, who was serving like a demon, had won their doubles and, in any case, winning was only part of the job Nastase was doing for WTT. The other part was simply being there—and being Nastase. Largely due to his presence, over three thousand people had turned out to watch a tennis-match that had absolutely nothing to do with Salt Lake City and, by the time he flew out of town, the WTT concept of the game had received twenty-four hours saturation coverage on Utah television and in the excellent local press.

Nor did the reporters try to tear Ilie apart as was to happen in some less tolerant cities. For, however strict Mormons may be in their own way of life, they do seem anxious to search for answers rather than to condemn people outright. Certainly Ilie was given a fair hearing in the local press, and Lex Hemphill of the *Salt Lake Tribune* let him down gently when he wrote, 'Ilie Nastase's tennis was not quite on the level of his acting Tuesday night ...'

That was true. But both Ilie and the reaction to him had been very mild in Salt Lake City compared with what lay in store further along the road. In Boston, it required the persuasion of Strings owner Jerry Buss to make him go back on court against Tony Roche after the crowd had bombarded him for several minutes with the most vicious abuse. Roy Emerson, the Boston coach, said he was not surprised Ilie walked off, especially as he had done little that particular night to warrant that kind of hate-filled reception.

Leaving aside for a minute the question of whether Nastase deserves that kind of treatment from the crowd—he is, to expand Valerie Ziegenfuss's point, getting paid more to put up with it—it might be worth considering how much courage it takes to go out and face an audience like that. To an extent public performers get used to it, but one still feels very exposed and alone on a tennis-court and in this age of crowd violence, being cast as the villain is a daunting prospect. A sensitive psyche must eventually grow callouses to protect itself from constant emotional bruising, and what effect it must have on the nervous system can only be guessed at by those of us who do not have to endure it night after night. For better or worse, Ilie handles it by fighting back.

'If a guy insults me,' Ilie told Stephanie Salter of the *San Francisco Examiner*, 'I have to insult him back.'

Nastase's visit to San Francisco for another match against the Gaters, which took place one week after his return from Paris and was in fact the sixth city he had visited in eight days, was extraordinary for the amount of publicity and interest it aroused in that cosmopolitan city. The Gaters are fortunate in that both the Oakland and San Francisco papers give tennis a great deal of space on their sports pages but 'The Coming of Ilie Nastase' was a happening that transcended the normal sports event.

The morning after the match, I switched on my car radio and quite by chance picked up a commentary that started out in tones of solemnity usually reserved for some deep political analysis: 'So now he has come and gone. And what conclusions can we draw from the visit to our town of Ilie Nastase? ...' This particular commentator adopted the extreme view of all those people in America whose moral and political convictions are so offended by the sight of a badly-behaved Communist (he plays for Romania, so he must be Communist, right?) that they become incapable of making a reasoned judgment.

One sentence typified the trend of his argument. 'If the Communist countries have to export anyone, do they have to send us Nastase?' Switching to the moral aspects of the matter, he then attacked the WTT owners for exploiting Nastase's image to boost their attendance figures. So it seemed he didn't approve of some of the more popular aspects of capitalism, either. Unhappy fellow.

In the *San Francisco Examiner* Stephanie Salter was more rational but no less scathing. She wrote: 'Last night, as Nastase was losing to the Golden Gaters' Tom Okker, 6–2, in the Oakland Coliseum Arena, he was insulted by the calls or non-calls of WTT linesman Bob Golton. The Romanian replied with a string of scatologies and a host of what are called "obscene gestures". The 9,387 fans, the Gaters' largest crowd of the season, lapped it up like thirsty winos.

'If Nastase's behaviour left a bad taste in the mouth of anyone present, he or she did not speak up. From his introductory ovation, right through his losing doubles match, Nastase kept the audience applauding, laughing, hollering and occasionally booing.'

Most commentators, however, were prepared to accept the publicly-voiced opinion of the Gaters' coach, Frew McMillan, that Ilie was 'an extremely complex person'. 'The good, the bad and the ugly,' was about as far as some analysts got and I don't blame them. Move over, Clint Eastwood.

Even though the Strings were still losing, Ilie's team-mates tended to see only the good. The thought of Nastase being in a team coached by Dennis Ralston would, a few months before, have seemed like asking the Pope to train a pagan prince. Dennis is a serious, very religious person who had a bad-boy image himself back in the early days of his career when he was the top-ranked player in America. But he is a reformed character now and, by accepting Nastase for what he was and making a real attempt to understand him, he proved that little of the old intolerance remained.

'Dennis finds it difficult at times,' said Valerie Ziegenfuss. 'Some of the things Ilie gets up to are beyond him. But he's been good with Ilie, not trying to order him about too much, letting him find his feet. And in turn Ilie has been great with Dennis, always calling him "coach" and little things like that. He gets on very well with the rest of us, especially Charlie. He respects Dennis and likes Rosie a lot.'

Bill Norris, the popular Strings trainer who looks more like singer John Denver than John Denver, had been favourably surprised by the way Ilie had fitted into the team.

'He's treated me excellently,' said Bill. 'The public only see one side of him on court, but with the people he has to work with he is far more cooperative and understanding than one would imagine. And he's proved himself a real team-man. He sits next to me out there on the bench and gets really nervous for us. He genuinely wants the team to win, which needn't necessarily be the case. After all, he's signed his contract. He's not going to starve.'

When the Strings settled down to a run of home matches at the Inglewood forum near Los Angeles Airport, I had a chance to talk to Ralston about this unlikely partnership.

'Sure I've been critical of Ilie in the past and I still would be,' Dennis said. 'I'm always critical of someone who breaks the rules but perhaps I am even more critical of the system that allows him to do it.

'I didn't really know Nastase when he joined the team, but I had already learned one thing—everybody's a person. We all have certain reasons for doing certain things and one must try to understand. My first responsibility is to see that we all get along, and so I was especially anxious not to let Ilie think that I was sitting in judgment on him.

'Actually, it's been a lot easier than I thought because he wants to be liked and accepted. And really as a team man he's been fine. I was a little concerned to start with, but he's been no problem at all. He doesn't put on airs or ask for any special favours and he turns up for practice on time.

'But on court he still needs to learn some discipline. He never forgets the linesman who gave him a bad call. He just can't block it out of his mind. He's got to realize that it can hurt the team if he loses matches because of it.'

Charlie Pasarell, a passionate and devoted worker on ATP rules committees, echoed one of Ralston's points when I spoke to him in London earlier in the summer.

'Ilie has done a lot of things he should have been kicked out of the game for,' said Charlie. 'But I almost don't blame Nastase for doing what he can get away with. His conduct just exemplifies the lack of good officiating in tennis. The main problem lies in the fact that the referees, umpires and linesmen are controlled by the tournament directors who have a vested interest in keeping the big drawing cards in the game, no matter what they do.

'We must get to the point where the game exists because of the game and not because of the stars. The referee shouldn't be appointed by the tournament director. You should have a referee who is totally independent and therefore doesn't give a stuff whether Nastase plays or not.

'If WTT has contributed anything to the game so far, it has been in officiating. I have been very impressed by it. They make mistakes, of course, but basically they are very professional.'

Wimbledon doubles champion Ross Case, who had been listening to this conversation, agreed with Pasarell. 'There was a dispute at the end of a match I had with Vilas last year,' Ross told us. 'I just felt Vilas was going to get the benefit of the doubt in a tight situation because he was the big draw of the tournament and obviously no one connected with the event wanted him to lose. There was a clear conflict of interest. But I understand the tournament director's attitude. I would feel the same way. It is just the system that is wrong and people like Nastase are the ones who benefit from it. I think that is what pisses people off more than anything about Ilie—that he is allowed to get away with it.'

By the end of the summer Pasarell had got to know Ilie a great deal better and the pair of them seemed to enjoy each other's company at matches.

'Charlie's a great guy,' Ilie told me when he looked back on his WTT season. 'It was great training with him. He really helped me.' Nastase was equally generous about Ralston, with whom he was never as close but whose technical expertise he respected.

At a party following the Gaters' match in San Francisco, someone fed Ilie some 'cookies' laced with marijuana. As he never smokes normal tobacco, let alone grass, the effect made him not merely high but ill as well.

'I tell you, I thought my head was going to burst,' he said after a couple of days recuperating in Beverley Hills. 'Even Mitch got sick.'

By some lucky chance, the Strings had three days off after the trip to San Francisco and, in a perverse way, the mind-blowing 'cookies' might have done Nastase some good. His whole system needed a good blow-out, something to bring it back to earth; something to stop it spinning on the never-ending merry-go-round of airports, hotels and tennis-courts. The passing illness, coinciding with some time in the comfort of the rented house on Beverley Crest with Dominique and the baby, seemed to do the trick, for by the end of the week his form had returned to something like its proper self.

In a third meeting with the Gaters, he finally got the better of Tom Okker, coming from behind to win in exciting style. He was enjoying the home matches at the Inglewood Forum.

'It's great to have a crowd behind you for a change,' he said. 'They really give me a lot of support and make me feel I want to play well for them.'

He played well for them on Sunday, 7 August, and to celebrate the occasion there were more people (8,883) than had ever watched WTT in Los Angeles before. It was not just Ilie pulling them in this time, but the appearance for the Cleveland Nets of the League's other male super-star—Bjorn Borg.

It was a match Ilie really wanted to win after the reversals he had suffered at the hands of the young Swede during the previous year and, in the end, he produced some of his finest tennis in months to fulfil his ambition. The victory was made all the more remarkable by the fact that Borg led 4–1 and 5–2 before Ilie broke back and finally clinched it 7–5.

Strings owner Jerry Buss was ecstatic. 'Isn't he fantastic?' he beamed happily afterwards. 'He's really starting to come through for us now.'

A few days later I spent some time chatting with Buss at his offices on Wilshire Boulevard in Santa Monica. It was in that ocean-side city that Buss, a former university teacher and chemist, had made his millions in the property market. As he and two partners own the Los Angeles Strings, the San Diego Friars and are part-owners of the Indiana Loves, Buss is the single most powerful man in World Team Tennis. If he had pulled out at any time during the critical period of 1975–77, the League would almost certainly have collapsed.

'The big losses are over,' Buss said confidently. 'Up to now I rekcon we have spent about one-and-a-half million dollars, but each season the attendance is increasing by an average of fifteen hundred and, if that increase is maintained again next year, we should be reaching the break-even point here in LA.'

Nastase is a major figure in Buss's plans for the future. He signed the Romanian to a five-year contract of a quarter of a million dollars a year, with an exit clause in Ilie's favour after two years. Why so much investment poured into one man?

'First, because for me, he is the finest player in the world and I want a winning team,' Buss answered. 'I am really fed up with losing.

'Secondly, there would be no LA Strings unless there was a WTT League and Nastase is good for the whole League, not just us. He draws record crowds on the road and by signing him for myself, I was also putting a lot of money into my fellow owners' pockets.

'Thirdly, of course, because of the effect he would have on our own attendances. In fact I may have underestimated him. Los Angeles crowds are very hard to impress, especially when you are bottom of the League, but Ilie has had a bigger effect than I thought.'

The proof of that came in the final match of the season when Sea Port, the second worst team in the League with no major draw card of their own, came to the Inglewood Forum for a totally meaningless match that would normally have drawn flies in a town like LA. In fact over four thousand people turned up. Nastase could have been the only reason.

Even when the Strings were not on the road and he was able to spend just a little time with his family, Ilie was not idle. Practically every day someone had a call on his time and at nights he tended to go to bed early while his brother-in-law, Bernard Grazia, hit the town with a group of friends who included the French pop star Michel Polnareff, a frequent spectator at Strings matches.

One Saturday, Ilie drove out to the Valley with Dennis and Charlie to play an exhibition match at a club calling itself Tennis Beautiful, in aid of Sugar Ray Robinson's children's charities. As another great showman, Sugar Ray appreciated Ilie who was in his element in this relaxed atmosphere. Teamed with either Charlie or Grand Masters star Hugh Stewart, Ilie struck just the right note of light-hearted comedy and had everyone in stitches.

The following week, Nastase was required to drive down to Annaheim for the Tennis Industries Trade Fair on behalf of Adidas who wanted him to make an appearance at their stand. It was an enormous exhibition that offered ample proof of the explosion that has taken place in the game in the United States over the past five years.

The Fair was also crawling with famous tennis faces. Apart from most of the Strings team, we ran into John Newcombe boosting the sales of his 'Moustache' line of clothing; Cliff Drysdale representing Kawasaki rackets; Jack Kramer maintaining the popularity of his best-selling Wilson Autograph racket; Arthur Ashe selling sun-glasses; Pancho Gonzales representing Spalding; and Pierre Darmon who had flown in from Paris. Everyone did a lot of business.

But Ilie's business was not finished. Mitch had arrranged for him to do two television shows at the NBC studios in Burbank that evening and, apart from being tired, he was starting to get a little nervous about it. Solo appearances on 'Laugh-In' and the 'Tomorrow Show' are a daunting prospect for a person who is still subject to extreme shyness outside a familiar environment and who still lacks confidence with his English. The conversation as we drove back down the freeway, sitting three abreast in Mitch's rented Pacer, reflected that mounting tension. As always, it started with a little humour.

Mitch had been complaining in his sarcastically funny way about the way some celebrities behaved when they were on show. Nastase was on to him in a flash.

'You're just a bloody hypocrite then,' he said. 'Why you always around celebrities if you don't like them?'

'I didn't say I didn't like them,' replied Mitch evenly. 'They just piss me off sometimes that's all.'

'You've never known any celebrities before me, anyway,' Ilie said deadpan, digging me in the ribs.

'Bullshit,' says Mitch, taking the bait.

'Oh yeah ... Who?'

'Well, Paul Newman and Joanne Woodward and I started a school together in Connecticut once.'

'You were at school with Paul Newman *and* Joanne Woodward? ' asked Ilie incredulously.

'No, dummy, if you learned English you'd understand what I said. We *started* a school together. A whole group of us tried to get the idea of a private school off the ground but unfortunately it didn't work out.'

Nastase's silence was his way of conceding that Mitch knew Paul Newman. But peace did not reign for long. Soon Mitch mentioned something about the next day's schedule and Nastase exploded.

'Shit, you've got more stuff for me to do?' he demanded angrily. 'God damn it, you're always doing this to me, scheduling me for all sorts of things I've never agreed to. Screw you and screw the TV tonight. You go and do it. Maybe you'll get more laughs than me.'

'That's bloody typical of you, Nastase,' Mitch shot back. 'You're either trying to get your own way by bullying or through pity.'

Mitch glared down the freeway at the slow-moving traffic that stretched for miles ahead and then, in a softer voice, went on: 'Listen I don't arrange these things for my benefit. You must realize that you have to grab your opportunities now while you are hot. You might break a leg tomorrow and your tennis career would be finished. They only want you because you can hit a ball.'

'They want me because I give the finger and get mad,' Ilie said without a hint of satisfaction in his voice. 'That's why they want me. I'm not the best player in the world. Borg, Connors, Vilas—they all win more than me. But they don't want them on 'Laugh-In'. They want me. Why? Because *I* give the finger.'

'Not just that,' said Mitch reassuringly 'Because you're funny, too.'

'Connors, he's funny as well,' said Ilie.

'Connors is contrived. He just apes you,' replied Mitch.

Ilie sighed. 'Oh, I know you are right but when am I supposed to relax? When do I see my daughter? Every day there's something else.'

Turning off the freeway at Sunset, they lapsed into silence, which allowed all that Balkan emotion to subside. But it was still bubbling below the surface when we got back to the house and Ilie emerged from the bedroom, ready to leave for the NBC studios, still dressed in his red T-shirt and jeans.

Mitch reminded him that the second show was a formal interview and that they might like him in a suit. But Nastase's belligerent mood had not subsided entirely.

'If you want me, you take me like this,' he said, standing defiantly in the doorway. 'I'm not changing. So what you want? We go or not?'

Mitch shrugged. 'OK, it's you who's making the ass of yourself. But at least take an Adidas racket this time for the 'Laugh-In' segment. They don't pay you all that money to have you waving a Dunlop around on nationwide TV.'

As we walked outside, Mitch gave me a despairing look. 'Last night he puts on his best Italian suit to go and have dinner with four friends and tonight he's looking like an ageing hippy for a national TV show. God, the artistic temperament. How perverse can you get?'

Plenty perverse—if your name is Ilie Nastase.

Apart from the fact that he played tennis with a chimpanzee—this time for a CBS Television Spectacular taped at Forest Hills—Nastase's contribution to the US Open was minimal. Still lacking the confidence to go for his shots, he allowed himself to be outsteadied in the second round by Corrado Barazzutti, who was destined to go all the way to the semi-finals.

That should have signalled the start of a two-week rest before the European autumn clay-court season started up, a rest that he needed badly both in body and mind. But, as one of their last efforts on his behalf, the McCormack Organization had fixed some exhibitions for him the week after Forest Hills and there was no way Ilie could get out of them. So he flew home to Paris for five days and recrossed the Atlantic yet again to play one-night stands in Tulsa, Oklahoma; Morristown, New Jersey; and finally at Madison Square Garden, New York, where he and Vitas Gerulaitis put on a curtain-raiser for the WCT Shakey's Tournament of Champions final between Harold Solomon and Ken Rosewall.

Then it was back to La Basoche for a few days before appearing at the Racing Club of Paris, who were staging a Colgate Grand Prix event for the first time. Guillermo Vilas and Nastase were the top seeds but Ilie did not last long—walking straight into the double-stringed racket controversy by losing to one of the new weapon's proponents, Georges Goven, in the first round. Ilie ran himself into the ground trying to keep Goven's top-spin drives in play, but the little Frenchman had been using the racket throughout the summer on the French Satellite Circuit and had perfected the art of making the ball swing through the air and leap off the red clay. Given all that movement, shots with the so-called 'spaghetti' racket were very difficult to attack. One needed a combination of steadiness, patience and power to combat the new threat as John Feaver had demonstrated at the US Open while beating Mike Fishbach, the only player to have used

229

the double-string job at Forest Hills. But Feaver had also been playing in France during the summer and had had some time to work out the problem during matches against Goven.

Nastase came to it cold and found Georges too clever by half. Ilie complained bitterly about the new racket afterwards and he was not alone. Nearly all the players who had come up against it were shocked by its effectiveness and the majority wanted to see it banned, not merely because they felt threatened by it but also for what they felt was the general good of the professional game.

'It is impossible to play good tennis with this thing,' said Paolo Bertolucci. 'It is too easy to keep the ball in play and if the best players start using it, the rallies will never end. We will bore ourselves and worse still we will bore the public. No one will want to watch.'

Barry Phillips-Moore, the veteran Australian who had been experimenting with the racket all year, insisted that it could be modified to suit any conditions of style of play. At the time of writing that still has to be proved, but one should not underestimate Barry's inventiveness nor that of the racket's originator, Werner Fischer.

A week after Vilas had been forced to work uncommonly hard to beat one of the spaghetti racket men, Christophe Roger-Vasselin (ranked 222nd on the ATP computer at the time) in the final at the Racing Club, Nastase decided to try it himself. Phillips-Moore persuaded him that he could cause havoc with the weapon with his great flexibility and touch and Ilie proved him right.

For the week at Aix-en-Provence, Nastase was like a child with a new toy. 'He had been stale and dispirited,' said his friend, Pierre Barthes. 'This racket helped him to change his attitude. It gave him something new and exciting to experiment with. Psychologically it was just what he needed.'

Pierre was right. Although it was unfortunate Goven had to pull out of a semi-final confrontation with Ilie because of injury, few people doubted that, armed with the racket himself, Nastase would have avenged his loss in Paris.

Certainly he proved too much of a magician for Vilas, who finally surrendered his incredible 51-match winning streak on clay by walking off against Ilie in the final at Aix when he fell behind by two sets to love in the best of a five-set match. Apart from suffering from a slightly sore wrist, Guillermo was mentally and physically exhausted after his long and triumphant summer that added the US Open title to the French crown he had won in June. Explaining his decision to default, Guillermo said, 'The racket and Nastase—you understand the combination is just too much.'

The racket and Nastase would probably have been too much for just about everybody had not the ITF stepped in and put an immediate banning order on the controversial instrument. Announcing their decision after a meeting in Barcelona, ITF secretary David Gray said that a technical committee would be set up to test the racket and that in the meantime it would be officially banned from all competitive play. It was probably a wise decision, although it is hoped that modifications of the racket will be given a limited airing in proper tournament play sometime in the future.

Having had his toy snatched away from him so quickly, one might have expected Ilie to slump back into a state of depression, but that was far from the case. It proved just the tonic he needed, and he was more optimistic about his game than I had seem him for a long time when Alain Deflassieux of *Tennis de France* and I met him for a coffee at a bistro on the Place Victor Hugo just prior to his departure for South America in October 1977.

'It was windy that day in Aix,' Ilie said. 'But still I was making the most fantastic shots. Top-spin lobs, drop shots; everything. It was unbelievable. Without the wind, I could have done things with the ball never seen before!'

Obviously his interest had been stimulated again and, even when he picked up his old rackets to play a round-robin tour in Switzerland and Holland for Tom Okker immediately afterwards, his enthusiasm carried him on to more success. He twice beat Vitas Gerulaitis, the only top player he had never defeated before, which was a big boost to his confidence. But of even greater importance was the reason for our meeting in the Place Victor Hugo. Dominique's gynaecologist was just round the corner. The Nastases were planning another baby.

14

CONCLUSIONS

By the end of 1977, it was becoming clear to Ilie and to those near him that he had reached a critical cross-roads in his career. Either he could concentrate solely on his tennis and buckle down to some serious training in a last bid to remain a member of the elite top half-dozen players in the world, or he could rest on the security of his fat contracts; diversify into areas like television, exhibitions and other side-shows and become more of an entertainer than a tennis-player. At heart, Ilie wanted to do the first. His competitive instinct was still too strong. Too often have I seen him grab the ATP's *International Tennis Weekly* to check on his latest computer ranking to believe this was a man who didn't care about his standing in the world. It is a source of considerable pride to him that he is one of only four players—Newcombe, Connors and Borg are the others—to have held the No 1 position on the ATP computer.

'And for four years I never went below No 7,' Ilie told me proudly one day.

But by October 1977 he had slipped to No 10. It had been a messy, exhausting year, constantly interrupted by too much poorly-planned and sometimes needless travel. As usual he had said 'yes' to too many people who wanted little pieces of his time. He had fragmented his mind and his talent to such a degree that he could no longer rely on either. He needed to rest and regroup; to zero in on one or two specific goals and tell everything else to wait. At thirty-one time was no longer on his side.

He realized that greater attention to practice was essential if he were to mount a serious assault on any of the big titles in 1978. Hopefully, he took heed of Pancho Gonzles.

'Nastase has the worst practice habits of any good players I know,' Pancho told me. 'He needs to spend four hours a day for two weeks before a big tournament ironing the bad habits out of his game. If you go on practising like a screwball, sooner or later you end up playing like a screwball.'

A properly-structured training routine is certainly something Nastase will have to adopt if he is to remain a major force in tennis. But that is not all. Physical fitness in general and speed in particular are two of the most vital aspects of his game. Is he starting to slow down? Some players think so. But the medical prognostications are good.

Dr Norman Rudy, who has looked after numerous American Davis Cup teams and is now physician for the Los Angeles Strings, found Nastase to be in good shape when he joined the team.

'He did have a touch of tendonitis which attacked the petalla tendon just below the knee,' Dr Rudy told me. 'I saw him slapping his thigh to break up the muscle spasms on court once or twice, but he did not show any great signs of discomfort. I would guess that he has a fairly high pain threshold. Ordinary aches and pains don't seem to bother him too much.

'But then he is naturally fit and is very strong in all the right places. He has great leg muscles, very strong wrists, a deep chest—a barrel chest, really—and pigeon toes which is not uncommon amongst athletes. O.J. Simpson, Jackie Robinson, and a lot of the great track stars have had pigeon toes. It gives the sprinter great facility to thrust off for quick acceleration.'

Dr Rudy found Nastase's heartbeat low even by athletic standards. 'Ilie has a heartbeat of 48 to 50, which is below average,' he said. 'Normally you would expect an athlete to have a reading of 60 or just under while the non-athlete is usually around 72. Actually tennis-players have the slowest heartbeats of any athletes I have examined. Marty Riessen's is 38 while I could hardly believe John Newcombe's which is down at 34.'

Bill Norris, who worked with professional basketball and baseball teams before switching to tennis, also found Nastase an exceptionally fit and supple athlete.

'Ilie reacts well to little injuries,' Norris told me. 'Generally he has so much fun playing that he is really relaxed and his muscles stay pretty loose. Once in a while he needs a massage, but in fact I think he'd respond better to a pat on the back. He always needs encouragement. But from a purely physical point of view he has the kind of body that has enabled Rosewall to go on for so long. As Ilie looks after himself pretty well, not drinking much and eating the right foods, there is no reason why he should not remain in top shape for a long time yet.'

But whether he can maintain that razor-edge sharpness, that extra burst of speed that makes him so exceptional is, perhaps, something else again. And what of the technical aspects of his game? Are they good enough to take him back to the very top? A lot of players think not. Most, like Charlie Pasarell, are in awe of him as an athlete.

'His physical ability is even better than Borg's,' says Pasarell. 'He has powerful running legs and incredible quickness with his hands. He is also smoother than Borg. He expends less energy. It is almost too easy for him, which might be a handicap because now he tends not to work hard enough. But he has such great anticipation—sometimes you find him just standing there waiting for the shot. But he can crack under pressure. His inability to handle tight situations is probably his biggest weakness.'

But Harold Solomon sees more basic structural defects. 'Of course he's a very talented athelete,' says Solomon, 'But he's not quite as talented as some people think. Connors has more *tennis* talent. Nastase is very fast and agile and has great racket control, but his back-hand is the worst of all the major players. He doesn't have a punishing volley, either, although I'm not one to talk about that. But he's developed a huge first serve which is now his biggest weapon.'

The Pole, Wojtek Fibak, is another player who finds Ilie's talents a little over-rated. 'It makes me mad when writers say Ilie can win anything just so long as he controls his temperament,' Fibak said. 'That's just not so. It suggests he has everything else necessary to win. But in fact he has fewer big shots than any top player. He just pushes his backhand and tries to go cross-court with it all the time. Also he pushes his volley even though he is a volley player.'

'What he does have is a great first serve and that incredible speed which makes him so difficult to catch out of position.'

The big first serve to which both Solomon and Fibak refer is something Nastase has developed over the past couple of years, mainly as a result of using a heavier racket since he switched from Dunlop to Adidas. In fact, for the first several months of his Adidas contract Ilie was using disguised Wilsons—he painted on the brown Adidas stripes himself—until the Strasbourg-based company came up with a wood racket to his liking.

'I suddenly decided that I might as well hit the first serve as hard as I could,' explained Ilie. 'If you are going to miss you might as well miss while going for an ace. And the heavier racket gave the shot more power.'

Some poeple now feel that Ilie's best chance of doing well lies on fast surfaces like grass or concrete, partly because of that big serve but more especially because everything happens so fast that he can play purely by instinct.

'Everyone keeps telling me I'm thirty-one and now I start to worry about my strokes,' Ilie complained recently. 'Now I'm thinking twice and three times before I hit each shot. Before I just used to play and everything came naturally.'

It was Socrates who pointed out that it is not only by wisdom that poets write poetry but by a kind of genius and inspiration. If that is true of sedentary artists, how much more so of active ones whose perfectly tuned bodies flow in a natural rhythm. For in searching for one word that describes the uniqueness of this multi-coloured, many-faceted human being called Ilie Nastase, it is the title of artist that fits him best. Of course he is an extraordinary athlete as well but that is not so rare and, in any case, few of them possess the true instinct and temperament of the artist. Nor can

Nastase claim special status among tennis-players as a champion, competitor or technician. Rod Laver was a greater champion; Pancho Gonzales a better competitor; and Lew Hoad was endowed with a far bigger arsenal of killer shots, to name just three of several examples.

But no matter how you wish to paint him, be it in Bacon's contorted images of rage and despair or the young Picasso's sad-faced Harlequin clown, Nastase himself provides as complete a portrait of the athlete as an artist as tennis, or any other sport, has ever known.

Laurie Pignon, a sensitive observer of men and their moods, has written of him: 'Never has sport produced such an enigmatic man. For while Nature endowed him with the golden gift of instinctive athleticism, she left him a little short in stability. This giving with one hand and taking with the other is a feature shared by many of the greatest men in the classical arts.'

For Gerald Williams, the BBC's tennis correspondent whose Welsh spirit moves in concert with passion and emotion, Nastase is also 'the ultimate enigma'.

When Williams was involved in the administration of the Dewar Cup in 1969, Nastase committed himself to play the whole circuit but pulled out halfway through with a minor injury. He knew he had disappointed the organizers and promised Lady Elizabeth Dewar, 'One year I'll come back and win your Cup'.

'And, of course, he was as good as his word,' says Williams. 'And it wasn't just his tennis that captivated everyone. In Edinburgh he dressed up in a kilt and fell in love with the city. And when he did win the Cup, he told the Hon. John Dewar "Now you can call me Lord Nastase". When he's in that kind of mood and playing his best tennis, he is magic. But at other times he can be as bad as anyone I have ever seen.'

Dan Maskell, the gentle and authoritative voice of tennis on BBC Television, offers similar sentiments concerning Nastase. 'I get letters from people complaining about Ilie, but somehow I always find myself defending him. No great talent is perfect. One must remember that Bill Tilden was no angel. But I do get very upset when Nastase goes too far. It's such a shame because he has so much charm and ability.'

The great talent, the artistic streak of genius—always it is the only common factor running through any attempted analysis of Nastase. For in every other facet of his personality there are contradictions that surface from within; not merely masks being glibly interchanged, but the real forces of this double or even triple nature taking temporary hold of the man himself.

He can, for instance, be unnecessarily generous to those less fortunate than himself, as was the case when a destitute Romanian long-distance walker turned up at Stade Roland Garros during the French Championships one year. Ilie had never met the man before. But, on hearing his

235

story, he bought him a new bicycle so that he could fulfil his ambition of cycling from Paris to Bucharest. Yet on a tennis-court he can play the part of the callous bully and apparently enjoy it. Bob Kreiss who has now retired to help run the family furniture business on Santa Monica Boulevard in LA, remembers playing Nastase once at the Albert Hall. Kreiss, it should be said, had a rather extraordinary style based on an extreme continental grip and Ilie was quick to exploit it.

'I was hitting the ball well when I went on court,' Kreiss recalled. 'But almost immediately, Ilie started imitating my strokes. I was so embarrassed, I daren't hit any top-spins for the rest of the set and lost it 6–0. The problem with Ilie is that you never know what he's thinking. Is he fooling around? Is he really angry? Is he tanking? He's like Muhammad Ali. You just never know what he's up to and it psyches you out.'

Author George Plimpton, who has shared the sweat of many an athlete's labours, agrees with the Muhammad Ali analogy.

'There are some wonderfully strange people in sport,' Plimptom said when we discussed the whole subject of sporting eccentrics in the Forest Hills locker-room one day. 'But in trying to find comparisons with Nastase, I can only come up with three I know of—Ali, Bobby Fischer and, to a lesser extent, Lee Trevino. You can't really put golf into the same context because basically a golfer is playing the course and therefore you miss that vital head-to-head personality clash on which Ali and Ilie thrive. As, of course, did Fischer who was always finding niggling little things to complain about which drove Boris Spassky wild during their matches in Iceland.

'But Muhammad Ali certainly has things in common with Nastase, largely in the ability to get inside people's heads and disturb them. But also he shares Ilie's shyness. He can be very uncertain of himself in a one-to-one situation although, of course, he can be very good with crowds.'

As there is no professional sport so governed by the ability of its participants to gain mental dominance over each other, this question of 'getting inside people's heads' is obviously of considerable importance and there is no doubt that some players allow themselves to be psyched out before they even walk on court against Nastase. It is all a matter of attitude.

'It's very easy to get to the point of anger when you are playing him and not the ball,' says Roger Taylor. 'I enjoy watching Ilie play other people, but when I am up against him myself I can get as furious as anyone else.'

However, Frew McMillan's sardonic outlook on life enables him to approach Nastase in a more relaxed manner.

'I think I have always accepted his antics a bit more readily than some,' Frew told me. 'A few of the things he does really amuse me.

Somehow it gives me an excuse to let my hair down and fool around a bit myself, which isn't always a bad thing. But we have had our rows, of course. Once during a WTT match it became quite personal and after he hit a few balls at me, I tried to get him chucked out of the match.

For McMillan's South African Davis Cup colleague, Ray Moore, there are similarities between Nastase and one of the greatest talents soccer has produced, George Best.

'I was constantly reminded of Nastase when I read Michael Parkinson's fascinating biography of Best,' Moore told me. 'Of course Best had to deal with even greater pressures than Nastase, like IRA threats on his life, but he, too, found it all too much to handle. The spotlight became too bright for him. Just as it has for Ilie. I think Nastase has lost his nerve. He can't compete any longer.'

People sympathetic to Nastase often talk about the need for him to reform for his own sake just as much as for the good of a sport that is constantly trying to find methods of curbing its *enfant terrible*. This naturally raises the primary question about Nastase. How much of his disruptive behaviour is deliberate?

Some years ago he was quoted in the *Daily Mail* by columnist Lynda Lee-Potter as saying, 'Everybody do something on court to win. It is a tactic. Sure, it is a tactic. They should not let it worry them. All the other players are too tight.'

But it is the next couple of lines that reveal just what kind of mood Nastase was in when he gave that interview. He goes on: 'If they (the other players) don't like me, OK, I don't mind. I don't care what they say about me behind my back.'

Like hell he doesn't. I would wager that he was feeling cornered, defensive and hurt when he was interviewed by Miss Lee-Potter, not because of the lady herself, but probably over some incident that had occurred just before. And so, of course, he lashes out in a mood of defiant belligerence. 'Sure, it is a tactic.' This is Nasty taking perverse enjoyment from seeing just how Nasty he can be. This is Nasty after the bad line-call and the abusive shout from the crowd, giving the finger to the world. It is a real part of him, make no mistake about that. But, in my opinion, it is not the dominant part nor a part he would readily be able to explain. If one asks him how often he acts up deliberately, his reply in quieter and more reflective moments is rather different.

'Sometimes I make the most of a situation that develops,' he says. 'But mostly things just happen. I never know when or why. They can happen any time. Mostly, of course, when I am nervous because then I get angry very easily. Sometimes I am just trying to have some fun and someone gets pissed because of what I do and then everything goes crazy. But now they expect me to go crazy anyway so I say, "OK, I'll show you how crazy I am".'

In his book *Man Watching*, Desmond Morris makes the point that after a certain length of time people start behaving the way others expect them to behave, and this is certainly becoming true of Nastase. Although it becomes an instinctive reaction it is not subconscious. Ilie is aware of this compulsive, almost bloody-minded, desire to give the public what they expect, just as he is aware of many other things that swirl about him, seemingly unnoticed.

Caroline Barthes, Pierre's Canadian-born wife who has known the Nastases for many years, feels that many people under-estimate Ilie's powers of observation and awareness.

'Nobody should be misled into believing that Ilie does not notice what goes on about him,' she says. 'In fact he's very acute. One evening recently he launched into a long description of the behaviour of some of his family and friends, mimicking them in precise and vivid detail. It was hilarious and it proved that nothing had escaped him.

'I think that he is rather like Pierre in that a lot of the time he just doesn't care how much people take advantage of him until suddenly he's had enough and puts his foot down.'

Often that doesn't happen soon enough for his own good, but, just like his good friend Vitas Gerulaitis, Ilie is one of life's givers and nothing is going to alter that. Arthur Ashe has said of him, 'Unless Nastase can emote, he can't play.' One might also add that unless he can give, he can't live—not, at any rate, in the manner and spirit that is most comfortable for him.

'Every time we have dinner with the Nastases I just know there's going to be a fight over the bill,' says Caroline Barthes. 'Both Ilie and Pierre hate letting the other one pay and there's nothing forced about it. It's just in their nature.'

Ilie, of course, is now a rich man and that tends to make his generosity all the more rare. But in case anyone should imagine Nastase is the original soft touch, they should be aware that he has a very clear understanding of the value of money and pretty sharp antennae for 'friends' and strangers who sponge. When that foot comes down, it comes down awfully hard.

However, for the next three years at least, Ilie can afford his generosity. Before Lamar Hunt signed an agreement with the Pro Council to bring his World Championship Tennis circuit into the Colgate Grand Prix and thus do away with guarantees against prize-money for the players he signs, Ilie landed the only contract WCT now has with a player—and it will ensure him a quarter of a million dollars a year for three years to play from January until the beginning of May.

From May until the end of August he has another quarter of a million-dollar contract with the Los Angeles Strings, which leaves four months of the year free to add to the $500,000 plus he will already have earned. And that is just on court.

The Japanese electronics company Akai pay him $35,000 to wear their flash on his sleeve just in Europe; he will get at least as much again from a hotel deal that is now in the works; and then, of course, there is the Adidas contract which will soon be earning him an annual six-figure sum.

Adidas think he is worth it. Dickie Dillon, the former Yorkshire county player who now heads the company's tennis division in Europe, finds him very easy to work with. 'We get a lot back from Ilie,' says Dillon. 'Whenever we really need him at a trade fair or store exhibition, he'll get there, no matter how tight his schedule. That's why all that bad publicity last summer about him being unreliable hurt him so much. It was totally unfair.

'Of course, he's a tough guy to supply, for two very good reasons. On the one hand he's so generous that he's always giving away shirts and shorts to people he meets around the world, and on the other he's very meticulous about what he wears himself. He'll never go on court looking scruffy. All the stripes have to match, all the colours have to coordinate. Naturally that's good for our image, but it also means we have to keep on our toes to be sure he has everything he needs.

'He also loves anything new. Sometimes we'll give him a sample that may never go into production just to satisfy this desire he has for something different.'

This search for something new does not, at the moment, extend further than the familiar world of tennis. But I suspect that it is only a lack of confidence—that basic shyness again—which makes him wary of experimenting in other fields. After half an hour's careful direction on the 'Laugh-In' programme Ilie was thoroughly enjoying himself, and it seems inevitable that a few years from now he will branch out to other forms of public entertainment.

Already the name of Ilie Nastase has become instantly recognizable far beyond the confines of his sport. Ali, Pele, Nastase, there are not many others who can claim the same level of global fame, and if Ilie's achievements do not quite match those of the other two, he is no less a superstar for that.

He is also all those other things I have tried to trace: villain and hero; tragedian and clown; and always, for me, an artist. But the story is not over yet. And until more chapters can be written, let me leave you with an assessment by the only player who made Pancho Gonzales pause in his prime; possibly the only player who had it all: the power and the personality, the skill, the looks and the killer touch. His name is Lew Hoad and, as he sipped a beer at Forest Hills last year, he said, 'Listen, Ilie does a lot of things I don't approve of—that's his problem. But ask me which player I'd most like to watch and I'll tell you Ilie Nastase.'

BIOGRAPHY

1946, 19 July	Born in Bucharest
1958	Wins first junior tournament in Bucharest
1959	Decides to concentrate on tennis instead of football
1963	First trip abroad to Sofia, Bulgaria
1965	Ranked No. 9 in Romania
1966	Wins Bucharest International
1967	Wins first tournament abroad at Cannes
1969	Wins first big international title at Baranquilla, Columbia
1970	Wins Italian Open
1971 December	First Masters title in Paris
1972 July	Become engaged to Dominique Grazia in Dusseldorf
1972 July	Loses Wimbledon final to Stan Smith
1972 September	Defeats Arthur Ashe to win US Open at Forest Hills
1972 December	Retains Masters title in Barcelona
1972 December	Marries Dominique first in Brussels and again at La Basoche, France
1973 May	Defeats Nikki Pilic to win French Open
1973 June	Defeats Manuel Orantes to win Italian Open
1973 June	Defies ATP boycott and plays at Wimbledon
1973 December	Retains Masters title at Boston
1974 July	Defaulted at US Clay Court Championships at Indianapolis
1974 December	Loses Masters title in Melbourne final to Guillermo Vilas
1975 February	Fined by ATP for stalling against Ken Rosewall in American Airlines Tennis Games at Tucson
1975 August	Fined by Pro Council for behaviour against Manuel Orantes in final of Canadian Open
1975 December	Beats Bjorn Borg to win Masters title for fourth time in five years
1976 April	Begins playing for Hawaii Leis in World Team Tennis
1976 May	Quits WTT and returns to Europe
1976 July	Loses to Borg in Wimbledon final
1976 July	Re-joins WTT in Hawaii after threat of law suit
1976 September–October	Makes an estimated $80,000 playing exhibitions during three week suspension
1977 April	Defeats Jimmy Connors to retain WCT Challenge Cup at Caesar's Palace, Las Vegas
1977 July	Begins playing for Los Angeles Strings in WTT
1977 September	Defeats Guillermo Vilas to win Aix-en-Provence with double-string racquet which is banned the following week.

NASTASE'S OVERALL RECORD

Compiled by Joe McCauley

	WORLD'S MAJOR CHAMPIONSHIPS							TOURNAMENTS		RANKINGS	
YEAR	Australia	Italy	France	Wimbledon	U.S.A.	WCT Masters	Grand Prix Masters	NO. PLAYED	NO. SINGLES WON	ROMANIA	WORLD
1966	*	*	3 Drysdale	1 Koch	*	*	*	11	1	7	—
1967	*	3 Mulligan	Kodes	Curtis	*	*	*	20	3	2	—
1968	*	4 Okker	Crealy	*	*	*	*	20	3	1	—
1969	*	3 Roche	1 Matthews	4 Graebner	Rosewall	*	*	31	8	1	—
1970	*	Won Kodes	Q.F. Richey	4 Graebner	*	*	*	30	4	1	6
1971	*	*	Final Kodes	2 Goven	3 Carmichael	*	Round Robin	28	11	1	10
1972	*	S.F. Kodes	3 Panatta	Final Smith	Won Ashe	*	Won Smith	32	12	1	3
1973	*	Won Orantes	Won Pilic	4 A. Mayer	Pattison	*	Won Okker	32	16	—	1
1974	*	Final Borg	Q.F. Solomon	3 Stockton	Tanner	Q.F. Kodes	Final Vilas	29	9	1	6
1975	*	S.F. (Ret.) Ramirez	3 Panatta	2 S. Stewart	Q.F. Orantes	*	Won Borg	31	10	1	6
1976	*	*	*	Final Borg	S.F. Borg	*	*	30	9	1	3
1977	*	Q.F. Dent	Q.F. Gottfried	Q.F. Borg	Barazzutti	Q.F. Dibbs	*	22	3	—	

THE ABOVE CHART SHOWS NASTASE'S FINAL OPPONENT AND ROUND REACHED IN THE MAJOR CHAMPS. (E.G. IN 1967 HE LOST IN THE 3RD ROUND IN ITALY TO MULLIGAN BUT WON THE TITLE IN 1970 BEATING KODES IN THE FINAL.)

In all Nastase has played 314 tournaments, winning 88 singles titles (28%) and 75 men's doubles (39 in partnership with Tiriac). Up to and including Jan. 1st 1978.

Note: The world rankings indicated above are my own as published in World Tennis, Rothmans Year Book and Tennis Australia, Asia, the Pacific.

DAVIS CUP RECORD

YEAR	ROMANIA'S OPPONENTS	VENUE	RESULT	NASTASE'S SINGLES RESULTS	MEN'S DOUBLES RESULT	PARTNER
1966	France	A	1–4	P. Darmon 1–6 2–6 2–6 F. Jauffret 1–6 3–6 6–8	Lost	I. Tiriac
1967	Belgium	H	4–1	P. Hombergen 6–3 5–7 6–1 6–0 E. Drossart 6–2 5–7 10–8 6–2	Won	I. Tiriac
	Spain	H	2–3	M. Santana 6–0 3–6 3–6 3–6 J. Gisbert 3–6 6–4 7–9 4–6	Won	I. Tiriac
1968	Denmark	H	4–1	T. Ulrich 6–4 6–4 6–2 J. Ulrich 6–2 11–9 4–6 4–6 6–4	Lost	I. Tiriac
	Norway	A	5–0	M. Elvik 6–2 6–3 6–1 F. Prydz 4–6 6–0 8–6 6–0	Won	I. Tiriac
1969	U.A.R.	H	3–2	M. Sonbol 6–4 6–0 6–4 I. El Shafei 2–6 6–1 3–6 1–6	Won	I. Tiriac
	Israel	H	5–0	E. Davidman 6–0 6–2 6–4 J. Stabholz 6–2 6–2 6–0	Won	I. Tiriac
	Spain	A	4–1	J. L. Arilla 6–4 8–6 6–2	Won	I. Tiriac
	U.S.S.R.	H	4–1	T. Lejus 4–6 6–3 6–2 6–2 A. Metreveli 6–4 6–2 7–5	Won	I. Tiriac
	India	H	4–0	J. Mukerjea 6–2 6–4 4–6 4–6 6–1	Won	I. Tiriac
	Gt. Britain	A	3–2	G. Stilwell 4–6 6–4 1–6 2–6 M. Cox 3–6 6–1 6–4 6–4	Won	I. Tiriac
	U.S.A.	A	0–5	S. Smith 6–4 6–4 4–6 1–6 9–11 A. Ashe 2–6 13–15 5–7	Lost	I. Tiriac

(cont.)

YEAR	ROMANIA'S OPPONENTS	VENUE	RESULT	NASTASE'S SINGLES RESULTS	MEN'S DOUBLES RESULT	PARTNER
1970	Iran	A	4–1	H. Akbari 6–2 4–6 6–2 6–3	Won	I. Tiriac
				T. Akbari 10–8 6–0 6–8 5–7 6–3		
	Greece	H	5–0	N. Kalogeropoulos 6–2 7–5 6–4	Won	I. Tiriac
	Yugoslavia	A	2–3	Z. Franulovic 3–6 6–3 2–6 1–6	Won	I. Tiriac
				N. Spear 5–7 6–8 2–6		
1971	Israel	A	5–0	J. Shalem 6–1 6–2 6–3	—	—
				J. Stabholz 6–0 6–0 6–1		
	Holland	H	5–0	J. Hordijk 6–2 6–2 6–3	Won	I. Tiriac
				F. Hemmes 6–0 6–2 6–4		
	Yugoslavia	H	4–1	Z. Franulovic 7–5 6–2 6–3	Won	I. Tiriac
				B. Jovanovic 4–6 6–4 (Ret.) (Won)		
	Germany	H	5–0	W. Bungert 6-2 6–3 6–2	Won	I. Tiriac
				C. Kuhnke 6–0 6–4 6–4		
	India	A	4–1	J. Mukerjea 6–3 6–3 6–4	Won	I. Tiriac
				P. Lall 6–3 8–10 6–1 6–1		
	Brazil	A	3–2	E. Mandarino 6–4 6–1 6–1	Lost	I. Tiriac
				T. Koch 6–4 6–0 8–6		
	U.S.A.	A	2–3	F. Froehling 6–3 6–1 1–6 6–4	Won	I. Tiriac
				S. Smith 5–7 3–6 1–6		
1972	Switzerland	H	5–0	M. Burgener 6–1 6–2 6–3	Won	I. Tiriac
	Iran	H	5–0	T. Akbari 6–1 6–1 6–3	Won	I. Tiriac
	Italy	H	4–1	C. Barazzutti 7–5 6–2 6–0	Won	I. Tiriac
				A. Panatta 4–6 6–0 6–3 6–1		
	U.S.S.R.	A	3–2	A. Metreveli 6–4 6–0 6–4	Won	I. Tiriac
				T. Kakulia 6–2 6–2 6–3		
	Australia	H	4–1	C. Dibley 6–3 6–0 6–2	Won	I. Tiriac
				M. Anderson 6–2 6–2 4–6 6–3		
	U.S.A.	H	2–3	T. Gorman 6–1 6–2 5–7 10–8	Lost	I. Tiriac
				S. Smith 9–11 2–6 3–6		
1973	Holland	A	3–2	J. Hordijk 6–3 6–3 6–2	Lost	D. Haradau
				T. Okker 6–4 6–2 6–4		
	New Zealand	H	4–1	O. Parun 6–1 8–6 6–2	Won	I. Santeiu
				B. Fairlie 4–6 6–0 6–3 6–0		
	U.S.S.R.	H	3–2	T. Kakulia 6–0 6–3 6–0	Lost	I. Santeiu
				A. Metreveli 6–0 6–2 6–4		
	U.S.A.	A	1–4	M. Riessen 6–2 6–4 6–2	Lost	I. Santeiu
				S. Smith 7–5 2–6 3–6 6–4 3–6		
1974	France	H	3–2	P. Barthes 6–2 6–2 6–3	Won	I. Tiriac
				F. Jauffret 6–2 4–6 3–6 2–6		
	Italy	A	2–3	C. Barazzutti 9–7 6–0 6–1	Lost	I. Tiriac
				A. Panatta 6–0 6–0 7–5		
1975	Spain	A	2–3	J. Higueras 6–0 8–6 4–6 6–1	Lost	I. Tiriac
				M. Orantes 6–2 6–2 6–4		
1976	Austria	A	4–1	P. Fiegl 6–1 6–3 7–5	Won	V. Marcu
				H. Kary 6–3 7–5 6–1		
1977	Belgium	H	5–0	J. P. Richer 6–2 6–2 6–2	Won	I. Tiriac
				B. Boileau 6–1 6–4 6–1		
	Czechoslovakia	H	3–1	J. Kodes 6–2 6–2 6–4	Won	I. Tiriac
				J. Hrebec 6–2 1–0 (Ret.) Won		
	Gt. Britain	H	4–1	J. Feaver 6–1 6–2 4–6 6–4	Won	I. Tiriac
	France	A	2–3	F. Jauffret 6–3 6–0 4–6 3–6 1–6	Won	I. Tiriac
				P. Proisy 6–4 4–6 8–6 6–1		

Nastase played 74 singles rubbers winning 59 and losing 15. Surprisingly, he never managed to beat F. Jauffret (0–3) or S. Smith (0–4) in cup matches although enjoying an advantage over both men during his career. In Davis Cup doubles Ilie won 29 and lost 10; in partnership with Ion Tiriac he won 27 and lost 7.

Nastase's aggregate total of 113 rubbers places him fourth in the all-time lists behind Pietrangeli (164), Brichent (121) and Santana (119). His success percentage is currently 77.8%.

COMPLETE RESULTS

1965 RANKED NO. 9 IN ROMANIA.

1966 PLAYED 11 TOURNAMENTS—WON 1 SINGLES AND 3 DOUBLES

SINGLES: Won Bucharest International.

DOUBLES: Won Nottingham (partnered by Tiriac), **Travemuende** (Tiriac) and **Bucharest** (Tiriac). R/up French (Tiriac).

Win/Loss Record; B. Butcher, J. Kodes, B. Montrenaud, M. Riessen and G. Sara, 1–0; C. Zeeman 1–1; I. Tiriac 1–2; R. Crealy, P. Darmon, C. Drysdale, K. Fletcher, F. Jauffret, T. Koch, L. Pawlik, J. Saul and W. Tym, 0–1. RANKED NO. 7 IN ROMANIA.

1967 PLAYED 20 TOURNAMENTS—WON 3 SINGLES AND 6 DOUBLES

SINGLES: Won Cannes, Travemuende and Romanian Nats. R/up Alexandria, Carlton, Riccione.

DOUBLES: Won Belgian, Senigallia, Travemuende, Viareggio, Mamaia and Romanian Nats.—all with Tiriac.

W. Bungert, D. Contet, J. P. Courcol, E. Drossart, Z. Franulovic, W. Gasiorek, M. Holecek, P. Hombergen, R. Howe, V. Korotkov, R. Kuhlmey, J. Leschley, S. Likhachev, J. E. Lundquist, P. Marmureanu, F. Pala, H. Pohmann, R. Russell, M. Sangster, M. Sonbol, P. Strobl, S. Tacchini, R. Taylor, 1–0; P. Curtis, I. Tiriac, 1–1; C. de Gronkel, C. Drysdale, I. El Shafei, J. Gisbert, G. Maioli, A. Metreveli, B. Montrenaud, M. Mulligan, J. Pinto-Bravo, H. Plotz, M. Santana, G. Stilwell, 0–1; J. Kodes and N. Pietrangeli, 0–2. RANKED NO. 2 IN ROMANIA.

1968 PLAYED 20 TOURNAMENTS—WON 3 SINGLES AND 8 DOUBLES

SINGLES: Won Viareggio, Mamaia and Romanian Nats. R/up Parioli (Rome), Reggio Calabria.

DOUBLES: Won Calcutta, Bombay, New Delhi, Parioli, Catania, Viareggio, Mamaia (all with Tiriac) **and Belgrade** (Holecek).

E. Castigliano, M. Di Domenico, S. Dron, P. Marmureanu, 2–0; J. Alexander, W. Bowrey, P. Curtis, P. Dent, G. di Maso, E. di Matteo, M. Elvik, J. Fassbender, Z. Franulovic, W. Gasiorek, B. Jovanovic, T. Lejus, G. E. Maggi, S. Minotra, J. Paish, O. Parun, B. Phillips-Moore, J. Pinto-Bravo, A. Stone, P. Toci, D. Viziru, M. Werren, 1–0; R. Crealy, M. Mulligan, 1–1; E. Mandarino, A. Metreveli, J. Mukerjea, T. Okker, N. Pietrangeli, 0–1; P. Lall, M. Riessen, I. Tiriac, 0–2. RANKED EQUAL NO. 1 IN ROMANIA.

1969 PLAYED 31 TOURNAMENTS—WON 8 SINGLES AND 6 DOUBLES

SINGLES: Won East India H.C.; Indian H.C., Indian Nats., Barranquilla, Ancona, Travemuende, La Corogne, Budapest. R/up Palermo, Stockholm Inds.

DOUBLES: Won East India H.C. (Lall), **Indian H.C.** (Marmureanu), **Indian Nats.** (Marmureanu), **St. Petersburg** (Franulovic), **Palermo** (Tiriac), **Bastaad** (Tiriac), **Ancona** (Tiriac).

I. Gulyas, 3–0; J. Kodes, 3–0; P. Lall, M. Rybarczyk, 2–0; M. Cox, S. Smith, 2–1; G. Andrew, J. Arilla, S. Baranyi, J. C. Barclay, P. Beust, M. Carlstein, I. Crookenden, E. Davidman, P. Dent, V. Dhawan, E. Drossart, S. Dron, B. Fairlie, W. Gasiorek, T. Gorman, T. Koch, T. Lejus, G. Maioli, V. Marcu, P. Marzano, A. Metreveli, S. Misra, G. Mulloy, H. Plotz, H. Pohmann, R. Ruffels, M. Santana, M. Sonbol, R. Taylor, J. Ulrich, T. Ulrich, G. Varga, H. Zahr, V. Zednik, 1–0; P. Barthes, I. El Shafei, Z. Franulovic, J. Mukerjea, T. Nowicki, N. Spear, I. Tiriac, 1–1; A. Roche, 1–2; A. Ashe, A. Gimeno, G. Goven, C. Graebner, R. Holmberg, R. Lutz, S. Matthews, M. Mulligan, J. Newcombe, M. Orantes, N. Pilic, G. Stilwell, 0–1; K. Rosewall, 0–2. RANKED NO. 1 IN ROMANIA.

245

1970 PLAYED 30 TOURNAMENTS—WON 4 SINGLES AND 9 DOUBLES
SINGLES: **Won U.S. Inds., Italian Open, Naples and Catania.** R/up Palermo, Belgian Open, German Open, Romanian Nats.
DOUBLES: **Won Philadelphia Inds., Reggio Calabria, Catania, Palermo, Italian Open, Belgian Open, French Open and Western Open (USA)**—all with Tiriac, **Naples (Pala). Also won Wimbledon mixed (Casals).**
N. Kalogeropoulos, 4–0; R. Crealy, A. Gimeno, J. McManus, M. Mulligan, B. Phillips-Moore, H. Plotz, G. Stilwell, R. Taylor, I. Tiriac, 2–0; I. Gulyas, 2–1; T. Addison, H. Akbari, T. Akbari, G. Battrick, B. Bertram, J. Borowiak, A. Bouteleux, R. Carmichael, E. Castigliano, L. Coni, I. Fletcher, T. Gorman, G. Goven, F. Guzman, R. Hewitt, R. Howe, J. Hrebec, P. Jemsby, J. Kodes, J. Kukal, M. Lara, M. Leclerq, J. Lloyd, V. Marcu, A. McDonald, R. McKinley, J. Osborne, J. Paish, F. Pala, O. Parun, A. Pattison, N. Pietrangeli, P. Proisy, F. Robbins, A. Roche, T. Ryan, T. Ulrich, S. Warboys, A. Zugarelli, 1–0; C. Richey, 3–3; J. Alexander, A. Ashe, A. Panatta, N. Pilic, 1–1; Z. Franulovic, 2–2; J. Cooper, P. Hutchins, H. Kary, D. Lloyd, P. Marmureanu, D. Ralston, K. Rosewall, N. Spear, 0–1; J. Fillol, C. Graebner, R. Laver, T. Okker, 0–2. RANKED NO. 1 IN ROMANIA.

1971 PLAYED 28 TOURNAMENTS—WON 11 SINGLES AND 8 DOUBLES
SINGLES: **Won Ancona, Omaha, Richmond, Hampton, Nice, Monte Carlo, British Indoors, Swedish Open, Champions Cup (Sweden), Istanbul and Pepsi Grand Prix Masters.** R/up French Open, Madrid, Belgian Open and South American Open.
DOUBLES: **Won Omaha, Nice, Monte Carlo, Belgian (shared), Madrid, Swedish, Istanbul**—all with Tiriac, **and South American** (Franulovic).
F. Froehling, T. Gorman, T. Koch, 4–0; J. Leschley, 3–0; Z. Franulovic, 3–2; B. Jovanovic, J. Kukal, E. Mandarino, J. Newcombe, M. Orantes, P. Proisy, C. Richey, R. Ruffels, R. Russell, 2–0; J. Kodes, S. Smith, 2–1; W. Alvarez, A. Ashe, S. Baranyi, R. Barth, J. Bartlett, O. Bengtsson, J. Borowiak, W. Bungert, J. Clifton, J. Connors, P. Cornejo, R. Crealy, P. Curtis, M. Di Domenico, E. Drossart, T. Edlefsen, R. Emerson, O. Escribano, J. Fillol, W. Gasiorek, A. Gimeno, F. Hemmes, M. Holecek, J. Hordijk, F. Jauffret, K. Johansson, R. Keldie, C. Kuhnke, P. Lall, R. Laver, J. Loyo-Mayo, V. Marcu, B. Mignot, J. Mukerjea, M. Mulligan, T. Nowicki, T. Okker, L. Olander, C. Pasarell, A. Pattison, J. L. Rouyer, M. Santana; J. Shalem, J. Stabholz, 1–0; R. Carmichael, R. Taylor, I. Tiriac 1–1; C. Graebner, 2–2; P. Barthes, C. Drysdale, G. Goven, 0–1. RANKED NO. 1 IN ROMANIA.

1972 PLAYED 32 TOURNAMENTS—WON 12 SINGLES AND 9 DOUBLES
SINGLES: **Won Baltimore, Omaha, Monte Carlo, Madrid (Melia), Nice, Dusseldorf, Canadian Open, S. Orange, U.S. Open, Seattle, Dewar Cup and Comm. Union G.P. Masters.** R/up U.S. Inds., Hampton, Wimbledon, Swedish Open.
DOUBLES: **Won Omaha, Kansas, Hampton, Italian Open and Canadian**—all with Tiriac, **Melia** (S. Smith), **German Open** (Kodes), **Dusseldorf** (F. McMillan) **and Edinburgh** (R. Howe). **Also won Wimbledon Mixed** (Casals) and r/up Mixed (Casals).
T. Gorman, 9–1; J. Connors, 6–0; S. Baranyi, J. Fassbender, F. Pala, 3–0; M. Orantes, 3–2; C. Barazzutti, G. Battrick, M. Belkin, C. Dibley, P. Dominguez, P. Gerken, I. Gulyas, J. Fillol, B. Jovanovic, G. Masters, A. Pattison, P. Proisy, P. Szoke, I. Tiriac, T. Ulrich 2–0; P. Barthes, T. Edlefsen. J. Gisbert, C. Graebner, A. Panatta, 2–1; T. Akbari, A, Amritraj, K, Andersson, M. Anderson, A. Ashe, J. C. Barclay. J. Bartlett, B. Borg, M. Burgener, E. Castigliano, M. Collins, J. Cooper, P. Cornejo, I. Crookenden, J. Clifton, C. Drysdale, H. Engert, H. Elschenbroich, I. Fletcher, B. Gottfried, L. Hoad, J. Hrebec, T. Kakulia, N. Kalogeropoulos, H. Kary, T. Koch, A. Kurucz, B. Mackay, A. Mayer, F. McMillan, K. Meiler, A. Metreveli, R. Moore,

J. I. Muntanola, A. Olmedo, J. Osborne, O. Parun, J. Pinto-Bravo, H. Rahim, R. Ramirez, C. Richey, N. Spear, H. Stewart, F. Stolle, B. Taroczy, R. Taylor, J. Velasco, J. Zabrodsky, 1–0; R. Hewitt, J. Kodes, 2–2; O. Bengtsson, R. Tanner, 1–1; P. Cramer, A. Gimeno, T. Okker, 0–1; S. Smith, 1–4.   RANKED NO. 1 IN ROMANIA.

1973 PLAYED 32 TOURNAMENTS—WON 16 SINGLES AND 13 DOUBLES

SINGLES: Won Omaha, Calgary, Merrifield, Barcelona (T.C. Polo), Monte Carlo, Madrid, Florence, French Open, Italian Open, Queens Club, Gstaad, Istanbul, Western Open, Barcelona (Godo Cup), Paris Inds., and Comm. Union G.P. Masters. R/up Hampton, British Hd. Cts. and Dewar Cup.

DOUBLES: Won Monte Carlo, British Hd. Cts., Istanbul and Paris Inds.—all with Gisbert, **Calgary** (Estep), **Madrid** (Norberg), **Hampton and Charleston** (Graebner), **Godo and Melia** (Okker), **Wimbledon, S. Orange and Stockholm Inds.** (Connors). R/up French (Connors).

J. Connors, 4–1; P. Cramer, M. Estep, J. Gisbert, F. Jauffret, J. Kodes, R. Moore, M. Orantes, N. Pilic, P. Proisy, 3–0; A. Panatta, 3–1; J. Alexander, P. Bertolucci, J. B. Chanfreau, P. Dupre, J. Fassbender, B. Fairlie, J. Hrebec, N. Kalogeropoulos, E. Mandarino, A. Metreveli, J. Paish, J. Pinto-Bravo, J. Singh, S. Stewart, R. Taylor, M. Vasquez, 2–0; A. Amritraj, G. Battrick, M. Caimo, R. Case, E. Castigliano, J. Cooper, M. Cox, P. Dent, E. di Matteo, P. Dominguez, H. Elschenbroich, I. El Shafei, R. Emerson, H. Fitzgibbon, I. Fletcher, N. Fleury, J. Ganzabal, G. Goven, J. Guerrero, Z. Guerry, J. Higueras, M. Holecek, H. Hose, T. Kakulia, R. Kreiss, M. Lara, G. Masters, R. Maud, I. Molina, M. Mulligan, J. Newcombe, W. N'Godrella, O. Palmer, B. Phillips-Moore, H. Plotz, H. Rahim, M. Riessen, J. L. Rouyer, T. Sakai, S. Siegel, J. Simpson, G. Stilwell, R. Stockton, P. Szoke, J. Thamin, I. Tiriac, P. Toci, A. Zugarelli, 1–0; B. Borg, P. Gerken, T. Gorman, O. Parun, S. Smith, 1–1; B. Gottfried, C. Graebner, A. Mayer, K. Meiler, A. Pattison, R. Ramirez, 0–1; T. Okker, 3–4.   UNRANKED IN ROMANIA DUE TO INSUFFICIENT PERFORMANCES.

1974 PLAYED 29 TOURNAMENTS—WON 9 SINGLES AND 4 DOUBLES

SINGLES: Won Kingston, Richmond, Washington Inds., Portland, British Hd. Cts., Cedar Grove, Madrid (Melia), Barcelona (Godo) and Hilton Head. R/up Toronto, Hampton, Monte Carlo, Italian Open and Comm. Union G.P. Masters.

DOUBLES: Won British Hd. Cts. and Godo (Gisbert), U.S. Clay Cts. and Dewar Cup (Connors). R/up Italian (Gisbert).

G. Goven, R. Taylor, 4–0; H. Solomon, 3–1; R. Crealy, R. Dowdeswell, F. McNair, M. Orantes, N. Pilic, K. Warwick, 2–0; C. Barazzutti, P. Barthes, B. Borg, B. Gottfried, T. Okker, R. Ramirez, M. Riessen, A. Stone, 2–1; V. Amritraj, R. Barth, O. Bengtsson, P. Bertolucci, M. Claitte, P. Dominguez, C. Drysdale, P. Dupre, J. Fassbender, I. Fletcher, J. Gisbert, T. Gorman, G. Hardie, J. Higueras, J. Hrebec, L. Johansson, T. Koch, A. Korpas, M. Lara, R. Laver, A. Mayer, J. McManus, F. McMillan, A. Metreveli, M. Mulligan, J. Newcombe, A. Panatta, U. Pinner, O. Parun, B. Prajoux, H. Rahim, R. Reid, M. Robinson, R. Ruffels, E. Scott, S. Smith, E. van Dillen, J. Velasco, 1–0; J. Alexander, F. Jauffret, R. Maud, A. Pattison, R. Stockton, R. Tanner, 1–1; G. Vilas, 1–2; W. Brown, J. Connors, J. Kodes, C. Richey, 0–1.   RANKED NO. 1 IN ROMANIA.

1975 PLAYED 31 TOURNAMENTS—WON 10 SINGLES AND 5 DOUBLES

SINGLES: Won Barcelona, Valencia, Madrid, S. Orange, Dutch Round Robin, Hilton Head, Graz, Helsinki, Comm. Union G.P. Masters and Uppsala. R/up Swiss Inds., Tucson, Louisville, Canadian Open, Charlotte.

DOUBLES: Won U.S. Inds., S. Orange, U.S. Open, Hamilton—all with Connors, Melia (Kodes). R/up Italian (Connors).

M. Orantes, 4–3; P. Dent, I. El Shafei, W. Fibak, H. Kary, V. Pecci, 3–0; B. Borg, 3–2; J. Andrew, M. Cox, E. Dibbs, J. Higueras, S. Krulevitz, R. Laver, I. Molina, A. Munoz, B. Phillips-Moore, H. Pohmann, M. Riessen, G. Stilwell, B. Taroczy, I. Tiriac, 2–0; R. Ramirez, 2–1; Anand Amritraj, Ashok Amritraj, B. Andersson, J. Andrews, O. Bengtsson, P. Bertolucci, D. Crawford, J. Delaney, C. Dibley, P. Dominguez, R. Dowdeswell, Z. Franulovic, J. Gisbert, T. Gorman, B. Gottfried, J. Herrera, R. Hewitt, N. Holmes, L. Johansson, T. Kakulia, T. Koch, R. Kreiss, R. Lutz, R. Machan, E. Mandarino, W. Martin, G. Mayer, F. McNair, B. Mignot, Z. Mincek, B. Mitton, R. Moore, M. Mulligan, R. Norberg, T. Okker, J. Pinto-Bravo, H. Rahim, M. Robinson, A. Stone, R. Taylor, S. Turner, E. van Dillen, J. Velasco, T. Waltke, 1–0; J. Alexander, A. Panatta, K. Rosewall, S. Stewart, G. Vilas, 1–1; V. Amritraj, J. Connors, J. Fillol, J. Hrebec, J. Kodes, K. Meiler, P. Proisy, C. Richey, 0–1; A. Ashe, 1–2; V. Gerulaitis, 0–2. RANKED NO. 1 IN ROMANIA.

1976 PLAYED 30 TOURNAMENTS—WON 9 SINGLES AND 1 DOUBLE;
SINGLES: **Won Atlanta, U.S. Inds., La Costa, WCT Avis Challenge Cup, shared Nottingham, Pepsi Grandslam, S. Orange, Caracas Round Robin, Argentine Round Robin.** R/up Baltimore, Hampton, Caracas, Stockholm, Wimbledon, Hong Kong.
DOUBLES: **Won Stockholm WCT** (Metreveli).
R. Laver, G. Vilas, 4–0; J. Connors, 4–1; J. Borowiak, R. Stockton, 3–0; A. Panatta, 3–2; J. Alexander, M. Cahill, J. Fillol, Z. Franulovic, W. Martin, S. Menon, R. Moore, J. Hrebec, C. Pasarell, H. Rahim, E. van Dillen, 2–0; M. Orantes, H. Solomon, R. Tanner, I. Tiriac, 2–1; L. Alvarez, V. Amritraj, J. Andrews, S. Ball, O. Bengtsson, P. Dent, C. Dibley, M. Edmondson, I. El Shafei, B. Fairlie, P. Fiegl, P. Fleming, C. Hagey, H. Kary, C. Kirmayr, J. Kodes, Tom Gullikson, C. Lewis, J. Loyo-Mayo, J. Lloyd, E. Montano, O. Parun, H. Pohmann, R. Reid, M. Riessen, W. Scanlon, S. Smith, N. Spear, A. Stone, B. Taroczy, B. Walts, K. Warwick, 1–0; A. Ashe, B. Mitton, R. Ramirez, K. Rosewall, 1–1; V. Gerulaitis, T. Gorman, B. Gottfried, 0–1; W. Fibak, 1–3; B. Borg, 3–4. RANKED NO. 1 IN ROMANIA.

1977 PLAYED 22 TOURNAMENTS—WON 3 SINGLES AND 4 DOUBLES
SINGLES: **Won Mexico WCT and WCT Challenge Cup, Aix-en-Province.** R/up Rotterdam, Virginia Beach and Rye.
DOUBLES: **Won St. Louis, Earls Court and River Oaks**—all with Panatta. **Aix-en-Provence** with Tiriac.
J. Kodes, R. Moore, A. Panatta, 3–0; V. Gerulaitis 3–2; V. Amaya, C. Drysdale, W. Fibak, J. McEnroe, F. McMillan, T. Okker, 2–0; J. Alexander, L. Alvarez, L. Baraldi, B. Boileau, R. Cano, R. Case, M. Cox, J. Feaver, Z. Franulovic, Tim Gullikson, Tom Gullikson, R. Hewitt, J. Higueras, J. Hrebec, R. Laver, B. Manson, W. Martin, K. Meiler, A. Pattison, B. Prajoux, P. Proisy, J. Richer, R. Tanner, E. Teltscher, 1–0; C. Barazzutti, K. Rosewall, 1–1; V. Amritraj, B. Borg, P. Dent, E. Dibbs, B. Gottfried, G. Goven, F. Jauffret, H. Pfister, A. Roche, R. Stockton, 0–1; W. Scanlon, 1–2; J. Connors 1–3; G. Vilas, 1–5. UNRANKED IN ROMANIA DUE TO INSUFFICIENT PERFORMANCES.

ALPHABETICAL LIST OF OPPONENTS AND CAREER WIN AND LOSS RECORD

The statistics of Nastase's win/loss record show the remarkable consistency of the man. Since his first year on the world circuit in 1966, he has played over 1,000 tournament singles matches for a success percentage of around 78%.

Ilie is the one player in the world who can regularly tame Jimmy Connors as is clearly illustrated by his imposing 16–7 record against the American.

Note: These records exclude one set matches, World Team Tennis and exhibition matches.

Records are up to and including Jan. 1st 1978.

Addison, T	1–0	Cano, R	1–0	Engert, H	1–0
Akbari, H	1–0	Carlstein, M	1–0	Escribano, O	1–0
Akbari, T	2–0	Carmichael, R	2–1	Estep, M	3–0
Alexander, J	9–3	Case, R	2–0		
Alvarez, L	2–0	Castigliano, E	5–0	Fairlie, B	4–0
Alvarez, W	1–0	Chanfreau, J	2–0	Fassbender, J	7–0
Amritraj, An.	3–0	Claitte, M	1–0	Feaver, J	1–0
Amritraj, Ash.	1–0	Clifton, J	2–0	Fibak, W	6–3
Amritraj, V	2–2	Collins, M	1–0	Fiegl, P	1–0
Amaya, V	2–0	Coni, L	1–0	Fillol, J	5–3
Anderson, M	1–0	Connors, J	16–7	Fitzgibbon, H	1–0
Andersson, B	1–0	Cooper, J	2–1	Fleming, P	1–0
Andersson, K	1–0	Cornejo, P	2–0	Fletcher, I	4–0
Andrew, G	1–0	Courcol, J. P	1–0	Fletcher, K	0–1
Andrew, J	2–0	Cox, M	6–1	Fleury, N	1–0
Andrews, J	1–0	Contet, D	1–0	Franulovic, Z	13–5
Arilla, J. L	1–0	Cramer, P	3–1	Froehling, F	4–0
Ashe, A	5–5	Crawford, D	1–0		
		Crealy, R	6–2	Ganzabal, J	1–0
Ball, S	1–0	Crookenden, I	2–0	Gasiorek, W	4–0
Baraldi, L	1–0	Curtis, P	3–1	Gerken, P	3–1
Baranyi, S	5–0			Gerulaitis, V	3–5
Barazzutti, C	5–2	Darmon, P	0–1	Gimeno, A	3–2
Barclay, J. C	2–0	Davidman, E	1–0	Gisbert, J	7–2
Barth, R	2–0	De Gronkel, C	0–1	Gorman, T	18–3
Barthes, P	5–4	Delaney, J	1–0	Gottfried, B	4–4
Bartlett, J	2–0	Dent, P	7–1	Goven, G	6–3
Battrick, G	4–0	Dhawan, V	1–0	Graebner, C	4–7
Belkin, M	2–0	Dibbs, E	2–1	Guerrero, J	1–0
Bengtsson, O	5–1	Dibley, C	4–0	Guerry, Z	1–0
Bertolucci, P	4–0	Di Domenico, M	3–0	Gullikson, Tim	1–0
Bertram, B	1–0	di Maso, G	1–0	Gullikson, Tom	2–0
Beust, P	1–0	di Matteo, E	2–0	Gulyas, I	7–1
Boileau, B	1–0	Dowdeswell, R	3–0	Guzman, F	1–0
Borg, B	10–9	Dominguez, P	5–0		
Borowiak, J	5–0	Dron, S	3–0	Hagey, C	1–0
Bouteleux, A	1–0	Drossart, E	3–0	Hardie, G	1–0
Bowrey, W	1–0	Drysdale, C	4–3	Hemmes, F	1–0
Brown, N	0–1	Dupre, P	3–0	Herrera, J	1–0
Bungert, W	2–0			Hewitt R	5–2
Burgener, M	1–0	Edlefsen, T	3–1	Higueras, J	5–0
Butcher, B	1–0	Edmondson, M	1–0	Hoad, L	1–0
		Elschenbroich, H	2–0	Holecek, M	3–0
Cahill, M	2–0	El Shafei, I	6–2	Holmes, N	1–0
Caimo, M	1–0	Elvik, M	1–0	Homberg, R	0–1
		Emerson, R	2–0		

Hombergen, P	1 0	McMillan, F	4–0	Rouyer, J. L	2–0
Hordijk, J	1–0	McNair, F	3–0	Ruffels, R	4–0
Hose, H	1–0	Meiler, K	2–2	Russell, R. A	3–0
Howe, R	2–0	Menon, S	2–0	Ryan, T	1–0
Hrebec, J	8–1	Metreveli, A	4–2	Rybarczyk, M	2–0
Hutchins, P	0–1	Mignot, B	2–0		
		Mincek, Z	1–0	Sakai, T	1–0
Jauffret, F	5–3	Minotra, S	1–0	Sangster, M	1–0
Jemsby, P	1–0	Misra, S. P	1–0	Santana, M	2–1
Johansson, K	1–0	Mitton, B	2–1	Sara, G	1–0
Johansson, L	2–0	Molina, I	3–0	Saul, J	0–1
Jovanovic, B	5–0	Montano, E	1–0	Scanlon, W	2–2
		Montrenaud, B	1–1	Scott, E	1–0
Kakulia, T	3–0	Moore, R	10–0	Shalem, J	1–0
Kalogeropoulos, N		Mukerjea, J	2–2	Siegel, S	1–0
	7–0	Mulligan, M	8–3	Simpson, J	1–0
Kary, H	5–1	Mulloy, G	1–0	Singh, J	2–0
Keldie, R	1–0	Munoz, A	2–0	Smith, S	8–7
Kirmayr, C	1–0	Muntanola, J. I	1–0	Solomon, H	5–2
Koch, T	8–1			Sonbol, M	2–0
Kodes, J	16–8	Newcombe, J	4–1	Spear, N	3–2
Korpas, A	1–0	N'Godrella, W	1–0	Stabholz, J	2–0
Korotkov, V	1–0	Norberg, R	1–0	Stewart, S	4–1
Kreiss, R	2–0	Nowicki, T	1–0	Stockton, R	5–2
Krulevitz, S	2–0			Stolle, F	1–0
Kuhlmey, R	1–0	Okker, T	9–9	Stone, A	5–1
Kuhnke, C	1–0	Olander, L	1–0	Strobl, P	1–0
Kukal, J	3–0	Olmedo, A	1–0	Stilwell, G	5–2
Kurucz, A	1–0	Orantes, M	16–7	Szoke, P	3–0
		Osborne, J	2–0		
Lall, P	3–2			Tacchini, S	1–0
Lara, M	3–0	Paish, J	4–0	Tanabe, K	1–0
Laver, R	9–2	Pala, F	5–0	Taroczy, B	4–0
Leclerq, M	1–0	Palmer, O	1–0	Taylor, R	13–1
Lejus, T	2–0	Palmieri, S	2–0	Tanner, R	5–3
Leschley, J	4–0	Panatta, A	15–6	Teltscher, E	1–0
Lewis, C	1–0	Parun, O	6–1	Thamin, J	1–0
Likhachev, S	1–0	Pasarell, C	3–0	Tiriac, I	13–8
Lloyd, D	0–1	Pattison, A	6–2	Toci, P	2–0
Lloyd, J	2–0	Pawlik, L	0–1	Turner, S	1–0
Loyo-Mayo, J	2–0	Pecci, V	3–0	Tym, 4	0–1
Lundquist, J	1–0	Pfister, H	0–1		
Lutz, R	1–1	Phillips-Moore, B	6–0	Ulrich, J	2–0
		Pietrangeli, N	1–3	Ulrich, T	5–0
Machan, R	1–0	Pilic, N	6–2		
Mackay, B	1–0	Pinner, U	1–0	Van Dillen, E	4–0
Maggi, G. E	1–0	Pinto-Bravo, J	5–1	Varga, G	1–0
Maioli, G	1–1	Plotz, H	4–1	Vasquez, M	2–0
Mandarino, E	6–2	Pohmann, H. J	5–0	Velasco, J	3–0
Manson, B	1–0	Prajoux, B	2–0	Vilas, G	7–8
Marcu, V	3–0	Proisy, P	9–1	Viziru, D	1–0
Marmureanu, P	3–1				
Martin, W	4–0	Rahim, H	6–0	Waltke, T	1–0
Marzano, P	1–0	Ralston, D	0–1	Walts, B	1–0
Masters, G	3–0	Ramirez, R	8–4	Warboys, S	1–0
Matthews, S	0–1	Reid, R	2–0	Warwick, K	3–0
Maud, R	2–1	Richer, J. P	1–0	Werren, M	1–0
Mayer, A	2–1	Richey, C	6–5		
Mayer, G	1–0	Riessen, M	7–3	Zabrodsky, J	1–0
McDonald, A	1–0	Robinson, M	2–0	Zahr, H	1–0
McEnroe, J	2–0	Robbins, F	1–0	Zednik, V	1–0
McKinley, R	1–0	Roche, A	2–3	Zeeman, C	1–1
McManus, J	3–0	Rosewall, K	3–6	Zugarelli, A	2–0

INDEX

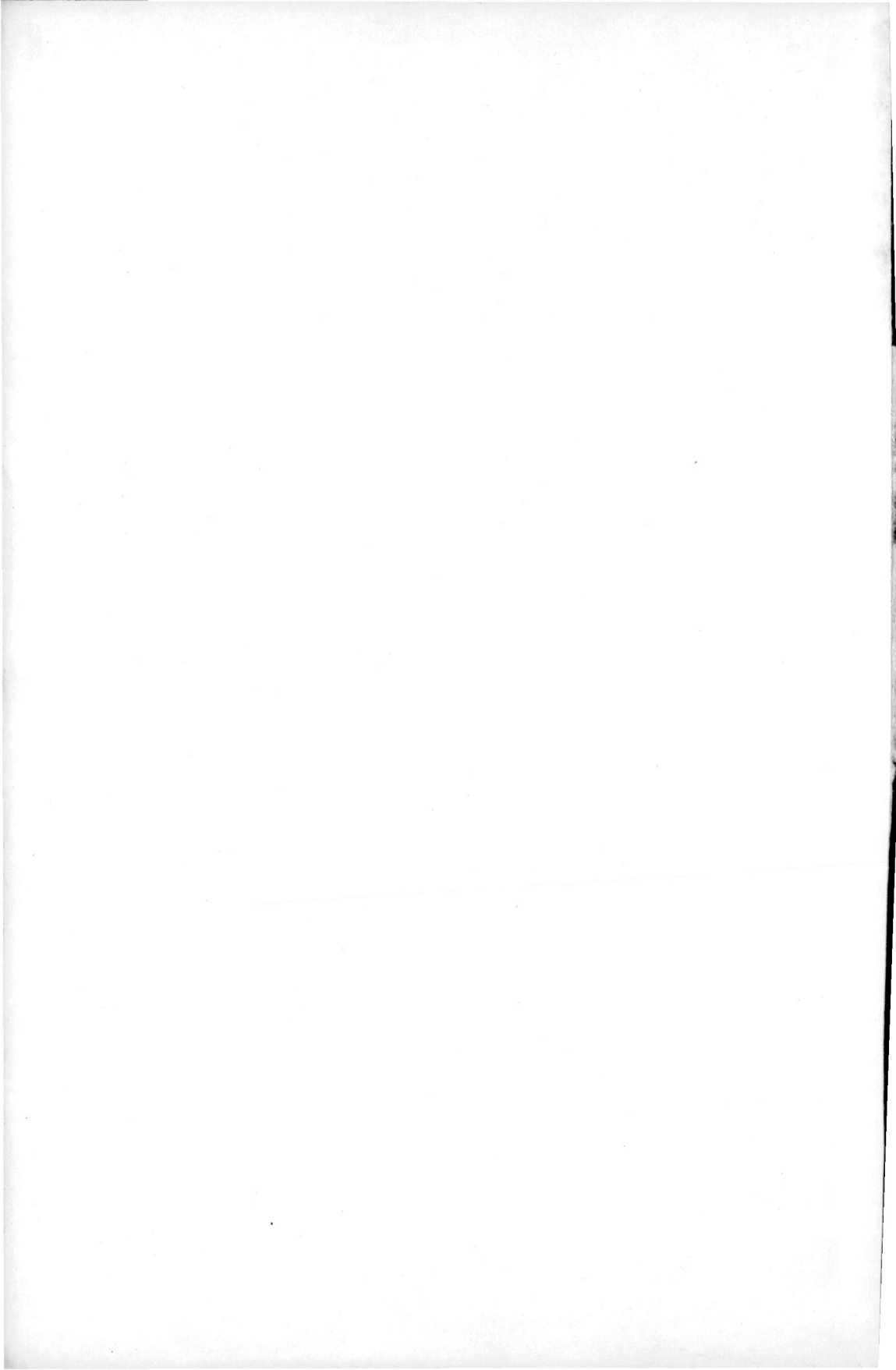